The Politics of
Welfare

The Politics of Welfare

Continuities and Change

Nicholas Deakin

HARVESTER
WHEATSHEAF

New York London Toronto Sydney Tokyo Singapore

First published 1994 by
Harvester Wheatsheaf
Campus 400, Maylands Avenue
Hemel Hempstead
Hertfordshire, HP2 7EZ
A division of
Simon & Schuster International Group

Typeset in 10/12 pt Ehrhardt
by Columns of Reading

Printed and bound in Great Britain by
Biddles Ltd, Guildford and King's Lynn

British Library Cataloguing in Publication Data

A catalogue record for this book is available from
the British Library

ISBN 0–7450–1430–5

1   2   3   4   5   98   97   96   95   94

For H.R.C.
who would not have approved

CONTENTS

ACKNOWLEDGEMENTS

This book had its distant origins in a game of children's football on Hampstead Heath. During the half-time break in a match, Bernard Crick (who coached one of the teams) asked me (the referee) if I would consider contributing to a series of short books on current political issues that he was editing. By the end of the game I had decided to decline; but to take a raincheck, in the hope that the right subject would come up. Several years later, I thought I had found it, in the Conservative Government's 'New Beveridge Report' – the major review of social security conducted by Norman Fowler in 1985–6. Although, for reasons explained in the text, this review did not turn out to be quite the event I had anticipated, by then I had persuaded Bernard, and through him Methuen, that the subject would fit. My first thanks therefore go to him.

The immediate opportunity for writing was provided by taking sabbatical leave from the University of Birmingham for the Spring Term of 1986. My colleagues in the Department of Social Administration there (now the Department of Social Policy and Social Work) kindly took over my teaching responsibilities during my absence. I spent the term's leave at the Suntory-Toyota Centre for Research in Economics and Related Disciplines (otherwise STICERD), at LSE, where Tony Atkinson and Julian Le Grand were most generous and considerate hosts.

Six years after first publication, I find myself revising the text for a second edition. Much has changed in the interval since the first version appeared, on the eve of the 1987 general election. During the third term of Conservative Government the hesitations over engaging in full-blooded reform of welfare that I (and other commentators) had identified were cast aside. A positive frenzy of legislative activity directed to achieving fundamental change was concentrated into the three years 1987–90, before the abrupt departure from power of Margaret Thatcher signalled a slowing up in the tempo (though not the direction) of change. I have added a new chapter to cover these events (Chapter 6) and have substantially modified the content of the previous chapter, though not the interpretation that I gave in the original version. Observant readers of both editions (if there be any such persons) will notice that the new material relies much less heavily than the earlier version on press stories for the background to policy developments. The reason is simple: most of the ministers involved in policy-making over the 1980s have now given us their memoirs (fifteen in total at the last count). We therefore have primary sources – though not necessarily wholly reliable ones – to draw upon where once we had to rely upon leaks. However, the memoirs also confirm the general accuracy of those leaks – and their usual origins. As Nicholas Ridley complains, 'Margaret Thatcher couldn't trust her Cabinet to keep matters to themselves' (1992, p. 37).

The other major alteration is substantial modification in the final chapter (Chapter 7) though not in the overall conclusions. I have changed my mind about a number of detailed issues but find little to alter in my judgments at midway point on the Thatcher experiment overall. Nicholas Ridley in his closing assessment (needless to say, a highly favourable one) nonetheless asks rhetorically whether Thatcherism 'might seem as if it was a gigantic experiment, which ultimately failed – like some vast science fiction concept which missed out one vital consideration and was never heard of again' (p. 2). I hope that my account may help to identify what was missing.

The revised edition ends in 1992, with the general election that returned John Major to power. The temptation to continue the story until the present to cover the nemesis of electoral Keynesianism was strong; but with the help of my new editor, Clare Grist, I have been able to resist it.

There remain some further acknowledgements. My departmental colleagues at Birmingham were again generous in allowing me time off to write and revise. All those mentioned in the earlier text were once more involved and helpful, with the sad exception of Victoria Baird, who left us in 1988 and is much missed. Catherine Jones Finer kindly read the revised text at a difficult time and made many shrewd and helpful comments, for which I am particularly grateful. Lucy Gaster taught an elderly dog one or two important technical tricks. Mark Cox at Bristol

University performed the indispensable feat of translating 1986 technology into 1993 form. Jack Donaldson, generous as always, supplied much important official documentation.

I would also like to thank the following who have kindly given permission for the use of copyright material: The Central Statistical Office for tables and figures from *Social Trends* and *Urban Trends*; Gower Publishing Limited for tables from *British Social Attitudes*; HMSO for material from Department of Social Security and HM Treasury Annual Reports and Briefings; The Office of Population, Censuses and Surveys for material on lone parenthood; The Policy Studies Institute for figures from various Policy Studies Institute reports; The Institute of Public Policy Research for figures from *The Justice Gap*, the first publication of the independent Commission on Social Justice; and The Royal Institute of Public Administration for a table from Jackson, *Implementing Government Policy Initiative: The Thatcher Administration*, 1985. Every effort has been made to trace all copyright holders, but if any have been inadvertently overlooked, the publishers will be pleased to make the necessary arrangements at the earliest opportunity.

Finally, I would like to acknowledge the help I have had from many friends and colleagues too numerous to name with whom I have discussed at various times the issues with which this book deals. I have drawn heavily on their views, written and spoken.

This book is dedicated to the memory of my dear friend H.R. ('John') Calmann, whose death in 1981 left a gap in the lives of all his friends which has never been filled.

Nicholas Deakin
Birmingham, 31 July 1993

INTRODUCTION

> We need a new set of convictions which spring naturally from a candid examination of our own inner feelings in relation to the outside facts.
>
> J.M. Keynes, *The End of Laissez Faire* (1926), in *Essays in Persuasion*, 1931.

This is a time of revolution in public policy. The machinery of government is being subjected to the most drastic overhaul it has experienced in recent memory. And prominent on the revolutionary agenda is fundamental questioning of the goals and performance of the Welfare State and the introduction of a whole series of measures designed to change them.

This process of change represents a decisive break with the past, as incarnated half a century ago in the Beveridge Report on Social Security. That, too, was revolutionary in its day: though Sir William was anxious to reassure the faint hearted that this would be a *British* revolution that would lead 'neither to Moscow nor to New York' (1943, p. 77). Now, his approach is to be put on one side, along with the rest of 'old Attlee's welfare state', as part of a process that has been reflected in, and fed upon, changes in political attitudes towards welfare and the way in which it is provided in our society. As a result, from being a ghetto topic, relegated to that limbo in which subjects that are both highly technical and complex but raise no partisan issues between the major parties are despatched to linger, welfare has moved to the centre of the political debate.

The reason that is commonly advanced for this fundamental departure from the postwar pattern is that the Welfare State has entered a period of 'crisis'. As presented by ministers in successive governments, and most notably by Conservative Chancellors and Treasury Chief Secretaries, this crisis consists of three interrelated elements. First, there is the constantly rising cost of providing welfare and its consequences for public expenditure; second, the likely increase in the burdens already being carried by the economy as a result of demographic changes both already occurring and yet to come; and finally the overload that these changes are producing both on the current system of administering and providing welfare and on the taxpayers who are ultimately footing the bill. Added to this (they argue) there is the ever-present risk of encouraging dependency, induced by the role played by the State in this field, which inhibits the spirit of individual enterprise on which the chances of economic recovery largely rest.

However, the concept of a crisis brought about by the workings of these factors is unsatisfactory, in the most direct sense, because it is not an accurate representation of reality. The evidence for this assertion will be presented later in the book. Briefly, the conclusions it suggests are that the cost of welfare does not place an intolerable burden on the economy; that many of the demographic changes now taking place are favourable, in social and economic terms, and that most taxpayers are willing at least to consider trading off paying higher taxes against receiving improved services.

If the main grounds commonly advanced for believing in a 'crisis' of the Welfare State do not hold water, why is it necessary to take up further time and paper exploring the fundamental purpose that welfare performs in our society? Paul Johnson has rather cynically observed that 'since the roots of the current critique of the welfare state are ideological, the way in which the system operates and its measurable economic and social effects are largely irrelevant to the critics' (1985, pp. 37–8). If true, this suggests that the task of refutation can never be finally accomplished. Moreover, there is the risk that in order to make themselves heard those setting out to offer a defence of welfare will be reduced to tedious repetition of the same few good old tunes. Though I do not seek to disguise my liking for many of them, I do not find turning the handle of the welfare barrel-organ a very rewarding activity.

However, far more important than the immediate criticisms now on offer are the broader concerns that lie behind them. For there is now widespread anxiety, covering all shades of opinion, about the future of welfare and the objectives that it should be seeking to achieve. Insistent pressure generated by government interventions in economic and social policy over the past decade has opened up a whole series of issues previously left largely unexplored and also provided the opportunity for the expression of concerns once dismissed as irrelevant.

Some of the questions opened up in this way are about the changing relationship between social policy and the broader policy goals of government and the conflicts that have been exposed by successive crises in the economy. Some relate to the objectives that the State's presence in the field of welfare are intended to serve. Some are about means; whether the State is capable of carrying out the tasks with which it has been entrusted, or whether welfare can be better provided through the market or informally. Then there are questions about the form and procedures through which welfare is provided and the role of those who deliver it, about the capacity of the statutory sector to work with other agencies and changing relationships created as a result. Others are about ends; whose interests welfare is intended to serve and who has really gained from its expansion – not just from the statutory services but also from the huge array of benefits provided through the tax system or by employers: the 'middle-class Welfare State'. Finally, there are questions to be asked about the persistent bias against women that was built into the structure of the Welfare State at the outset and perpetuated by the attitudes of those who have administered it and the subsequent reluctance to admit the claims of minorities of all kinds, which still defies all attempts at change.

Out of the answers to these and other questions, there may be some prospect that what Rudolf Klein and Michael O'Higgins call 'the deterministic fatalism inherent in the use of crisis rhetoric' can be rejected and the scope for policy intervention and innovation reaffirmed (1985, p. 4). But in order to achieve this outcome and make the case convincingly, it is necessary to return to first principles and uncover not just the factors at work in the current situation but the stages by which the present structure of welfare and the complex web of relationships between different agencies and individuals came into existence.

Here, another difficulty arises – that of the concepts commonly employed in discussion of these issues. The key central term in the debate is the 'Welfare State', and that term is often used as shorthand for the whole range of services and activities falling under the broad definition of welfare. But there are good grounds for supposing that the unqualified use of the term 'Welfare State' grossly distorts discussion. A very high proportion of what we usually think of as 'welfare' is not in fact directly delivered by the state at all. It is provided by individuals, separately or collectively, by families, by informally or formally organised voluntary associations, or purchased in the market. Furthermore, discussion that equates welfare with State provision accentuates the link between welfare and provision for the poor and risks both separating off the poor from the mainstream of society and concealing the large proportion of welfare that is consumed by the better off.

The very common description of the debate that has been taking place about the objectives of welfare as a contest between 'individualism' and 'collectivism' is another example of the kind of simplification that blurs and eventually obscures the fundamental issues at stake. If two such clear-cut categories actually exist, it is only at the extreme ends of the spectrum of opinion. Hardly anyone outside the hardest members of the hard-core 'libertarian' right actually believes in the total abolition of State welfare; and only on the militant left is there any remaining affection for the concept of the all-encompassing state. Any analysis that talks in terms of two all-embracing sets of opposing views is bundling together a whole set of disparate opinions of uneven shape and length, spread out along a continuum with many overlaps and discontinuities.

This is also true of many of the other concepts customarily employed to explain shifts in the balance of political forces: 'Thatcherism', 'Fabianism', 'Social Democracy', 'Liberalism', 'Marxism'. On closer examination, these constructs turn out to have very little internal consistency or explanatory value; with overuse, they have degenerated into convenient labels that absolve the user from the trouble of devising proper explanations of events. In extreme cases, they have become mere terms of abuse. Once again, the process of oversimplification has helped to obscure the variety and complexity of the processes at work.

To propose a re-examination of the place of welfare and its functions is therefore not just to call into question the underlying objectives that governments and their critics assign to it but also the terms in which the debate has often been conducted. The practical difficulty is that the project risks covering far more ground than can be contained within the limits of an exercise like the present one and requires a range of skills that I do not possess. To escape from this dilemma a choice must be made of a door, so to speak, through which to enter the debating chamber. I have chosen to consider the future of welfare as a political issue: hence my title.

I have three reasons for this choice. First, I am anxious to avoid the fragmentation of discussion that has marked some past contributions to the debate on welfare, in which the issues are explored service area by service area, and relationships between different parts of the political and administrative system are implied, at best, rather than examined. Second, a political perspective seems appropriate because the political arena is – or rather should be – the place in which the main decisions about the priorities to be attached to different forms of state activity and different items of expenditure are discussed and taken. Third, the political context is the one in which I feel most at home myself. This is not because I am, or ever have been a politician, except in the most marginal sense (my sole encounter with the electorate as a candidate is a distant and inglorious episode). However, I have had nearly fifteen years of experience of working in government at both central and local level. As a result of that involvement in the making and implementing of social policies of different kinds at different levels I am convinced that despite all its deficiencies (of which anybody with working experience of Whitehall or town hall cannot help being acutely aware) the State in one form or another should remain central to the provision of welfare in our society for the foreseeable future. There is room for almost infinite disagreement about the scope of that role and the form that it might take, but of the relevance of the State's involvement I have no doubt. Furthermore, my experience strongly suggests that the State as it exists in its varied forms in Britain today is neither an executive committee set up to serve the class interests of the bourgeoisie nor a device for gratuitous meddling with the sacred harmonies of the market. I am conscious, of course, that by making this confession I will immediately be categorised either as a 'reformist' (by one set of definitions) or a 'welfarist' (by another) – or even conceivably both.

The basic approach, therefore, will be through considering the various competing views of the function of welfare expressed in public policy and exploring their consequences. The first chapter is intended to clear the decks by defining with as much clarity as I can command the issues at stake in the current debates. This involves addressing the questions presently being discussed by political philosophers and welfare economists about the role of the State in public policy and its relationship to citizens, both individually and collectively. These are difficult and controversial issues but of such fundamental significance that we neglect them at our peril. The form in which the debate is conducted may appear abstract and general; but its applications are real and specific, as any European over the age of 50 can testify from personal experience.

Having examined the main issues in contention and established the terms on which the discussion of those issues can most helpfully be conducted, I set out to explain how we have reached the situation in which we now find ourselves and, eventually, how we can best move forward. Such an account necessarily begins with the Beveridge Report of 1942 and the set of views that crystallised round it, because that is justly seen as the point of departure for the development of the pattern of welfare as we now know it. In doing so, I have tried to set the Beveridge Report in its proper context – notably, the debate about the value of state planning and its limitations that began towards the end of the 1930s. Then, since I believe with the Michelin Guide that in attempting to understand – or even possibly enjoy – the architecture of any man-made structure *un peu d'histoire* comes in handy, I offer my account of the period that separates the creation of the modern Welfare State from the arrival of the 'crisis'.

Next, I explore in greater detail the various grounds upon which it has been asserted that the Welfare State is 'in crisis' and the various measures that have been taken by governments acting on that assumption. This account provides the context within which the present Government's successive initiatives in the field of welfare, leading up to the recent legislation, can be evaluated. Does the evidence, when fully examined, justify the action that has been taken or proposed: is it appropriate to the situation confronting successive governments? Are there alternative measures which might better answer the needs of that situation? It is still the Conservative Government's practice, at the time of writing, to maintain that the nature of the situation demands certain measures to which there are no feasible alternatives. That claim requires testing; although it is a fact beyond disputing that alternatives are on offer. Finally, I conclude by attempting to plant some signposts of my own to alternative directions for the future.

Two other points. First, it is frequently urged – and not without reason – that discussion of social policy in Britain is excessively insular. Although I will refer to relevant experience in other broadly comparable societies, the references that space permits are bound to be both brief and superficial. Second, any account written by an academic, even if it is not an academic account (and this is not) risks the standard accusation of being remote from the realities with which ordinary people have to live every day of their lives, and with which any study of the Welfare State should properly be concerned. Like most people who work in my subject area, I try to spend as much time as possible outside the study and the lecture hall and in the field. By that means, if no other, I hope to remind myself that behind the statistics and policy statements with which I deal there are individual human beings and often human suffering. To take a specific example, I know from direct experience that the apparently inexorable rise in the homelessness statistics means more families spending their lives in one filthy inadequate room and more of my fellow citizens sleeping out on January nights in cardboard boxes.

In sum, what I now offer is a cocktail. In mixing it, I have done my best to secure a blend, without making the product excessively bland. In particular, I have tried to make the subject matter accessible and avoid wherever possible the technical terms that creep in all too frequently whenever vigilance is relaxed. Much of the subject matter is complex; that cannot be helped. What can be helped is muddle and lack of clarity; and I have done my best to root them out.

Finally, I disclaim any originality in what follows. It is not based on original research. What I have attempted here is a synthesis, in which some ideas and opinions of my own are added to reading and discussion with a wide range of people of different backgrounds and points of view to make up what the Conservative philosopher Roger Scruton calls a work of dogmatics. That means that if this book has any merit it derives very largely from the work of others. Writing it has been a heartening experience in at least one sense; the variety and vigour of the work that I have been able to draw upon conclusively refutes – to me, at least – the suggestion that the subject matter of social policy is in any sense 'exhausted' or 'jaded'. However, I have preferred wherever appropriate to state arguments in my own words. In adopting this approach I hope at least to have avoided the failing that the novelist Samuel Butler observed in the professors of his imaginary Erewhon, 'who seemed to devote themselves to the avoidance of every opinion with which they were not perfectly familiar'. However, there will certainly be occasions where I have oversimplified or not done full justice to cases made with far greater elegance and eloquence by their originators. For these offences, and for other sins of omission and commission, I ask forgiveness in advance.

1

VALUES AND WELFARE

In showing that security can be combined with freedom and enterprise and responsibility of the individual for his own life, the British community and those in other lands who have been involved with the British tradition have a vital service to render to human progress.

W.H. Beveridge, *Social Insurance and Allied Services*, 1942.

Towards the end of The War (which is how people of my generation still habitually refer to the Second World War) my mother took to bringing home from our visits to the children's clinic that the local authority had recently established small brown bottles labelled 'welfare orange juice'. My brother and I gulped down the contents willingly enough: the flavour, bland, but with a slightly bitter chemical back taste, was in every way preferable to the only alternative on offer: cod liver oil. Now, forty years later, the ghost of the tang that the juice once left still appears unbidden on my palate whenever I first see the word 'welfare'; and illustrates in a trivial but (to me) highly immediate way how the terms employed in the debate about the future of welfare have developed associations and personal references which are lodged deep in the collective unconscious of the nation.

That, perhaps, is one reason why it needs an effort of will to remember that the concept of a 'Welfare State' is still a relatively recent one, at least as far as this country is concerned, and rests on a number of assumptions about the functions that the State can or should perform for its citizens that are not normally made explicit. Not merely has the notion that the State has responsibility for these functions come to be taken more or less for granted; until recently, the scale of State activities and steady

1

increases in the resources devoted to them have also been regarded as
given. This, very generally, was the pattern in all major developed
countries for the thirty years after the Second World War.

In retrospect, that situation now seems surprising. Both the concept of
the State itself and the responsibilities it has assumed and the place of
welfare among those responsibilities have in the past been highly
contentious issues. Seen in a longer time perspective, it is therefore
hardly unexpected that the assumptions about the Welfare State that we
have unconsciously absorbed and the values and institutions that
underpin them are now being subjected to a process of questioning and
scrutiny that has gathered momentum over the past few years. Some of
these are questions about the reasons for the present organisation of
welfare: Why has the State become involved in the provision of welfare?
Why does it perform the particular tasks that it has taken on and not
others? What are the explanations for the way in which these tasks have
been discharged – how they are funded and operate? Other questions are
about performance: How well does the State carry out these tasks? Can
other institutions or individuals (either collectively or separately) do
them better? Is there scope for collaboration between the State and these
other agencies? If so, what form should it take?

All these questions have radical implications, in the proper sense of
going to the root of issues that are now arousing widespread anxiety.
Some of those politicians who have been asking them most insistently
currently enjoy access to political power. This gives the questions
particular bite; it also means that the task of arriving at convincing
answers has become vitally important for all those concerned about the
future of welfare.

The debate that has resulted has not been by any means exclusively about
welfare; it has also focused on the State itself – the role that it plays in our
society and in relation to other centres of power and authority within and
outside our national boundaries. The State in its modern form is a highly
complex institution, containing within it, like a nest of Chinese boxes, a
whole series of subordinate institutions and linked in a wide variety of ways
with a series of other agencies and sources of power, including ultimately
the individual citizens from whom, in democratic theory, if not in practice,
the State ultimately derives its authority. These complexities are the result
of a long process of historical development, which differs substantially in
form and outcome from one country to another.

All States have in theory this much in common: their legitimacy is
accepted both by their own citizens and by other States and their

authority is capable of being asserted, if necessary, by the sanction of force. But in practice, the experience of the plethora of new States that have emerged in the twentieth century, latterly mainly as a result of the breaking up of the great colonial empires (including at the end of the 1980s the Soviet Union), shows how malleable that concept can be under internal or external pressure. The last few years have also seen the appearance of a number of supranational institutions which have led to some tentative moves towards the surrendering by nation states of some of the controls they customarily exercised – for example, over the movement of goods or people – and some exchange of services, not least in the field of welfare. The erratic progress of the European Community in this direction and the series of adjustments and adaptations that have proved necessary to already complex national systems aptly illustrates the diversity that exists in systems of law and government and the structure and functioning of institutions as between neighbouring states. The loss of the control that nation states are able to exercise over their national economies as a result of the growth in the period after the Second World War of the scale of operation and influence of multinational corporations is another crucial factor working for change in the environment within which States function.

Although the provision of welfare has become one of the functions that all modern states are expected to perform, the objectives of welfare policies have often been determined by the outcome of other debates, for example about priorities in economic policy. As a result, a variety of different forms of provision have appeared, even in countries with broadly similar histories and economic and social structures. This diversity of forms, in particular among the 'advanced capitalist' states of Western Europe and North America provides good grounds for caution before accepting oversimplified views of the 'inevitability' of certain developments leading to the emergence of the Welfare State at a particular time and in a particular shape.

An additional complication is that the single rubric 'Welfare State' brings together a large number of volatile elements which separately and together can assume a bewildering variety of forms at different times and in different places. To take only one example, the term 'state schools' can cover a range of educational institutions: those where teachers are direct employees of the Government and the content of the curriculum that they teach is laid down by officials of central government; schools funded from taxes but operated by other agencies according to priorities that they negotiate or set for themselves; 'self-managed' schools and those that are merely regulated or inspected by an official agency. The State agency concerned can also be either an organic part of central government or an independent local body. Their authority can derive from election, either at central or local level, from appointment or nomination, or a combination of all three. Similar – sometimes even greater – diversity exists in other fields, like housing or social security.

If there is one factor that helps to differentiate one society from another it is the particular values to which importance is attached and the public and political responses to major issues that stem from them. The question of the State's role in the field of welfare is one of these issues: it has provoked widely differing responses at different times and in different societies. In seeking to explain these responses, a logical way to begin is by attempting to identify the values that have assumed particular significance in this context in our own society, trace their historical and social roots and chart the shift in their importance over time.

THE DEBATE ON WELFARE

One of the striking features of the current political debate about welfare is that the whole range of views expressed since the first tentative steps towards intervention by the modern State were taken in the mid-nineteenth century can still be heard today. It is as if prehistory were rewritten so that dinosaurs and space shuttles coexisted, with no certainty about which would be likeliest to become extinct and which survive. Thus, the extreme libertarian position, which would expel the State not just from the field of welfare but from the whole range of functions that it has taken on is now being articulated in terms almost identical to those employed 100 years ago by the philosopher Herbert Spencer. True, the ranks of those prepared to advocate an all-encompassing role for the State in welfare as in the economy, which would define not merely citizens' needs but the manner in which they are to be satisfied, have thinned noticeably over the past thirty years; but they can still marshal a fair sized platoon. And in the vast acreage which separates the position of full-blooded State-driven collectivists from dogmatic desert-island individualists a whole series of stalls have been set out, staffed by eager hucksters. The problem is that their bids for territory and the symbolic landmarks upon it overlap and conflict and the rationale for their claims is often cast in confusingly similar terms.

The solution adopted by those attempting to present a tidy account of the state of the debate on ideas about the future of welfare has usually been to establish paradigm positions. This involves packaging and labelling different sets of views in three or at most four bundles and arranging them at regular intervals along a spectrum conceived in conventional political terms, and therefore stretching (naturally) from left to right. The difficulty with this procedure is its artificiality. The categories are imposed by the analyst, not chosen by those whose views they purport to describe (who may very well wish to reject them, if they are in a position to do so – the dead, of course, have no redress). And the constructs can only achieve full intellectual consistency if the views that divide those who have been grouped together are suppressed, together with the views that (often more interestingly) unite those who are supposed to be divided. Such an approach also often fails to take account of the intellectual ancestry of the ideas in question.

For example, the similarities both in form and in content between the free market and Marxist critiques of the postwar Welfare State in Britain have often been remarked upon (Offé, 1984); but are usually treated as coincidence or aberration on the part of one or other party. It may be more illuminating to treat these positions as having real significance – that is, as if both parties really intend what they say.

The brief account that follows is therefore cast in terms of the primary objectives identified for welfare in the debates that have taken place over the past hundred years, as described by the participants themselves. This procedure is also open to several objections. First, and most crudely, it can be argued that the positions adopted are not in fact those that their advocates are genuinely attempting to secure. For example, it is clear that Marxist critics could not accept their bourgeois rivals' commitment to freedom as a value within a mixed economy as genuine, since it is axiomatic that authentic freedoms cannot exist for the working class under any form of capitalism. Similarly, their adversaries would be unlikely to recognise that a defence of representative democracy in its electoral form can be honestly undertaken by a committed Marxist.

At a less elevated level, it can be suggested that politicians – who do, after all, have the ultimate responsibility for implementing policies and securing public endorsement of them at elections – may not attach the same order of significance to abstract concepts as political philosophers do. Third, a fixed categorisation of views leaves little room for changes of opinion on the part of individual advocates, which have often been of particular significance in this field – witness Beveridge's wobbling across the blurred boundary line between advanced liberalism and socialism and back again, the Webbs' journey from state collectivism without party allegiance, through parliamentary socialism to communism and (in the more recent past) Sir Keith Joseph's transformation from interventionist minister to the hammer of the collectivists. Finally, such categorisations suggest an arbitrary choice between values that may be equally prized or whose significance may vary according to circumstances (wartime conditions have a remarkable effect on people's ordering of their priorities, and theorists and practitioners of welfare are no exception).

With all these qualifications, and recognising that any selection is bound to appear arbitrary, the four values to which primary importance has been attached at one stage or another during the twentieth-century debate on welfare are: liberty (or in alternative definitions freedom), equality, democracy and efficiency. All have had powerful advocates – both those whose primary emphasis has been on the theoretical implications of the position which they advocate and those who have made the case in terms of practical policies they wish to see adopted. Most are based on the assumption that in any advanced society basic human needs will be met. These needs are most often defined in material form (shelter, subsistence), sometimes as a general sense of well-being in society as a whole, less frequently in terms of personal emotions and what the framers of the American constitution called 'the pursuit of happiness', important though this is to many people in the late twentieth century. Because these four broad values interact and at times conflict with one another a simple choice between them is neither feasible nor desirable. Rather, it is a question of emphasis and a recognition that the task of reconciling objectives that are – potentially – mutually opposed may prove a difficult one.

For those who have identified liberty as the major value with which welfare policies should be consistent, the main outcome that such policies should be designed to secure will be the widest feasible range of choices for the individual, exercised under the least possible restriction. The stress is likely (though not certain) to be on the individual's autonomy and capacity to act without illegitimate constraint; physical security of person and property is also likely to be a major policy goal. The test of the success of policies will more often than not be the level of satisfaction of individual needs and aspirations.

But there are a variety of ways of achieving that outcome. The simplest and most straightforward statement of this position is the minimalist one; its advocates in the current debate, the 'libertarians' (the choice of term is their own) would argue for a total exclusion of the State from the sphere of welfare, on the grounds that individuals should take full responsibility for their own situation, entering where appropriate into contractual arrangements enforceable at law. Care of dependants would be the responsibility either of their family or if no family ties remained would need to be purchased in the market. Some, though not many libertarians would go so far as to include public order in the range of goods that the State should no longer provide, but which the individual should instead purchase or secure for themselves. Though it has ample historical precedents, this position, in its full-blown form has not been prominent in more recent political debates in Britain, although echoes of the extreme libertarian position can be heard in some of the critiques of welfare bureaucracy and the allegedly inevitable disabling consequences for those that resort to it for help. For historical and cultural reasons, these arguments have until recently been more prominent in the debates in the United States than those in this country; but over the past decade their transfer and application to the British situation has become something of a cottage industry.

Wholesale exclusion of the State is not the position of those economic liberals like Milton Friedman and his British avatars at the Institute of Economic Affairs, who place their faith in the market and its mechanisms for allocation of resources. From their perspective, State intervention is admissible for two purposes: to police the boundaries of the market and to provide where necessary the essential minimum of resources that the market cannot for a variety of reasons secure for those in extreme poverty. The form of relief that should be provided is financial, since cash enables individuals who receive it to function as consumers in the market, whereas care may disable them from doing so by removing any need to make choices. The condition is that assistance should be strictly confined to those who can demonstrate that they are poor: this in turn implies means testing (or, in the 1980s vocabulary, 'targeting') of provision.

Friedrich von Hayek, whose work contains the most substantial treatment of these themes in the current literature and who has been demonstrably influential on recent government policies both in Britain and the United States, is also prepared to allocate a significant role to the State. His major preoccupation has been with the conditions in which the State should be permitted to operate, under the rule of law, with constitutional provisions and with rules deriving from custom. These provide the guarantees that liberties will not be infringed by State action. His famous attack on State planning in *The Road to Serfdom* was heavily influenced by the rise of totalitarianism in Europe between the two

World Wars, but extends the attack to cover the means as well as the ends, so that planning becomes by definition tyrannical as well as inefficient as soon as it begins to impinge upon freedom of choice within the market (Hayek, 1944).

Latterly, Hayek became concerned with the interaction between liberty and another of the crucial values, democracy, and the possible conflicts that may arise as a result of demands articulated by groups operating within the pluralistic political system that has become characteristic of advanced industrialised societies. The most notorious example of these are the trade unions and their demands for modifications of the free operation of the labour market. These are transmitted through the political arena by means of the links that the trade unions enjoy with political parties of the left. But the unions are only the extreme example of the pressure group in action; all sorts of other demands – crucially, for increased spending on welfare – are expressed by producer interests and other pressure groups formed to argue for increased resources to be devoted to the cause they were established to promote. In a democracy, politicians must necessarily respond to these pressures, as a result of the way in which the electoral system now functions and the development of sophisticated techniques of persuasion. At best, this produces progressive overload upon the machinery of government and pressures upon available resources; at worst, it perverts the whole system since it involves making concessions that can only be granted at the expense of the interests of other citizens – characteristically, by requiring penal levels of taxation to fund them.

These measures are usually legitimated by reference to concepts like 'social justice' that have (Hayek argues) no substantial existence. The term has no meaning because, in a free society based on the market, inequalities are not imposed but arise naturally as a result of the interaction of circumstances over which no individual exercises control. Nor can the State provide redress; to do so requires knowledge about individual preferences – and the capacity to satisfy them – that governments cannot legitimately acquire without fatal interference with the functioning of the free market. Hayek looks to the legal system and to the rules established by custom to defend the citizen against these intrusions, and has proposed constitutional reforms that would defend the general good against the demands of sectional interest groups. At the same time, his economic liberalism, which descends directly from Adam Smith, does not exclude the possibility of substantial interventions by the State in areas of morality, where custom and the stability of society require the prescription of certain activities or forms of behaviour. This form of qualified liberalism has particular attractions for contemporary governments of the right, who are concerned to preserve the State's role, while redefining its range of responsibilities – a leaner, but in many respects fiercer State. As Margaret Thatcher put it in 1980: 'In our party we do not ask for a feeble State. On the contrary, we need a strong State to preserve both liberty and order' (Heald, 1983, p. 322).

By contrast, there have been Liberals to whom liberty is a key value but who regard the market not as a guarantor of freedom but a potential threat to it. For them, the State occupies a key position, and its role needs expanding as the range of interventions which they see as necessary to secure liberty increases. Beginning with the New Liberals at the end of the nineteenth century, this strand in liberalism extends the freedoms that the citizen can legitimately expect from the State into the economic arena, most strikingly by defining a 'right to work' (Hobhouse, 1964, p. 83). The initial interventions of the Liberal Government of 1905 were eventually extended to cover the full range of freedoms implied in Beveridge's famous image of the five giants from whom citizens could legitimately expect the State to deliver them: want, disease, ignorance, squalor and idleness. Positive liberalism of this kind has accepted that the provision of welfare will be costly and require the creation of new executive agencies to oversee and deliver new services. This, in turn, will involve some element of direct intervention by the State in the mechanisms of the market, of the kind proposed by J.M. Keynes, most distinguished of the Liberal theorists of the interwar period.

The problems associated with the growth of bureaucracy produced by an expansion of the responsibilities of the State are met by the assumption that bureaucracies will be staffed by public servants whose probity, efficiency and lack of interest in personal reward will guarantee the delivery of an equitable and cost-effective service. If this should not suffice, the link is made with democracy and the forms of oversight that the political system will provide. In order that liberty shall remain a central feature of such a system, it is essential that the element of choice should be preserved; most of those associated with this line of approach would see the market as the main device for achieving that outcome, provided that all consumers are equipped with the means of making unconstrained choices. The State's task is to ensure, through appropriate interventions – management of demand in the economy as a whole, redistribution of income and support for individuals in need – that this is the case. Tony Crosland, whose robust defence of consumer preference has been overshadowed by his misreading (subsequently corrected) of the prospects for sustained economic growth was one of the most prominent of postwar democratic socialists to take this view; though to him, as to most of those who accepted the mixed economy, equality was an even more significant objective.

The 'strategy of equality' (the phrase is originally R.H. Tawney's) necessarily implies a strong – indeed, a central – role for the State, though it does not prescribe the form that this role should take. The spectrum of views among those that endorse this value is therefore narrower than in the case of liberty. To implement the strategy of equality requires redistribution of material resources and reallocation of power. The forms of intervention required therefore extend across economic and social policies, and beyond the limits of welfare policies in the strict construction of that term. It also follows that its advocates accept the legitimacy of adopting policy objectives which if implemented may adversely affect the interests of some individual members of society.

For its critics, the 'strategy of equality' is by its nature coercive and therefore best pursued in state socialist societies, where problems of consent and consistency with law and custom do not arise – or at least not in a form that need immediately concern those who exercise power in such societies. However, as has been frequently observed, these societies in fact moved only very unevenly in the direction of greater equality. Many of them have preserved both material privileges for a defined elite (the *nomenklatura* in the former USSR, for example) and their transmission between generations.

To its defenders, the strategy of equality rests upon consent, expressed in the free exercise of choice through the democratic political system. The ballot box legitimates this approach, which does not require the explicit consent of all those likely to be affected. Nor does it demand for its implementation (its defenders maintain) the introduction of a full-blooded command economy. However, they accept that it is difficult to conceive of a fully egalitarian society in which the market plays a decisive role in the allocation of resources. In most advanced industrial societies that have consciously attempted to achieve greater equality, in peacetime circumstances (the conspicuous exception is the United States), the approach rests on a compromise in which the State's role is to exercise some kind of direction over the economy and the general pattern of distribution of resources; but scope is left for individual citizens to exercise choice over the way in which they satisfy their individual preferences for goods and services.

Such a compromise implies continued tension between the goals of equality and those of liberty. The importance of the general adoption of the Keynesian approach to the management of the economy after the Second World War was that it appeared to offer the means of resolving these tensions by providing the guarantee of additional resources which would enable redistribution to take place without tears, because without losers. In order to secure this happy outcome, the State coopts into partnership representatives of the other main centres of power in the economy – the employers' organisations and the trade unions – with whom the distribution of these additional resources can be negotiated. The deal is blessed by the middle classes, who often stand to make more substantial gains from the settlement than those for whose benefit it is ostensibly intended. The introduction of this form of solution, collectively known as 'corporatism', has been a feature of several postwar welfare regimes, although compared with those in other European countries the British form was uncompleted and relatively inchoate (Middlemas, 1979; Mishra, 1984). The impermanence of this solution became clear as soon as the additional resources ceased to be automatically available and no 'dividend of growth' was available for distribution. Potential losers, especially in the middle class, became real ones, and dug their heels in. Taxpayers' (and ratepayers') revolts became a feature of the politics of many Western countries in the course of the 1970s, sometimes leading to the creation of new political groupings, sometimes expressed through existing ones. The ratchet of increased demands based on trying to keep up with past expectations produced pressures that severely damaged the electoral chances of social democratic governments in a whole series of European countries as social solidarity based on stability and prosperity was replaced by a struggle to satisfy individual needs.

Implementing any form of strategy of social equality raises other problems. Apart from the difficulties of implementation, there are issues of definition: establishing precisely what the objective of equality means in practice. The two are bound up together; rhetorical cloudiness about equality has opened those programmes that have been introduced to secure it to damaging criticisms about both their goals and their performance. On the weakest definition, what is being sought is equality of esteem: the style of society is egalitarian, and status within it is not directly related to the possession of material resources. Japan is an example of a society where prestige is ostensibly linked to age and seniority. It is not difficult to think of other societies that approximate to this definition – Australia, and in some respects the United States – which at the same time tolerate a wide degree of inequality between classes, ethnic groups and genders. These societies also place substantial emphasis on individual self-respect; and couple this with an emphasis on the importance of equality of opportunity, which is perceived as distributing life-chances evenly throughout society, regardless of class background. In the form advanced by the sociologist Michael Novak, the distinguishing feature of liberal capitalism as exemplified in American society is that any native-born American can legitimately aspire to become President, regardless of background or ability (a proposition whose validity Americans amply proved in electing Ronald Reagan twice to that office).

A stronger approach to equality of opportunity is one that attempts to equalise resources as between different sectors of society, variously defined; this approach, unlike the earlier example, requires substantial administrative intervention by government. One major difficulty here is that more even distribution of resources is no guarantee that they will be effectively used, perhaps as a result of incapacity or through lack of motivation. The strongest definition of equality requires parity of outcome, reflected in access to goods and services and – perhaps most important of all – in power. This is the definition of equality that has attracted particularly strong criticism recently, both on the grounds that it involves illegitimate coercion to an extent that is inconsistent with freedom of choice, and because it implies an unacceptable degree of paternalism on the part of the State as the agency responsible for implementation in restricting individual choice.

The case of education is often cited as an example of an area where a deliberate attempt at social engineering through uniform provision by the State has, in Britain at least, apparently failed to achieve the objectives set by its advocates, having proved neither effective in improving standards nor redistributive, since the middle classes proved to be disproportionately highly represented among those who gained from State investment (Le Grand, 1982). In addition, egalitarianism tends to be centralising; the State claims the right, on behalf of the citizen body as a whole (sometimes described as 'the community') to redistribute resources according to general principles decided at the centre. The outcomes of the process may well have disproportionately severe consequences for particular localities and individuals; yet in most instances these localities or people do not have the right to opt out of the system that produced such consequences. In Albert Hirschman's distinction, they do not enjoy the right of 'exit', or it is only available on financially unfavourable terms; their remedy lies only in the exercise of 'voice' and this may be of limited use (Hirschman, 1970).

The issue of equality arises with particular force in the case of groups that have suffered the consequences of past unequal treatment, on grounds of race, class, religion or gender. In particular, feminist critics have argued that the structure of the postwar Welfare State contains built-in discrimination against women, based on illegitimate assumptions about their role in providing welfare and the terms on which they are prepared to provide it – the 'compulsory altruism' that the State requires of women (Land and Rose, 1985). More recently, the exposure of the extent of persistent discrimination on racial grounds has led to the introduction of a series of measures designed to eradicate inequalities of treatment (Brown, 1985). If these past negative discriminations are to be corrected, it is argued, positive action in favour of those groups suffering from the effects of historical burdens must form part of any egalitarian programme – 'equal opportunities policies', in the terms employed in contemporary social policy. These programmes are also likely to give rise to conflicts, to the extent that they redistribute goods (jobs, houses, places in higher education) for which there is strong competition, on the basis of values that may not be universally accepted (Edwards, 1986).

An alternative way of formulating the goal of equality is in terms of a basis for the membership of civil society; and welfare is seen as a binding force securing this common membership by conferring rights: rights to health care, education and relief from poverty and more controversially the right to work. The badge of citizenship, implying entitlement to this range of benefits is available universally and unconditionally to all citizens regardless of circumstances or desert. To some egalitarians welfare should also be available on the same basis to newcomers to the society, even if they are not yet recognised as full members of it. Beveridge conceived his scheme of social insurance, based on flat-rate contributions from all citizens, whatever their means, in these terms; and used it as the basis for some of his highest-flown rhetoric about a nation standing together in social solidarity, in the face of common dangers. To achieve the transfer of this conception of welfare as the integrating force holding society together to a peacetime environment was one of the main objectives of social policy in Britain immediately after the war. Equality of sacrifice in the common cause was one of the most frequently repeated (but diminishingly effective) slogans designed to secure that objective.

Common membership of society can be defined in other ways, by the possession of other rights; and the most significant of these in a modern democracy is the right to vote. All States exclude minors (variously defined). Some European statelets have only recently conceded the vote to women; others extend the disqualification to adults of particular origins or beliefs. Most exclude immigrants, either completely or selectively, from participation in the electoral process; and some Eastern Europe States newly restored to independence have excluded from the franchise residents with different ethnic, cultural, linguistic or religious affiliations. Others will deprive those convicted of criminal offences of the right to vote ('loss of civil rights'); the British remove it from those elevated to the peerage.

The vote is also potentially important in helping to decide the direction of welfare policies by giving the citizens the opportunity to articulate their demands ('voice' in Hirschman's definition). Democracy therefore has a potentially crucial relationship to welfare, in providing a means to signal preferences and make choices as parties are encouraged to offer the electorate competing social policies. The significance of this role has increased as public spending on welfare has grown both in absolute terms and as a proportion of total expenditure. But in practice the scope for exercising choices is limited, not just by exclusions from the electoral register or by reluctance (for whatever reason) to use the vote but also by the ways in which most Western political systems present them to the voter. The opportunity to choose comes irregularly, and the decisions are blurred and overlaid by the way in which issues are presented, through party programmes put forward on a simple, take-it-or-leave-it basis, and the differential weight attached to individual votes under many voting systems. The capacity of a parliamentary system to promote free discussion of alternative policies by elected representatives is also limited by the adversarial style of political discussion in Britain and by the domination here of the legislature by the executive.

In theory, the weaknesses of representative democracy can be at least partly remedied by extending the opportunities for the exercise of power through creating new institutions and extending or modifying existing ones to provide for greater citizen participation and control. But from the outset, the Welfare State in Britain has excluded all consumer and many producer groups from any significant share in decision-taking; this exclusion was based on the premise that parliamentary scrutiny would provide the necessary safeguards – Aneurin Bevan's assumption in the case of the health service. In practice, decisions have increasingly come to be taken outside the parliamentary forum by representatives of interests not subject to election, in arenas to which the individual citizen has no access.

Those now arguing for giving greater importance to democracy as a value in the provision of welfare are drawn both from among those collectivists who have become disillusioned by the deficiencies of the machinery created for the delivery of welfare and those to whom State-run mechanisms never held out any promise of providing a service that would be sensitive to the needs of individuals and adaptable to their preferences. The coincidence between the criticisms advanced by these two groups does not, however, extend to a corresponding agreement about the remedies on offer.

The result of these criticisms has been a shift towards closer scrutiny of welfare policies and a closer focus on how they are implemented at local level and increasing the accountability of those that deliver them. Increased accountability is held out as one of the chief rewards for moving towards a participatory model of democracy, linked with decentralisation, in the sense of devolving responsibility for delivery of services to the lowest efficient level. However, decentralised democracy has also been harshly criticised for obstructing the effective working of the machinery of government. The potential opposition that these criticisms reflect between the values of democracy and efficiency is another of the key pressure points in the politics of welfare.

Efficiency as a distinct objective is easy to caricature, but difficult to ignore. To the extent that it implies a testing of the effectiveness of alternative forms of welfare that are on offer and reaching a judgment between them based on objective criteria it is, in theory, neutral as between different concepts and the values upon which they are based. Measurement is a technical matter, innocent of any political intent. But in practice, this appearance of impartiality dissolves as as soon as choices are made about the criteria upon which judgments should be based and the way in which they are to be employed.

Tests of efficiency have had a long, and often uneasy relationship, not just with welfare policies but with the activities of government in general. This history stretches back to Bentham and the utilitarians at the beginning of the nineteenth century and continues through the work of the neo-classical economists to the application in the late twentieth century of new techniques of measurement and evaluation made possible by the introduction of new methods of collecting, storing and analysing data.

In principle, these developments open the way to treating welfare like any other commodity, in terms of marketing, delivery, profitability and consumer response. In practice, the complexities of the 'mixed economy' of welfare and the constraints that the limits on access and rationing of resources impose upon the range of choices open to the consumer make it difficult to employ abstract concepts of consumer behaviour developed in the context of a market economy which permits (in theory at least) complete freedom of choice.

Financial measures offer what seem superficially to be viable alternative means of measuring the costs and consequences of policy in a form that has objective validity and allows comparisons to be made between different forms of service and situation and assessments undertaken of the value obtained for investment of public money. Tests of cost-effectiveness have accordingly been applied to welfare services in most developed countries, but with mixed results. The problems of making every item 'visible' and devising some means of weighing non-financial costs – so important in a system where informal care makes up such a significant proportion of welfare – make clear-cut comparisons difficult to achieve (Glennerster, 1992).

Nevertheless, there has been much discussion recently in Britain about efficient financial management in government. The Welfare State has been prominent in this debate, largely because it is seen as a 'soft target' for economies in public expenditure, with the implication that much expenditure is potentially wasteful and ineffective, because insufficiently precisely focused (Lilley, 1993). Recent examples of attempts to address these issues are the search for excellence in management, as reflected in the use of new techniques of financial control – the creation of cost centres with identifiable budgets and clear tests of performance – and the introduction of new styles of management modelled on practice in the private sector, most conspicuously in the case of the 'internal markets' created in the National Health Service. The introduction of such techniques rests on the assumption that fixed goals covering a significantly long period of time can be set and agreed and that the effectiveness with which these policies are then implemented can be treated as a legitimate outcome in itself.

As a rationale for value-free professionalism, this approach has a long pedigree, and by no means all on one side of the political spectrum. However, the question remains: is the goal of 'pure' efficiency consistent with democratic accountability? In certain circumstances, it may also legitimately be asked whether efficiency is always wholly consistent with liberty. If the use of new information technology makes the process of administration more 'transparent' (to use a phrase currently popular with politicians) we may not like what we can now see. Much of the suspicion in England of the State's role during the early stages of the establishment of the Welfare State was due to concern felt about what was seen as regimentation practised by continental bureaucracies and the detailed control that some European States appeared to be able to exercise over the lives of their citizens. This suspicion was common to all social classes – not wholly without justification – and has arguably never fully disappeared.

Clearly, in setting out to devise an ideal system for the delivery of welfare in a modern society, the choice of the major values that the system should be designed to reflect ought to be a crucial factor in determining which functions the State performs, and how it performs them, and which are reserved for the private or informal sectors of welfare. In practice, however, no system is ever designed from scratch; and the choice between different priorities will never be clear-cut, even in abstract terms. Some of the broad goals set for policy will appear at certain times to be in conflict; at other moments they will be easy to reconcile. Some circumstances demand the imposition of particular priorities (an extreme example is health measures in an epidemic); others permit the luxury of debate and even experiment before settling on what appears to be the most favourable outcome. But eventually, in Pierre Mendès-France's phrase, 'to govern is to choose'. Most postwar administrations have chosen to tilt one way or another between the four main options for welfare policy – some stressing equality, others liberty. Their successors of whatever political colour are likely to have to concern themselves more closely with the incipient conflict between democracy and efficiency and ways in which they can best be reconciled.

FROM PRINCIPLES TO PRACTICE

The relationship of broad concepts like those discussed in the previous section to action is always likely to be controversial. Keynes once remarked that 'practical men, who believe themselves to be quite exempt from any intellectual influences, are usually the slaves of some defunct economist' (Keynes, 1936, p. 383). The degree and form of their servitude is, however, often quite hard to pin down. Examples of the straightforward translation of ideas from abstract formulation at the philosopher's desk to the statute book are hard to come by. Moreover, by no means all the crucial animating concepts are the outcome of profound philosophical consideration. In many cases (some would say almost all) it is the immediate material circumstances that set off the process and determine its outcome. Cause and effect are frequently inextricably tangled, with challenges to the existing system producing responses within it and correction of abuses generating their own unintended consequences.

In the simplest of terms, the events that will determine whether new policies can be introduced and what form and direction they will take can be located in four different spheres of activity: the economic, the political, the administrative and the personal. All of these interconnect; and in each of them powerful influences are already at work, deriving chiefly from the distribution of power and authority within them. All require some further elucidation.

Consistency with the form in which the economy of the society in question is organised is the most obvious example. Traditionally, Marxist doctrine has suggested that this alone will be sufficient to determine whether welfare policies are introduced at a particular time or in a particular place. Capital will determine whether the existence of such programmes is consistent with its interests; and then employ the State apparatus to introduce them or frustrate their introduction, as required. Similarly, the working class will make its own appraisal and respond according to its own class interests. Such a view rests on concepts of State and class that would not now command widespread acceptance either within or outside Marxism. It also faces the difficulty that in real life spokesmen for capital have often vigorously resisted the introduction and maintenance of programmes that should 'objectively' work to their own advantage, just as workers have campaigned to secure the benefits that in theory tie them even more tightly to serving the interests of the ruling class.

Nevertheless, what happens in the economy is self-evidently crucial to the future of welfare, in the sense that the welfare of individuals must always be directly affected by the amount of wealth generated within a society and the way in which it is distributed. What is in dispute is not the significance of the economic system but the extent to which the mode of production and the material outcomes that derive from it are in themselves decisive. An alternative view is that the linkages are less direct and in some circumstances the economy forms a distinct subsystem within which new developments occur and individuals act according to principles that do not necessarily have universal applicability. This subsystem interacts with other systems, notably the political; but their relationship changes according to the pressure of changing circumstances, most obviously when political power changes hands.

There is also the problem that national economies cannot be viewed in isolation. The form of their connections with the international economy and the degree of their dependence upon other economies with which they are linked can be crucial, as, for example, in the case of nations with a long history of trading relations with other countries, or former colonies. The sociologist Peter Townsend's comment that there cannot logically be social policies that are independent of economic policy must in any event hold true; but the form of the connection often remains problematic and the consequences for welfare policies not always easy to establish.

The political system is likely to be a crucial variable in determining the form in which welfare programmes are designed and delivered. Democratic systems, as has already been implied, impose constraints, but also provide opportunities that were not open to citizens in those totalitarian societies where central planning defined not only needs but the ways in which they are to be satisfied. Issues of choice and cost can be debated within a parliamentary system; but on terms that may distort rather than clarify. The emergence of other channels through which demands for public welfare provision can be articulated is a factor common to most modern democracies. Politicians' perception of what is desirable (or possible) may be fundamentally affected by the ways in which these demands are stated, through campaigns in the press, by direct approaches from constituents, through the reflection of public concern in opinion polls, or by a combination of all of these.

Any expansion of public provision will necessarily have administrative implications. These are also likely to affect the choice of means for the implementation of new policies and the extent and level of provision made. At a period of perceived shortage of resources, these factors are prone to lead to compromises and result in distortions in new programmes. Even when resources are not under immediate pressure, an accumulation of new initiatives can lead to overload upon the machinery of government and those who operate it. The ready availability of information to government in far greater quantity (though not necessarily better quality) than ever before can also bring additional pressure to bear. The involvement of powerful interest groups, like the employees of the State welfare system organised in trade unions to protect their members' interests, is liable to add edge to the resulting conflicts.

Such developments may tend to exclude – even alienate – the private citizen. This is something of a paradox, since the individual has always been central to the provision of welfare. Despite the steady increase over most of the twentieth century in the level of intervention by the State, there has always been, and continues to be in all Western societies, a vast amount of care not provided through any formal arrangements. This is given within the immediate family, across the extended family, in the locality or neighbourhood, and through mutual exchange in any one of the variety of different worlds through which people move in the course of a normal lifetime – through education, at work, in religious organisations and at leisure. Such care is virtually impossible to quantify and fatally easy to sentimentalise; but taken as a whole, it represents a vast range of activity. Yet to attempt to trap it in the net of formal analysis by treating it on the same basis as the care provided by State institutions, or those run by voluntary organisations or for profit is to risk begging a whole number of questions. For example, how far is such care always provided voluntarily? How often is there some form of coercion at work, in which the role of carer is assigned, however subtly and indirectly, rather than chosen? And how far is such care readily available to those outside the magic circle of kin, neighbour or co-religionist? Where, especially now, with the fading of the religious impulse, are strangers and their needs?

Richard Titmuss argued from the example of blood donors that the impulse to aid those in need extended even to unseen strangers, creating what he called the 'gift relationship' between donor and recipient (Titmuss, 1970). Furthermore, he suggested that such a means of supplying blood was more efficient than the alternative of purchasing it on the market, assessed in terms either of quality or cost. Perhaps not surprisingly, this conclusion earned him the epithet 'naive' from economists who disliked his conclusions. Another way of explaining the persistence of these forms of altruistic behaviour, 'irrational' in economists' terms because bringing no measurable material advantage, is to view them as evidence of the continued existence of what Beveridge once called a 'welfare society' – a term he chose to encapsulate his concept of a society in which welfare provision was shared between State, voluntary bodies and individuals and mutual aid was positively reinforced by such collaboration (Watson, 1957, p. 19).

This raises the issue of the general acceptance of the form that welfare services take and their consistency with values to which individual citizens attach particular significance – freedom from want, privacy, control over their own lives and possessions, family ties, friendships and enthusiasms. It is not only extreme libertarians who feel that the intrusion of the State into the domestic sphere, where disputes have customarily been mediated informally, cannot always be justified; nor is it only dogmatic collectivists who on encountering the latest example of abuse of the defenceless (usually women or children) in that sphere by those who possess power there (almost invariably men) conclude that the Government must do something about it. This debate, too, has been sharpened by the development of the feminist critique of the way in which welfare policies have exploited women without protecting them from abuses and by evidence of the ways in which these policies have excluded the legitimate claims of ethnic and religious minorities to full and equal access to services (witness the State's hesitancy in responding to Muslim parents' clear preferences over the education of their daughters).

So in order to understand why welfare policies have taken the form that they did and changed in the ways and at the times that they have, some understanding of the structures and processes at work as well as the basic concepts that lie behind the details of new policies is required. The interplay between them is best illustrated in action; in the next chapter, a brief (because selective) narrative account of the development of welfare policies is set out, concentrating on those episodes which most clearly illuminate this interplay.

2

KEYNES AND AFTER

The influence of Great Britain as a pioneer of political liberty has not been small; but the question which today, next to international anarchy, is the worm at the root, is less political than social. This country, if it grapples with it boldly and in time, might also lead the world some steps along the road to social justice.

R.H. Tawney, 1941, quoted in E.F.M. Durbin, *What Have We To Defend?*, 1942.

Reviewing as a 'croaking Cassandra' the political and intellectual dislocations of the period between the two World Wars, J.M. Keynes proclaimed the final death of *laissez-faire*; only to add in the same breath that, had he been born 100 years earlier, he, too, would undoubtedly have subscribed to that same doctrine.

This shrewd hit at those who take events and sentiments and judge them out of their context in time could be turned on Keynes himself, since the ghost of *laissez-faire* now walks again, to all appearances restored to rude health. But the general point stands: most investigators of policy are intellectual truffle-hunters and, faced with a past in which ideas and values pass in and out of fashion, will try to break into the cycle at the point at which the predominant ideas match most closely the temper of their own times. Until recently, belief in a secular myth of progress has been the strongest common value; hence the persistent interest in exploring the origins of the twentieth-century Welfare State in the reforms of the Liberal Government immediately before the First World War. But other students of social policy are temperamentally Jacobite: they pine (or in some instances plan) for the restoration of past glorious causes that have gone down to undeserved defeat and seize upon

22

evidence from the past to substantiate those hopes. In each case, the easiest of all ways of putting flesh on the bones of these aspirations is by seizing upon some individual who most aptly incarnates them in his or her life and work, so that, though long dead, they can be carried like El Cid into battle at the head of the army of the just.

Selection of a point of departure is therefore a political act in itself; but, given the present concern – both in government and outside – with the value of liberty, a possible starting point is the mid-nineteenth century, when attachment to that value and a constellation of individualistic beliefs associated with it was at an apogee. However, a major difficulty about seeking the roots of current political debates on social policy in Victorian England is the vast gulf that separates our society from theirs – not merely in time, but also materially and culturally. The central part played by religion in political and social life, the absence of a developed State apparatus, the limitations on the franchise, the undeveloped condition of the labour movement, the state of relations between men and women, both inside and outside the family, changing attitudes towards work in a newly industrialised society: the list could be extended almost indefinitely. Perhaps the most significant example of all, from the social policy perspective, is the situation of the poor: anatomised in the copious Blue Books of the period, dramatised by the great mid-Victorian novelists, preached upon by moralists, religious and secular and melodramatised in the case of the 'dangerous classes' on the margin of society. While there are fascinating (and intensely depressing) parallels to be drawn with current experiences of poverty, the circumstances of the Victorian poor bear little direct resemblance to those of our own time.

Hence, while it is not difficult to trace in mid-Victorian debates the lineal ancestors of some of the views now being expressed in discussions about the future of welfare in the late twentieth century, their applicability to the detailed issues with which we are now concerned is highly dubious. There is an additional difficulty, in that most of those most concerned with the 'Condition of England Question' (as that generation of Victorians termed it) were out of sympathy with the spirit of the age, and sought their own models for social change elsewhere: Carlyle in an idealised past, Ruskin in the future – where he imagined an expansion in the State's role 'which we can hardly dream of'– and William Morris in a fantasy Utopia which he aptly christened Nowhere. Of course there were the great figures whose analyses transcend the limitations of time and culture: Adam Smith in a previous generation and

Karl Marx in the mid-Victorian period itself. But Smith and Marx were mainly concerned with the construction of intellectual systems, rather than with their immediate applications.

In this sense, John Stuart Mill would be a more appropriate choice as a first reference point, because his own career took him between the worlds of theory and action – he served both as senior civil servant and as an MP, in which capacity he demonstrated conspicuous moral courage in advocating unpopular causes – and because he clearly still speaks directly to participants in the current debate with a wide variety of views: feminists, Socialists and neo-Liberals. His reputation as a man prepared to think through difficult issues in public and in terms accessible to the public earned him the nickname of the 'Purveyor-General of Thought'. Many of the questions in which he interested himself are still of direct contemporary relevance. Among the dilemmas which he anatomised were the tensions between the efficient conduct of the business of the State by a politically sophisticated elite and the need for the wider involvement of citizens (among whom he specifically included women) in the business of government; the definition of individual rights and their defence against the tyranny of majorities; and the virtues and limitations of representative democracy as a system of government. A recurrent theme, the importance of securing individual liberty at a time when the claims of the State are constantly expanding, leads to the well-known conclusion to *Liberty*:

> A State which dwarfs its men, in order that they may be more docile instruments in its hands, even for beneficial purposes, will find that with small men no great thing can really be accomplished; and that the perfection of machinery to which it has sacrificed everything will in the end avail it nothing. (quoted in Ryan, 1974, p. 142)

It might be objected that although the positions defined by Mill on these issues are of great interest in terms of intellectual history, their immediate application in present debates on welfare is limited. Nevertheless, the successive modifications of Liberal theories and attitudes towards State intervention exemplified in Mill's own work were demonstrably influential in determining the subsequent direction of social policy – witness Herbert Spencer's anguished attempt to reassert the values of classical liberalism – in his *The Man versus The State* as against the increasingly active role played by Liberal Governments from the 1870s onwards. This role was underwritten by the Oxford idealists – T.H. Green and his immediate followers, who Anglicised Hegel's concepts of the functions of the State and linked them to notions of social service to help create an intellectual climate favorable to the interventionist social policy of the 1906 Liberal Government. L.T. Hobhouse's elegant synthesis of old and new concepts of liberty, *Liberalism* (1911), appeared at the point when that government had embarked upon the programme of new initiatives generally taken to mark the first appearance of State welfare in its modern form and contains almost the complete twentieth-century social policy agenda, in a form and in terms still immediately recognisable to a late twentieth-century reader.

To point to the connection between trends in intellectual debate and developments in social policy is not necessarily to establish cause and effect. Most commentaries on the politics of welfare prefer to explore these connections through specific issues: poverty, for reasons already implied, being the strongest candidate. The long debate on the causes and consequences of poverty in our society is a tale that has often been told (e.g. Himmelfarb, 1984). The remedies adopted at various stages in the evolution of policy, most conspicuously the reform of the Poor Law in the early nineteenth century under the influence of Benthamite utilitarianism, also left permanent marks upon the machinery of government and attitudes towards it. To the nineteenth century's concern to find means to identify and reward desert among the poor, to stimulate self-help and discourage idleness and profligacy the early twentieth century added a concern with national efficiency. Beatrice Webb's attempt as a member of the Royal Commission on the Poor Law to link the two themes and by drawing on new techniques for the scientific investigation of poverty developed by Booth and Rowntree provide the basis for a new and more logical structure failed in its immediate objectives; but the Webbs' Minority Report remained an influential statement of the priorities for State action. At the same time, the accumulation of evidence about the impact of unemployment upon the condition of the working class pointed to another area in which State intervention (once unthinkable) might now be legitimate. The young William Beveridge makes his first appearance on the social policy scene as author of studies of unemployment and Churchill's adviser on the creation of the labour exchange system.

In the expansion of the State's functions launched by the Liberal Government and ranging from State pensions to health and unemployment insurance the position of the working class remained equivocal. Reservations about the content and objectives of State welfare policies, based on both experience of the workings of the Poor Law and equivalent schemes in other countries were frequently expressed by Labour spokesmen during the passage of legislation. With the expansion of the franchise, the working class had acquired a foothold in the political process and could express views on the issues of poverty through the ballot box and their elected representatives, in the active and expanding trade union movement and the impressive range of institutions of self-help and mutual aid established by the working class itself. This change in the status of workers from objects of debate to participants, however marginal to the centres of real power, altered the character of the debate itself. The Webbs were ambivalent about this development. Beatrice had earlier confided to her diary:

> We are not in favour of the cruder forms of democracy. And we do believe in expenditure on services that will benefit other classes besides the working class and which will open the way to working men to become fit to govern, not simply to represent their own class; and we are in favour of economy as well as expenditure. (15 March 1903; N. and J. MacKenzie, 1983)

Questions thrown up by Britain's erratic progress towards mass democracy went far wider than the issues of welfare, although these raised in particularly sharp form the implications of the participation of the beneficiaries of State action in the democratic process. The relationship between economic and political democracy and the form in which the potential power of the expanded electorate might be exercised preoccupied politicians of all parties and led to the appearance soon after the First World War of the first tentative attempts at informal reconciliation of the interests of the competing classes in the State – an embryonic corporatism, based in part upon the common sacrifices made during the course of that war (Middlemas, 1979).

These initiatives are not only of importance in themselves but reflect one persistent tendency among politicians in their approach to social policy, towards the collective identification of common problems, for which mutually acceptable solutions can be devised, capable of being implemented by non-political experts. The supreme example at this period is the Webbs' constitutional proposals for a separation of powers within the legislature to permit social and economic issues to be examined under a committee system constructed along the lines developed by the London County Council, free from the distractions of adversarial politics (Webb and Webb, 1920). In the event, the identification of Lloyd George, who wished to carry consensus to the point of creating a new centre party, with this approach to postwar problems helped to damn it. After the collapse of his Coalition Government in 1922 the country relapsed into a vain attempt to recapture the lost glories of the pre-war world, symbolised by the decision of Winston Churchill, as Conservative Chancellor, to return the pound to the Gold Standard. But even before this, the Government's flirtation with social reform had been interrupted by a sharp recession, to which it responded with drastic cuts in social programmes, thereby illustrating another characteristic of twentieth-century governments in Britain. This has been to regard social policy as necessarily subordinate to economic priorities – in this instance despite the acute anxiety generated in the Cabinet by fears that the British working class might be on the point of being infected by the bacillus of Soviet revolution.

The failure of the orthodox economic policies pursued by successive Chancellors from both parties throughout the 1920s to eliminate unemployment placed a substantial strain on the economy, through the difficulty of maintaining payments under the unemployment insurance provisions introduced during the brief interlude of radicalism immediately after the war. It also placed the unemployment issue back in the centre of political debate, and in a disconcerting way, since it was evident that most of those who were out of work could not be categorised either as unenterprising or deliberately idle. The failure of the labour market to 'clear' and thereby spontaneously bring down the level of unemployment, as classical economic theory held that it should, presented governments with a dilemma to which the Treasury had no satisfactory answer. The departmental view, as articulated by Winston Churchill as Chancellor, was that 'whatever might be the political or social advantages, very little additional employment can, in fact, and as a general rule, be created by State borrowing and expenditure' (Winch, 1972, p. 118). To an increasingly wide range of people, this response was no longer convincing.

Among the most vigorous critics of the conventional wisdom was Keynes. Even twenty years ago, the publication of his *General Theory* in February 1936 could still be seen as the decisive turning point, the moment when the means became available for resolving the problem of unemployment – the issue that dominated the domestic political arena throughout the interwar period. Although the State apparatus did not then possess the powers or the analytical capacity to implement his proposals in full, and although the National Government elected in 1931 stubbornly refused to accept the logic of his case, the approaching war provided the opportunity for Keynes to translate theory into practice and (so the argument ran) illustrate the truth of his own proposition that there is nothing so powerful as an idea whose time has come. Now even that patch of apparently firm ground has begun to quake, as the validity of both Keynes' analysis and his solutions have come under question. Nevertheless, the ideas that he generated and helped both to disseminate and eventually to implement, and the connections made between them and the concurrent proposals for the relief of poverty and provision of adequate social services have had a fundamental influence in shaping the world that emerged from the Second World War. Since this is in most crucial respects still the world in which we now live it is essential to explore in further detail the political context in which those ideas were first advanced and tested.

My narrative proper therefore begins at the beginning of the 1930s, the 'Devil's decade'; it divides into four chronologically defined sections (recognising the essential artificiality of all such arbitrary boundaries), and takes the story up to the fundamental reassessment of the system of welfare that began a decade ago and is still under way.

FORWARD FROM LIBERALISM

In September 1931, the minority Labour Government of Ramsay MacDonald was bundled out of office after the Cabinet had hesitated to make the cuts in public expenditure – and in particular in payments to the rapidly growing numbers of unemployed – that the Prime Minister and his Chancellor, Philip Snowden, believed were necessary to restore confidence in the currency and the British economy. The Government's fall was compared satirically by Oswald Mosley, who had briefly been a member of it, to a Salvation Army taking to its heels on the Day of Judgment. The comparison, though sharp, is inept; the Labour Party had no Holy Writ to which reference could be made in addressing the complex series of problems that had arisen as a result of the failure of the British economy to recover from the traumas of the First World War. The patchwork of economic and social policies that had been stitched together over the course of the previous decade was clearly inadequate; yet, unlike its principal rivals on the left, the Labour Party had no conception of how the powers of the State, substantially increased as a result of the war, could be put to constructive use.

In the search for new ideas, the dominant political figure was Lloyd George. In government, a decade earlier, he had been responsible for a number of potentially important measures; ambitious plans for postwar reconstruction that included the creation of a Ministry of Health, the expansion of unemployment insurance and the beginnings of a systematic public sector housing programme. These programmes had been substantially modified or abandoned before he left office; but in opposition Lloyd George recovered his radical instincts and among other initiatives launched an important inquiry into the state of the nation, appointing to it not only some older Liberals with a long-standing concern with social issues, like C.F.G. Masterman and Seebohm Rowntree, but younger critics, including Maynard Keynes. The report of the inquiry (which came to be known as the Liberal Yellow Book) bore a clear impress of Keynes' thinking. In the introduction to the report the notion that liberalism and State action cannot be reconciled is vigorously disputed (Liberal Industrial Inquiry, 1928, p. xxi). In the main body an ambitious set of proposals for intervention in the economy is laid out, including substantial programmes of contra-cyclical public works, designed to stimulate economic revival and provide an efficient modern infrastructure of communications and public utilities (Skidelsky, 1992). Widely distributed in an alternative popular format as *We Can Conquer Unemployment* and strongly puffed by Keynes himself and his fellow economist Hubert Henderson, the Lloyd George programme nonetheless failed to convince the electorate, who preferred to install a second minority Labour Government under MacDonald.

The failure of this second Labour Government to make any substantial use of the new ideas about State intervention in the economy, either in the form advanced by Lloyd George, or in the alternative version put forward by Oswald Mosley, led directly to the imposition of a crisis programme of drastic cuts by the National Government that succeeded it, also under MacDonald's leadership. The 'Doctor's mandate' that he had obtained at the general election hastily called in the autumn of 1931 was interpreted as justifying the introduction of measures of strict financial rectitude, in the traditional sense: balanced budgets achieved through substantial cuts in social spending programmes.

Popular support for these measures was greeted with relief by those who believed that a mass electorate could never be persuaded to accept harsh remedies, even at times of economic crisis. The form of the remedies chosen also underlined the status of welfare programmes as potential burdens upon the economy, to be put aside at moments of emergency. The governments of the interwar period, in Bentley Gilbert's phrase, engaged in social politics, but had no social policy, as such (Gilbert, 1970, p. 304). In the aftermath of recovery from the worst effects of the international depression, the National Government did embark on some cautious interventions on both economic and social fronts: Neville Chamberlain, who had undertaken a substantial recasting of the Poor Law under the previous Conservative Government, sanctioned some limited programmes of public works; persistent high rates of unemployment in the North and Scotland were also addressed through a heavily circumscribed regional policy designed to bring industry back to selected 'special areas'. The system of unemployment insurance was also restructured and responsibility vested in a new Unemployment Assistance Board; although benefits were initially set so low that many claimants lost money, even by the stringent standards previously set. The successful revolt against this measure was one of the few substantial rebuffs suffered by the National Government. Despite the rising pressure of protest outside Parliament against its policies, MacDonald's successor, Stanley Baldwin, won an easy victory at the general election held in 1935. Nevertheless, a widespread feeling remained that the Government's policies were inadequate to the scale of the problems that the country still faced (Winch, 1972, p. 79).

Criticisms of the National Government's approach came from a number of different, but overlapping sources. Keynes had set to work to develop the ideas that he had first expressed in the debates of the late 1920s and refined in argument with the Treasury during the Labour Government's period in office. His critique of the inactivity of the Government in the face of the major economic and social problems of the Depression was matched by that of number of active politicians in all parties who were attracted by the notion of economic planning as a systematic and coordinated activity. This group, subsequently christened 'middle opinion', generated an effective propaganda organisation, PEP (Political and Economic Planning) and a manifesto of its own, *The Next Five Years*, published in 1935 and updating and extending the proposals in Lloyd George's Yellow Book. Enthusiasm for planning extended outside the boundaries of this group, to Oswald Mosley on the far right, now well advanced on his descent into fascism and political oblivion, through Harold Macmillan, whose book *The Middle Way* (1938) sums up much of the thinking behind the pressure for more effective State intervention, to John Strachey on the far left, a vigorous and effective polemicist for the Communist Party, although never actually a member. In addition, a number of younger socialist economists, Evan Durbin, Hugh Gaitskell and Douglas Jay, were attempting to construct their own synthesis between the ideas that Keynes was developing, the case for efficiency being made by the planning movement and their own preoccupation with the goal of securing greater equality through redistribution (E. Durbin, 1985).

The various strands interrelated as they developed, while remaining distinct; all those involved looked abroad for models for succesful interventions of the kind which they were advocating: Keynes and many of the enthusiasts for planning to Roosevelt's New Deal; Mosley to Mussolini and the Italian corporate state (which was by then clandestinely supporting his British Union of Fascists); Strachey to the Soviet Union's Five Year Plans and their apparently impressive record of modernisation through State direction – an enthusiasm in which he was (somewhat unexpectedly) joined by Sidney and Beatrice Webb. However, the form of intervention implied differed from one group to another.

Keynes' approach, as it emerged in his *General Theory* (1936), required governments to adopt policies of demand management which reversed conventional assumptions on the role of savings and consumer expenditure in an economic depression. It also challenged the ruling orthodoxies on the toleration of substantial budget deficits and the function of public works and their consequences. But his analysis did not imply a diminished role for the market – rather the contrary. Nor did he envisage the creation of comprehensive planning machinery with detailed responsibilities for direction of the economy (Budd, 1978, p. 35) The advocates of planning were more ambitious. The amorphous character of the movement makes generalisation difficult; but a broad distinction can be made between those, like Macmillan, who were chiefly concerned with planning as a means to achieve rationalisation and modernisation in industry; the social planners of PEP, who were concerned with the inefficiency of the patchwork of services and the consequences for the health of the nation and especially the present and future workforce; and the Socialists who believed that planning would enable them to take control of the economy and achieve a fairer distribution of wealth – the 'social justice and efficiency' which Evan Durbin defined as the essential socialist objectives (1940, p. 32).

The debate about the applications of planning was understandably dominated by unemployment and its impact on the health and welfare of those that had experienced it. However, the patchy recovery achieved by the National Government by the end of the 1930s, which with the help of a substantial programme of rearmament and a consumer boom in private housing reduced unemployment well below the crisis levels of the early part of the decade, did not close this debate. As it turned out, the reluctance of the National Government to adopt the remedies being urged upon it was a temporary, not a permanent check. Many of those involved in formulating these proposals found themselves shortly after the outbreak of the Second World War in a position to reverse the policies that they had criticised. As individuals, many of them were taken into government: Keynes as an adviser at the Treasury, Beveridge (who served during the 1930s as chairman of the Government's advisory committee on the unemployment insurance system) initially at the Ministry of Labour and a whole series of younger economists and academics scattered throughout wartime Whitehall, bringing with them what Keith Middlemas calls the 'sedimentary intellectual deposits' laid down in the pre-war debates.

BEVERIDGE AND BEYOND

The circumstances in which William Beveridge was first entrusted with the task of drawing up a report on Social Insurance and then given what amounted to a free hand to produce it in whatever form he thought fit would hardly have arisen except at a time of national emergency. An urgent diplomatic need had developed to shuffle Beveridge sideways from the Ministry of Labour, where he had the status of a former Permanent Secretary but no substantial job, mainly as a result of the 'pinched distrust' of his minister, Ernest Bevin. This need, combined with the pressure being brought to bear by the TUC on the insurance issue, presented Beveridge with an unexpected opportunity to pull together a whole range of ideas that he had developed for 'all-in' insurance into a single coherent scheme (Thane, 1982, p. 181).

Despite his initial disappointment, Beveridge seized his opportunity and made good use of it. He did not confine himself to the ostensible subject matter of the inquiry, but boldly set out a comprehensive long-term programme for the provision of security against need in all its forms – personified as the five threatening giants: want, disease, ignorance, squalor and idleness – and covering the entire population. To secure this objective, he argued, would require not merely a comprehensive scheme for income maintenance, but also the establishment of a national health service and the maintenance in the immediate postwar period of full employment. To these Beveridge added, as a long-standing supporter, his endorsement of Eleanor Rathbone's lengthy campaign for the provision of family allowances to provide supplementary support for the rearing of children. All these additional elements were fundamental conditions, Beveridge argued, without which his Plan for Social Security could not be implemented.

The Plan itself (Beveridge's own rhetorical capital letter becomes inevitable) would provide a national minimum, set at a subsistence level identified on the basis of the best available research. The benefits that would secure this outcome would derive from flat rate contributions to a compulsory insurance scheme, entitling contributors to equal benefits paid without means test. The scheme would be a national one, organised on a uniform basis without local variation, and administered centrally by Government. This approach eliminated both the private insurance companies and friendly societies which had featured so prominently in Lloyd George's original design and the residual but long-standing link with the locality and its specific circumstances which still survived from the Poor Law.

In putting these proposals forward, Beveridge was very conscious of his own radicalism. In private, he was urged on by his future wife, Jessy Mair, who wrote to him while the Plan was in preparation

> how I hope you are going to be able to preach against all *gangsters* who for their mutual gain support one another in upholding all the rest . . . the whole object of their spider-web of interlocked big banks and big businessmen [is] a frantic effort to maintain their own caste. (Thane, 1982, p. 246)

Thus fortified in his resolve, Beveridge accepted that his proposals would be redistributive – 'the Plan is first and foremost a means of redistributing income' (para 457) and would require an unusually strong degree of collective commitment to common objectives. He also acknowledged the risk inherent in diverting energies at a crucial moment from the paramount priority of winning the war (an anxiety that Churchill, for one, felt very strongly). Hence his famous formulation that implementation of the Plan would provide the basis for a 'British revolution' because it was simultaneously radical and built upon established foundations. At the same time, he was careful to stress that his proposals had been properly costed and based on realistic assumptions – though this did not prevent Treasury officials from expressing deep concern and the Chancellor, Sir Kingsley Wood, comparing expenditure on social security to throwing money 'down the sink' (Lowe, 1993, p. 129).

The strength of the chord that Beveridge struck in his Report surprised him and alarmed the Government. In Parliament, it led to the most substantial revolt of the war against the Churchill Coalition. Outside, 'Beveridge Now' became a popular slogan, taken to the electorate first by a succession of independent by-election candidates, running against the Government under the conditions of the wartime political truce and eventually by a new political grouping, Common Wealth, heir to pre-war 'middle opinion'. The popularity of Beveridge's proposals, as measured both at the ballot-box and in early opinion polls proved too great to resist. Converts were made in all sorts of unlikely quarters; the society host and backbench Conservative MP, 'Chips' Channon wrote in his diary: 'The Beveridge Report has been made public. It will revolutionise life in England – but at first glance I am in favour of it' (Channon, 1967, p. 345). Churchill's first instinctive response, to defer the issue and treat the question as one for long-term consideration as part of the general review of reconstruction policies, had to be set aside. Beveridge's proposals were submitted to scrutiny by a committee of officials, following which the Government issued their own White Paper.

Speaking in the debate on this White Paper in his new capacity as a Liberal MP, Beveridge formally acknowledged paternity of the proposals; but already modifications were being made that compromised the integrity of his original vision of a secure basis for the elimination of want. To the problems that Beveridge had himself experienced in dealing with the question of rents, with their substantial regional variations, and the concessions that he had made to the Treasury's concern about costs (in particular over pensions) the White Paper added further restrictions. These included reductions in the level of benefits (already arguably set too low by Beveridge himself), limitations on the duration for which sickness and unemployment benefit could be drawn and tighter restrictions upon the entitlement of women claimants to benefit, in particular in the circumstances arising from the breakdown of marriage (Field, 1982).

Nevertheless, further concessions were made by the Government to the principle of comprehensive action that Beveridge had proclaimed, despite the anxieties about costs that the Chancellor had set out in the original debate on the Report. The principle of family allowances having being conceded, legislation was introduced and enjoyed a relatively easy passage through Parliament, despite the anxieties of some trade unions about the implications for wage negotiations. Perhaps more significantly, the Government went on to make a formal commitment to the principle of sustaining full employment, in a White Paper of 1944. Although this document enjoys a status almost equivalent to the Beveridge Report as one of the founding documents of the postwar Welfare State, its radicalism stems chiefly from the simple fact that an undertaking had been entered into by the State. In most other respects it is a cautious statement, seeking to reassure its readers through a mixture of exhortation and instruction in the new doctrines of economic management that the means to the desired end of full employment, both intellectual and material, did actually exist. In producing the White Paper, the Government's mind was greatly concentrated by the knowledge that Beveridge himself was in the process of drafting with the help of a number of young economists, all enthusiastic Keynesians, his own unofficial report. This was subsequently published as *Full Employment in a Free Society* (1944) and pushes the argument considerably further than the White Paper's cautious platitudes. Nevertheless, the importance of the public conversion of the Treasury to the new doctrine cannot be understated. A new orthodoxy had to all appearances superseded the classic Treasury view, as Churchill had once expressed it. Not until much later did it become evident that those who had interred the discarded dogma had failed to provide against its resurrection with the traditional stake through the heart.

The change in the intellectual environment during the second half of the war would have been inconceivable without Keynes; not only had he laid out the principles on which the wartime economy could be run, in 'How to pay for the war' (1940) (an approach welcomed by his great intellectual opponent of the interwar years, Hayek), he had helped to ensure that they would be put into effect, as an adviser at the Treasury. In that capacity, he had been an enthusiastic supporter from the outset of Beveridge's proposals, a compliment that Beveridge returned through the endorsement given to Keynes' ideas in *Full Employment in a Free Society*.

A crucial precondition of the effectiveness of policies designed to secure full employment was the participation of the labour movement. This had been secured for the duration of the war through the tripartite alliance between the unions, reinforced by the strength of Ernest Bevin's personal commitment, the employers, who were in the process of

substantially modifying their pre-war scepticism about the implications
of the intervention of the State in the economy, and the Government.
Bevin himself was sceptical about some of the measures of social reform
that the Coalition Government had been asked to adopt. Apart from his
personal dislike of Beveridge, he had substantial doubts about the effects
of the introduction of family allowances. But he was in no doubt that a
bargain had been struck; the unions had been asked to play a full part in
the war effort and they were entitled to their share of the rewards of
victory. As early as July 1940, he told a union audience: 'if our movement
and our class rise with all their energy now and save the people of this
country from disaster, the country will always turn to the people that
saved them' (Middlemas, 1979, p. 275). If the working class wanted full
employment and social reform, they should have it.

The notion of a contract between the nation at war and its rulers was
established early in the conflict and is a pivotal concept in most
subsequent analyses of events, in particular by the official historians,
above all Richard Titmuss (1950). But at the time, there was considerable
scepticism about the capacity of the Government to deliver, especially
after the experience of the failure of reconstruction to provide the
promised rewards after the First World War. As a result, there was at
first also a disposition to pitch the objectives at a more modest level. Evan
Durbin had commented that a future Labour Government would need to
concentrate on economic measures, which in turn implied 'placing power
before benefits – the pill before the jam of social legislation' (Durbin,
1940, p. 298). In his revisionist history of the period, Corelli Barnett has
argued that the subsequent failure to adopt this line had consequences
that were eventually to prove ruinous for the British economy (Barnett,
1986).

Moreover, it is easy to overstate the novelty of the ideas that were
being floated and the extent of the change that they represented.
Middlemas and Thane both argue that the concept of the Welfare State
that emerged from the period of the Coalition Government was
essentially a *rechauffée* of the ideas of the progressive centre of the pre-
war period. Whether more fundamental reforms were ever a practical
possibility remains an open question; the attempts by Common Wealth
and its most prominent spokesman, Sir Richard Acland, to promote the
notion of a fundamental shift in the distribution of power and resources
were sufficiently disturbing, at least in some quarters, for Hayek to
describe him (quite unfairly) as the precursor of an English
totalitarianism. Something of the same anxiety can be detected in

Quintin Hogg's well-known remark in the debate on the Beveridge Report that if the people were not given social reform they would take social revolution. More soberly, the shift in attitude among major employers made explicit at the Nuffield conferences on postwar industrial policy and the progress made behind the scenes by politicians of all parties in the Government's Reconstruction Committee, reveal the extent and strength of the convergence of views on the importance of reform and the acceptance that the responsibility for initiating action lay with the State. The bridge that linked all these separate positions was the concept of the Welfare State, accepted by the victorious end of the war at every level in society as expressing

> something greater than a simple description of the activities of government in respect of one area of its activities. It expressed the desire for a more socially just, more materially equal, more truly democratic society, in short, everything that pre-war society had not been. (Thane, 1982, p. 253)

THE SHORT LIFE OF MR BUTSKELL

In the debate on the King's Speech immediately after the Labour Party's unexpectedly sweeping victory at the general election of 1945, Herbert Morrison attempted to distinguish Labour's policies from those of the preceding Coalition Government. 'Where the coalition failed' he observed, 'was that whilst we could agree to an extraordinary degree on such matters as the Education Bill and the White Papers on social policy, we could not agree when it came to land, economic control and the direction of industry' (Hansard, 21.8.45).

The initial reaction of the Conservatives on finding themselves in opposition was to soft-pedal the extent of division between the parties, tacitly accepting Morrison's contention that there was not much difference in principle between the form in which the Labour Government was carrying out social policy commitments and the Coalition's original conception of priorities in welfare. At the same time, the Opposition felt it necessary to stress the problems likely to be caused by the introduction of new spending programmes, especially in the light of the heavy debts incurred during the war and as a result of the American loan negotiated by Keynes. There was also the pressing problem of meeting the costs of discharging the role of full partner in the Atlantic alliance – what Conservative party documents chose to call the 'patriotic' foreign policy. R.A. Butler, who had been responsible in the Coalition for the passage of a major item of social legislation, the Education Act of 1944, was given responsibility by Churchill for overhauling Conservative policies to cope with this new situation.

Butler describes in his autobiography, *The Art of the Possible* (1971), how he decided to withdraw from outright opposition in Parliament to Labour's social legislation, retaining only, in an appropriately military image, a 'thin line of skirmishers'. Butler's own main energies, and those of the young men he recruited to the Research Department that he established at Conservative Central Office, were devoted to transforming attitudes within his own party. Thus the Conservative spokesman on the National Insurance Bill, Richard Law, dismissed the legislation as a necessary but tedious last step on a journey already completed in all but the final details. 'Now' he said, 'we are getting social security, and I hope that security will become less of an obsession than it has been over the past few years' (Hansard, 6.2.46). The sole exception, although an important one, was the National Health Service legislation; here, the Tories, perceiving the vital interests of the medical profession to be threatened by the form in which Aneurin Bevan had cast the legislation, divided the House and gave support to the attempts of the British Medical Association to undermine his approach. Outmanoeuvred by Bevan's shrewd handling of the profession through generous and well-timed concessions, the Conservatives subsided into grumbling protest about the style in which Bevan conducted the political controversies surrounding the legislation.

The remainder of the wartime Coalition's social programme passed into law with little controversy, despite the changed emphasis in Labour policy on egalitarian objectives and social justice sanctified by a perception – if not the reality – of equality of sacrifice. The immediate postwar atmosphere of planned austerity posed a tactical dilemma for their Conservative opponents. Labour appeared to be open to challenge both on the feasibility and efficiency of the planning process and on the drabness of the style of life that had resulted – a line of attack indicated in two influential works of the period, written from very different perspectives but containing surprisingly similar messages, Orwell's *1984* and Hayek's *The Road to Serfdom* (1944). However, the Government remained obstinately popular. Butler's response was subtle. By copious reference to the past history of his party, its undogmatic character and openness to new ideas, he laid the foundation for a substantial shift in the direction of policy. In essence, this shift brought the Conservatives closely into line with their opponents' position on all the major issues of social policy and most economic priorities besides. As Butler observed in a party document, 'the conception of strong Government policy in economic matters is, I believe, in the very centre of the Conservative tradition. Conservatives were planning before the term entered the vocabulary of political jargon' (Clarke, 1950, p. 48). A strong interventionist role of this kind could even encompass acceptance of a substantial role for the trade unions.

The vehicle by which this conversion was to be achieved was the Industrial Charter, a major statement of Conservative policy presented to – and accepted by – the party conference of 1947. To the extent that there was an internal debate, it was with the traditional right wing of the party, whose spokesman, Sir Herbert Williams, christened the new policy 'pink socialism'. However, the argument was one-sided and the outcome never in serious doubt; the 'New Conservatism' was formally adopted and became the new orthodoxy, an achievement sealed for Butler by the personal presentation by the party leader of a bottle of Pol Roger Champagne, Churchill's favourite. It was at this point if any that the postwar consensus became a reality. What is striking, in retrospect, was the ease with which the transition was managed and the absence of any attempt to articulate a free market critique of the implications of accepting a major role for the State in economic management.

A partisan facade was sustained throughout the period of the Attlee Government, with stress on attacks on the *dirigiste* aspects of Labour's economic policy, aptly summed up by Churchill in his speech on the devaluation debate of 1949, in which he accused the Government of perpetuating 'a mass of wartime controls in order to give them the power of interference in the life of the country which is a characteristic of socialism' (Hansard, 28.9.49). The rancorous climate of much of this discussion was greatly enhanced by the uninhibitedly critical line taken by the Beaverbrook press, with its continual attacks on 'snoopers' and Government 'grabs'. But despite public differences, the underlying tenacity of the convergence that had occurred during the war years is well caught in Quintin Hogg's lengthy polemic, *The Case for Conservatism* (1948). Hogg wrote:

> our cry must be 'Social Democracy without Socialism'. By Social Democracy I mean so-called equality of opportunity – and a basic minimum for all those who are handicapped in the battle of life or who from time to time are unavoidably prevented from making their own way. (p. 300)

When the Conservatives narrowly regained power in 1951, despite polling less votes than their Labour rivals, Butler was sent (after some hesitation on Churchill's part) to the Treasury. The conduct of the economy had increasingly come to be an area of divergence between the parties, in contrast to social policy. The brief Chancellorship of Hugh Gaitskell had been a difficult one; the rash British commitment to a substantial rearmament programme after the outbreak of the Korean War in 1950 had placed new strains on an economy that had earlier shown signs under Stafford Cripps' Chancellorship of strong revival. The decision to impose health charges had divided the Labour Party and led to the resignation of Bevan, Harold Wilson and John Freeman. The changes were limited and the charges themselves small; but the breach in the principle of free delivery of health care set off reverberations within the party that persisted throughout the following decade. Labour had devoted much energy during the election campaign of 1951 to reminding the electorate about the mass unemployment of the 1930s and invoking the potential danger to the Welfare State of electing a Conservative government that might not be fully committed to maintaining it. As Harold Macmillan testifies in his memoirs, this attack struck home, at least to the extent that the incoming Conservatives were concerned to reassure the electorate that there was no substance in their opponents' accusations.

In practice, Butler, the standard bearer of the New Conservatism, established his own distinctive style as Chancellor without greatly altering the substance of policy. Greater reliance on monetary policy and the abandonment of a range of subsidies and, eventually, the remnants of the rationing system that Labour had retained from the war could be – and were – represented as substantial changes. But the abandonment of controls had been to a large extent anticipated by Labour; contrariwise, their own commitment to planning had steadily diminished after 1947, when Cripps had moved with his economic planning staff to the Treasury. Had Butler accepted an early proposal to float the pound, under the codename 'Robot', things might have been different: as Butler himself comments 'the word Butskell might never have been invented' (Butler, 1971, p. 160). But as it turned out, the continuities of policy – and, indeed, of the influence of key Treasury officials – outweighed the changes, and *The Economist*'s casual coinage gained a currency which has outlived its real value. Neither of the two men whose names it linked much cared for it; Butler comments in his autobiography:

> I shared neither his [i.e. Gaitskell's] convictions, which were unquenchably Socialist, nor his temperament, which allowed emotion to

run away with him rather too often, nor his training, which was that of an academic economist. Both of us, it is true, spoke the language of Keynesianism. But we spoke it in different accents and with a differing emphasis. (1971, p. 160)

In a situation where great play had been made of the country's economic problems, it might have been legitimate to expect that the welfare services would be at risk. *The Times*'s correspondent, referring portentously to a 'crisis' in the Welfare State, speculated about the possibility of moving towards means-testing, if it could be introduced without damaging civic solidarity (26 February 1952). The principle of charging in the health service having been admitted by Labour, some scope for expansion of charges existed. There was also some interest among younger Conservatives in the backbench One Nation Group, notably Iain Macleod and Enoch Powell, in systematic direction of resources towards those in greatest need – what later came to be called 'targetting'. However, as Lowe comments, 'on its own admission, the group never succeeded in fully squaring the circle of market economics and state welfare' (1993, p. 82). The Conservatives handled the situation with extreme caution. Pledges had already been given in the devaluation debate in 1949 that no drastic cuts would be made in welfare services, despite the heavy burdens on the economy. In practice, the only significant reductions that were made in public expenditure were in education; talk of eliminating waste in the health service faded away after research undertaken for the Guillebaud Report by Richard Titmuss and Brian Abel-Smith demonstrated that the NHS made good use of limited resources. As the economic climate improved, the opportunity was taken to upgrade the level of benefits, although attempts to reinstate the Beveridge principle of a national minimum providing full subsistence were brushed aside. The spectre of intolerable strain on the economy through the growth in numbers of those of pensionable age was faced out. In short, the mantle of the New Conservatism, admittedly a trifle thin in some places and brief in others, was thrown around the Welfare State.

The only sector in which the Conservatives developed an independent set of policies was the built environment; their reservations about the land-use planning system introduced by Labour were exacerbated by the need to meet the pledge to construct 300,000 new houses per year which had been pressed on the leadership by their party conference. By delivering on that pledge, Harold Macmillan gave his own career a decisive upward push; and through the emphasis on the role of the private sector in the provision of new homes helped to develop the theme of 'property owning democracy' that was to serve the Conservatives well later in the 1950s. Even when the economic pressures returned in 1955, with the 'overheating' of the economy after Butler's pre-election budget, the Treasury spared the social services in the Chancellor's emergency autumn measures. Seldon rightly maintains that the Conservatives made 'little attempt to work out a coherent and balanced social policy' (1981, p. 246); but the content was less significant than the visible commitment to the principle of state responsibility. The Welfare State had, it appeared, been firmly established as an essential part of the apparatus of government, whose proven popularity with the electorate would protect it against all but the keenest winds.

The venom of Gaitskell's attack on Butler in the debates on the 1955 emergency budget, precipitated partly by the anxieties he had expressed about the potential dangers to the Welfare State in any recession, swept away any real basis for consensus in economic policy-making. In this speech, deeply resented and sharply refuted, Gaitskell observed of Butler that 'he began in folly, continued in deceit and ended in reaction. He is a sadly discredited Minister' (Hansard, 28.11.55). From this point onwards, the Labour Party was concerned to develop its own approach, in which the revived concept of planning played an increasingly prominent part. Nor was Labour prepared to accept the Conservatives in the role of patrons of the Welfare State and protectors of the *status quo*. Hampered by the fratricidal strife that had broken out immediately upon leaving office, and by the disappointment of losing the 1955 general election, the party embarked upon a substantial overhaul of policies after Gaitskell's accession to the leadership, immediately after the election.

In social policy, the main theme was unfinished business. In the most substantial analysis produced during this period, *The Future of Socialism* (1956), Tony Crosland set out to demonstrate why 'Keynes-plus-modified-capitalism-plus-Welfare State' did *not* by itself constitute socialism. Despite its substantial merits, he suggested, this formula fell decisively short because it failed to provide for the achievement of greater equality, the prime goal of Socialist policy (p. 148). The critique of Conservative social policy therefore focused first of all upon its failure to bring about redistribution in favour of the less well off (a line of attack opened up by Gaitskell, in a censure debate in December 1954) and then on the growing inability of specific services to keep up with the pressure of demand, in health, in housing and in pensions, where Labour laid particular emphasis on the importance of their new plan for national superannuation.

Richard Crossman subsequently described how he had brought in the three Fabian academics, Titmuss, Abel-Smith and Townsend to join the National Executive's working party ('one of the most useful decisions of my life') to work on pensions and benefits, and in so doing 'evolved what was then a new approach towards the whole Beveridge philosophy', moving away from what he saw as 'the pessimistic determination to ensure that since poverty was endemic, poverty must at least be fairly shared' (Crossman, 1966, p. 1). In retrospect, this apparent shift by Labour away from universalism in welfare, based on social solidarity, seems like a clear departure from the original Beveridge principles. But at the time, the main focus of debate had moved to the field of education and the inadequacy of the Butler Act and the tripartite system of education that it had created to deliver equality of opportunity. An even sharper critique of Conservative policies was developed by Richard Titmuss: in a series of polemics he attacked what he saw as the willingness of the Conservatives to abandon the redistributive elements in the postwar settlement (which he saw as crucial) and move towards a means-tested service for the poor, while the rich increasingly enjoyed access to welfare benefits of their own, through the parallel systems of fiscal and occupational welfare, providing them with support through the tax system and additional 'fringe' benefits in contracts of employment (Titmuss, 1958).

All these different strands in the Labour critique rested upon the assumption that the postwar settlement was incomplete, and required not merely the addition of further policy initiatives but a fundamental shift in objectives, in order to secure the outcome of greater equality. However, the assumption that the State should play the central role in the organisation and delivery of welfare remained one common to both the two major parties, even if the tasks that the State should perform were differently defined. To the extent that there was an alternative perspective on offer, it was provided not by the Conservatives, but the Liberals. In near-political eclipse, after a humiliating rebuff at the general election of 1950, the Liberal Party, reviving some of the libertarian ideas put forward before the First World War by Hilaire Belloc in his eccentric but engaging polemic, *The Servile State*, produced a series of pamphlets, and ultimately a complete book, both under the title of *The Unservile State* and subtitled, *Essays on Liberty and Welfare* (Watson, 1957). In these essays the case for a minimal – and diminishing – role for the State in welfare was set out. These statements of a neo–Liberal position anticipated the subsequent polemics of the Institute of Economic Affairs with which some of the group that produced *The Unservile State* later came to be associated.

Conservative social policy was fully set out by Iain Macleod, who served as Minister of Health in Churchill's Cabinet. In a speech on the future of the Welfare State made at a Conservative summer school, held at Oxford in 1957, Macleod set out to rebut the accusation that the ghost of Butskell still walked. Under the rubric 'The Political Divide', he offered the delegates a comprehensive review of policy, reassuring them that the party would continue to give active support to the social services, but on a basis that stressed opportunities before 'crass egalitarianism' (CPC, 1958, p. 10). Whether the mixture as provided was intellectually coherent was much debated, both at the time and subsequently (cf. Lowe, 1993, p. 82); but it was evident that it had impressed the voters, and in particular the skilled working class. Harold Macmillan, who had become Prime Minister in 1957 after the premature retirement of Anthony Eden, discredited by the failure of the Suez invasion, made shrewd use of the theme of greater opportunity provided by increased prosperity. Even when economic setbacks in the following year provoked strong disagreement within the Cabinet about the right measures to adopt, Macmillan was not prepared to abandon his commitment to maintaining established levels of social expenditure and with them the 1944 White Paper goal of full employment, preferring instead to sacrifice his Chancellor (Peter Thorneycroft) and the whole Treasury ministerial team, who resigned with him. Shrugging off the whole episode as a 'little local difficulty', the Prime Minister rode out the storm skilfully – although Thorneycroft and his colleagues earned themselves an honoured niche in subsequent right-wing revisionist accounts as monetarism's first martyrs. Economic recovery enabled Macmillan to go to the country on the basis of an expansionary budget in October 1959. He was rewarded with a third successive Conservative win, and a parliamentary majority in three figures. The New Conservatism appeared to have entered into its full inheritance.

PLANNING REVISITED

Labour's move away from the weak but pervasive consensus on economic and social policies that had persisted through the first four years after the Conservative return to power was based mainly on the attempt to identify a viable alternative approach that would eliminate the 'stop–go' cycle that had characterised the Government's economic management. This concern was linked to the critique of the inadequacies of Conservative social policies, as Labour conceived them, through the common element of planning.

Increasingly, the model to be followed for this approach to planning under central State direction was identified as being those Western European countries that had adopted systematic planning techniques as an integral element in their postwar reconstruction programmes. The example that increasingly found favour in Britain was that of the French system of 'indicative' planning. Such an approach stressed the importance of institutional reforms; the creation of an enhanced capacity for State direction through new techniques of analysis; an extended role for the expert – not merely the academic economist or social scientist but also the bureaucrat with professional skills – and stress on the economies of scale that could be achieved through mergers and amalgamation of smaller (and presumptively less efficient) units. An economy run in this way would be able to guarantee a higher level of growth, together with more efficient mechanisms for distribution: hence the social services could expect to be major beneficiaries of the new approach to planning.

This particular fashion did not find favour only on the Labour side of the policy divide. A number of younger Conservatives, and in particular some members of the Bow Group (a pressure group broadly to the left of the party) were concerned to explore new approaches to the organisation and functions of government. The most prominent of these younger Conservatives was Sir Keith Joseph, who in a speech to the British Medical Association at Winchester summarised the concern of those in his party who believed that government lacked the capacity to identify and implement new priorities in welfare, and therefore needed to be provided with new instruments. Calling for the appointment of a minister to coordinate the social services, and create 'policy in the light of the best research that could be done', he commented that the Welfare State had extended the opportunity for choice that the upper and middle classes enjoyed to the working class. In this way, it 'had increased personal freedom and the scope for responsibility' (*Times*, 10.4.59).

The Conservative victory in 1959 was followed by a post mortem debate on the Labour side of quite unusual length and bitterness even by the party's customary standards. The attempts of the revisionists to move the party towards the model of European social democracy were passionately opposed by those fundamentalists who believed that the principles embodied in the 1918 party constitution still represented a viable basis for the party's programmes. The ferocity of the debate was considerably accentuated by the strong suggestion that a secular shift in attitudes might be taking place among the skilled working class. The switch of allegiance in this group had produced a number of Labour election losses in predominantly working–class constituencies and appeared to suggest that a move away from class politics toward a more instrumental view had occurred. The notion that affluence might be a solvent of traditional political loyalties and that voters might punish or reward strictly on grounds of material advantage was one element in the common belief at this time that the political system might be experiencing a decline in the significance of ideology, as part of a general process affecting all advanced democracies (Rose and Abrams, 1960; Bell, 1962).

But within two years it had already become clear that the Conservatives had not succeeded in breaking away from the stop–go economic cycle. The volume of criticism began to mount again; from this period dates a quite unusual quantity of self-questioning literature, seeking to establish the causes and consequences of Britain's relatively poor postwar performance (cf. Hartley, Koestler, Thomas, Shonfield, Brittan, Shanks). Macmillan's response was to break away from previous policies and adopt wholesale the planning devices that Labour had previously proposed. Selwyn Lloyd, his Chancellor, announcing the setting up of new institutions for the planning and overall direction of the economy, the National Economic Development Council (NEDC), announced that he was not afraid of the word planning (Budd, 1978, p. 91). Macmillan went further; after all, as he rather coyly pointed out, he had once written a book on the subject. A new emphasis was laid on the importance of growth; and substantial increases in public expenditure were identified for the major welfare services – notably health, where Enoch Powell as minister was to preside over a particularly rapid expansion in his department's hospital construction programme under the 1962 Hospital Plan.

The new policies changed the character of the political dialogue, but failed to check the country's economic or the Conservatives' electoral decline. An unexpected but vigorous Liberal revival was followed at a more stately pace by the political recovery of the Labour Party. Macmillan's subsequent gambits – the peremptory dismissal of one-third of the Cabinet, followed by a British application for admission to the Common Market, vetoed by General de Gaulle – proved no more successful. Despite the unexpected death of Hugh Gaitskell, at the beginning of 1963, and Macmillan's own resignation later that year, the Conservatives narrowly lost power to Labour at the general election of 1964.

Read with hindsight, the documents on which Labour fought and won that election have an innocence which is almost breathtaking. The New Frontiers, to be stormed by the systematic application of new technology and cultivated through the creation of new structures and institutions fit for late twentieth-century men and women were at last within reach; the golden key was to be the application of the new techniques of economic planning. Within three years all these hopes were in ruins. The new structures that were to provide the direction: the Department of Economic Affairs and the Regional Economic Planning Councils, the specialists brought in to ensure that the break with past practice would be decisive and above all the centrepiece of the structure, the National Plan proudly unveiled by George Brown in 1965 – all crumbled away in the face of an old-fashioned sterling crisis. Some of the modernising reforms left a more enduring mark: successive inquiries reviewed the functions and performance of the civil service, local government, all the various sectors of education and eventually the personal social services. A substantial overhaul of social security was undertaken, which united under the same department pensions, the national insurance function and national assistance. Many of the structural changes introduced as a result are still in place, though in an increasingly precarious state.

For here, too, there has been substantial disillusionment. Both the quality of much of the new provision and the scale and manner in which it was provided have attracted criticism from all directions. Reflecting in his diary on the nature of the housing problems that he confronted as minister, Richard Crossman concluded that nothing short of sweeping central intervention would suffice – 'a Labour Minister should impose central leadership, large scale State intervention, in these blighted areas of cities' (quoted in Hadley and Hatch, 1981, p. 51). The main legacy of those decisions, and similar programmes of comprehensive redevelopment on other major cities, was the inner-city high-rise housing estates – the characteristic urban form of the 1960s, along with the shopping mall, the system-built primary school and the off-street parking facility. All were constructed in the same limited range of unsuitable materials, none reflected any individuality or sense of place. Many of the deficiencies in the physical provision were also reflected in the services located in them. The rapid expansion in the numbers of those entering what came to be known as the caring professions and in the tasks facing them and the pressures on the training provided precipitated large numbers of young people into situations with which they were ill-equipped to cope.

At the same time, expectations had been raised by two decades of uneven but sustained growth. Evidence of disillusionment with the standard of public services began to appear, assiduously chronicled by the Institute of Economic Affairs, whose simple but increasingly effective message about the superiority of the market as a means of providing welfare had begun to reach an audience outside the confines of the far right. On the other side of politics, the message of the widespread student unrest of 1968, in Europe as in Britain, was that the postwar compromises held little attraction for a generation that took security for granted and a steadily increasing standard of living as its birthright. Viewed as an event, alongside the great upheavals of the past, the Student Revolution was more than a little farcical; but the ideas disseminated in the process struck root in some unexpected quarters and eventually flowered.

Specific issues in social policy attracted particular criticism during Labour's term of office (1964–70). Housing, one of the areas of particular partisan conflict in the 1950s, remained controversial, both through Labour's emphasis on building new public sector housing and strict control of private landlords as the main means for improving housing circumstances, and also as a result of the Government's failure to meet its ambitious construction targets. But the major cause of dissent, chiefly between the Government and its own supporters, was over the persistence of poverty. References to the 'rediscovery' of poverty at this time are misleading; the problems resulting from the failure of successive governments to set the level of benefits high enough to provide a proper national minimum as Beveridge had intended were well known – the steadily increasing number of those dependent on national assistance (known after 1966 as supplementary benefit) was clear enough proof of that. But Townsend and Abel-Smith's *The Poor and the Poorest* (1965) had rammed these lessons home, and served as the basis for a campaign designed to achieve fundamental policy changes. This campaign, which produced in the Child Poverty Action Group, one of the most effective lobbying organisations in the whole area of welfare policy, provided a blueprint for a series of campaigns on other social policy issues (Banting, 1979).

As part of this process, the Labour Government's record was subjected to well-informed and critical scrutiny and found wanting.

Faced with the response that economic circumstances meant that ambitious plans would have to be postponed or even abandoned, Brian Abel-Smith retorted: 'it is a terrifying fallacy to pretend that economic and social aims are wholly competitive. Why do we want economic growth if it is not to promote social and not economic ends?' (Abel-Smith, 1966, p. 10). Richard Crossman's retort, delivered through the same medium of a Fabian pamphlet was that 'I feel no doubt that we shall, in the lifetime of this Parliament, complete the task we set ourselves in Opposition, of breaking away from Beveridge and creating a system of social security which abolishes poverty in affluence' (Crossman, 1966, p. 24). But this response, and others like it, did not convince the critics. On race, on poverty, on inner-city deprivation, they saw the tendency as being to respond rather than initiate, to allow lobbies to make the running and intervene only when the political pressures made action inevitable. Despite the steady growth in public expenditure on welfare over this period, progress towards the egalitarian goals set before the Government came to office was slow.

At the same time, the enthusiasm of the Conservative Party for social reform had become markedly less strong. One of the issues that the incoming Labour Government had to confront in 1964 had been the sudden outbreak of hostility towards the then relatively recently arrived immigrants from the Caribbean and Indian sub-continent, which was exposed by the successive electoral defeats of Labour's Foreign Secretary, Patrick Gordon Walker, first in Smethwick, then at Leyton. The Government responded by tightening immigration control (which they had opposed in Opposition) and introducing limited measures to outlaw racial discrimination. Enoch Powell's apostasy in 1968, when with his 'rivers of blood' speech he fractured the precarious understanding that had developed between the major political parties not to allow the issue of race to be exploited for partisan ends and earned himself dismissal from Ted Heath's Shadow Cabinet as a result, was the most spectacular example of an attempt to change the agenda. But other, less dramatic shifts of opinion were taking place across the whole policy spectrum, and found expression at the end of the 1960s in the Conservative Party's turn towards a market-based approach to the economy and selectivity in the social services, known as the 'Selsdon' programme after the hotel in which the Shadow Cabinet had met to devise it. This approach was widely seen as the first instance of a reversal of a general trend in postwar politics; instead of moving toward the centre in opposition, the Conservatives (and subsequently Labour in

1971/2), were moving further out to the wings. This tendency – and the associated process of moving back into the middle in Government – was subsequently labelled by the economist Michael Stewart the 'Jekyll and Hyde' syndrome (1977). But the concept rests on an imputation of virtue to centrist Jekyll and vice to radical Hyde that would have many fewer takers now than when Stewart coined it in the mid-1970s.

Moreover, after the unexpected Conservative victory in the 1970 election, continuity was more evident than change. There was brave talk of fundamental change in government – the so-called 'quiet revolution' – and a flurry of executions of ideologically unacceptable quangos. On the industrial relations front, the Conservatives took up the issue of trade union law reform; but could (and did) claim that they were applying the principles laid down in the Donovan Commission on Industrial Relations, on which Labour had flinched from legislation. The entente between Government, employers and unions, severely damaged by the 1972 Act and the mass protests that it generated, nevertheless survived.

On the social policy front, common elements were even more evident. Structural reforms in local government and the health service took a different form but embodied the same principles: economies of scale through creation of larger units; introduction of new management techniques and the application of technical and professional expertise to issues of policy priorities and resource allocation. Ministers in the main spending departments competed tirelessly for a larger share of an expanding welfare budget – conspicuously successfully in the case of Sir Keith Joseph at the new Department of Health and Social Security and Margaret Thatcher, whose White Paper on education policy bore the striking title *A Framework for Expansion* (1972). Among Joseph's innovations was the introduction of a new benefit, Family Income Supplement, designed to address the problems of the working poor. Attending the annual general meeting of the Child Poverty Action Group to explain his approach, Joseph was warmly applauded. Both the event itself and the response would have been unthinkable a decade later. Greater controversy surrounded the attempts of Peter Walker at another of the new large ministries, the Department of the Environment, to reform the chaos of housing finance and impose central government control over rents of council housing; and, once again, the issue of pensions divided the parties, with the Labour plans, lost as a result of the timing of the 1970 election replaced by another set of new proposals. Yet arguments continued to be about means, within the context of increased public expenditure on the existing structure of welfare.

It was the unexpected reappearance of the issue that had dominated the pre-war debates, unemployment, that transformed the situation. It was an article of faith common to all parties in the postwar period that any government that permitted unemployment to reappear on any scale would instantly forfeit the support of the electorate; and a claim ritually repeated at successive elections that the 'bad old days' would never be allowed to return. In 1972, the unemployment figures reached a postwar record level of one million; the response of the Heath Government was to abandon hastily its tentative experiments in economic liberalism and return to the classic Keynesian recipe of recovery through stimulating demand in the economy. The application of this formula by the Chancellor, Anthony Barber, was coupled with the creation of a new agency, the tripartite Manpower Services Commission, to address the problems of the labour market. The successful consummation of Britain's long-delayed entry into the European Community was widely seen as another stimulus to improved economic performance, providing the spur of emulation of our new European partners. Instead, a sharp rise in inflation compounded by the drastic increase in oil prices imposed by the oil producing states after the Yom Kippur War of 1973 propelled the Prime Minister into a statutory pay policy and, eventually, an unsuccessful showdown with the miners.

The narrow defeat of the Conservative Government at the general election of February 1974, called ostensibly on the issue of the respective powers, responsibilities and rights of governments and trade unions was in the broader sense a defeat for the second consensus, which had for a decade sought with diminishing conviction solutions for social and economic problems in better planned and organised interventions of the State. In particular, the ignominious failure of the Barber boom to achieve either its economic or its political objectives fatally discredited the use of Keynesian techniques for planned change. From this moment onwards intellectual fashions began to shift; in a new and more sceptical environment the old certainties were held up for close scrutiny and in many cases found wanting.

CONCLUSIONS

The initial conception of the Welfare State and the complex of economic and social policies that brought it into being and sustained it have been subjected in retrospect to all manner of mythological reinterpretations.

The main myth is the secular one of progress – the Victorian concept of organic development of society through change and adaptation, dressed up in modern clothes. Beveridge's 'British revolution' is best understood in this sense: his Plan represents an attempt to draw upon past experience and distil those elements in it which offered the best prospect of achieving the objective defined: the elimination of want. This goal, in turn, could be linked to the heightened sense of common purpose – the solidarity produced by the collective experience of war, however differently it may have been experienced in practice. Neither in form nor in rhetoric was Beveridge's Plan revolutionary, as that term is commonly understood: it presupposed no violent changes in institutions, nor did it seek to reverse the balance of power between classes, still less genders in society. Yet rarely has a measure of social reform acquired so many claimants to parenthood: from the left, who could represent the Plan as the culmination of two generations of pressure by the working class to achieve social justice; to the right, who portrayed the wartime Coalition Government as striking a judicious balance between the claims of various interests and resolving them in the name of One Nation. The centre, whose claim to parenthood is probably most convincing, could see in the postwar settlement the systematic adoption of the principles of scientific rationality in administration and the impartial, apolitical application of rules derived from commonly accepted values for which 'middle opinion' had argued before the war. Beveridge (whose brief flirtation with party politics was not for him a happy experience) spoke for this group when he observed during his short membership of the House of Commons that social insurance should be kept out of politics – since it was 'not a controversial issue, but it does lend itself fatally to be the subject of political auction' (Hansard, 3.11.44).

This sense of common ownership is reflected in a second sort of myth: that of a golden age. True, the precise location of that happy moment varies: the left would prefer to see it in the radical moment immediately after the publication of the Plan, when the strength of the popular response to its proposals frustrated the Government's intentions to delay implementation, or in the struggles of the Labour Government in the hard years after the war to deliver on their compact with the working classes. Conservatives, until recently, would point to the statesmanship of Churchill on his return to office in 1951 and the blend of economic expansion and social compassion achieved by the New Conservatism. Both these accounts are now coming under increasingly sharp critical scrutiny, notably in Barnett's study (1986) and later by Tory revisionists anxious to write the Macmillan–Butler period out of the canon of true Conservatism (Willetts, 1992). But they still retain some of their original force and help to explain the reluctance of both major parties to reopen issues that had apparently been resolved for good.

Nor is the notion of the golden age wholly mythical. Even the most superficial comparison between the situation confronting the minority Labour Government elected in February 1974 with that of its predecessor of 1929 (with whose fall this narrative began) will demonstrate what an immense distance separates the two. Not that all the problems were so dissimilar. The 1974 Government faced major difficulties – a rapidly rising rate of unemployment and inflation on the verge of getting out of control – with the additional anxiety that the tools that had once provided reliable means of addressing these problems had proved fallible. But the continued presence of the Welfare State still seemed assured; and the poor of 1974 could call upon a level of support and a range of services of a quality and accessibility of which the poor of 1929 could only dream. Rodney Lowe's authoritative analysis of the performance of what he calls the 'classic' Welfare State between the end of the Second World War and 1975 provides solid corroborative evidence of the progress that had been made over the whole period. Although the goal of greater equality had not been secured– in part because it had not been wholeheartedly pursued:

> the redistribution by the classic welfare state of both social status and power is nevertheless undeniable. Freedom from fear of absolute poverty and universal access to services such as the NHS and secondary education dramatically improved the quality of the lives of many. So too did the comparative job security and, above all, the sustained rise in average living standards that emanated from full employment. (Lowe, 1993, p. 293)

On the issue of the performance of government, Lowe's verdict is that 'despite particular instances of inefficiency . . . the classic welfare state represented a general gain in efficiency in relation to both expenditure and the distribution of resources' (p. 295).

The achievement that these outcomes represent is customarily put down to the existence of a consensus. As this account of the development of the politics of welfare should have indicated, it is wholly misleading to speak, as Tony Benn has done, of a universally held and undifferentiated block of beliefs extending over the whole period from the formation of the Coalition Government in 1940 to the election of Margaret Thatcher in 1979 (*Guardian*, 14.2.86). Conservative acceptance of the Welfare

State in the 1950s was often a grumbling acquiescence, despite Butler's brilliant sleight of hand. Labour's reluctance to accept that the various separate structures they had left behind in 1951 did not make up a permanent edifice of welfare, complete for all time, led to acrimonious debate in the later 1950s. The subsequent conversion of both parties to the principles of planning took place at different stages and for different reasons, as did their respective recantations. Coincidence rather than conjunction of views is more often than not the true hallmark of the postwar period; as is the inconsistency of many of the protagonists, whose positions were modified drastically by changing circumstances and political imperatives – as were those of Joseph, Powell and Benn (all of them true believers whose beliefs passed through a series of sea changes). Finally, the vocabulary of crisis was frequently employed throughout the period, both in defence of the Welfare State and as a criticism of the level of expenditure it absorbed and the consequences of State involvement for other institutions, for the family and for the situation of individuals (cf. Robson and Crick, 1970)

Nevertheless, it is possible to identify a minimum position that extends throughout the period. This comprised acceptance of the legitimacy of the central role of the State in welfare; tacit agreement that debate on detail of social policies belonged at the margin of the political system, while questions of public expenditure must necessarily lie at the centre; and the assumption that, since the individual issues concerned had tended to become highly technical, a substantial role in the initiation and implementation of policy should be entrusted to professional experts and technicians. Outside critics, pressure groups and other interests were also recognised as having a legitimate part to play, if a subsidiary one. But, crucially, the whole approach rested on a belief that the Welfare State enjoyed widespread popular support.

Yet within five brief years from 1974, this apparently solid edifice of common assumptions had been riddled through and through by a fusillade of criticisms from every point of the political compass. In its place, there was widespread acceptance that the Welfare State was inefficient, unpopular and on the verge of disintegration. The processes through which this change was brought about and the basis for the beliefs from which it drew its motive force are the subjects of the next chapter.

3

THE CRUMBLING OF CONSENSUS

> There is nothing more conservative than an old reforming party, and particularly one which has repeatedly achieved political success by pressing for a programme of political improvement.
>
> E.F.M. Durbin, *The Politics of Democratic Socialism*, 1940.

Why were the critics of the postwar settlement able to mount such a vigorous and successful assault on the set of beliefs and practices bundled together under the label of 'consensus'? And why did the structure that they were besieging prove to be not a New Jerusalem but a Jericho, its walls collapsing – and in some instances gates flying treacherously open – at the first sound of the trumpets outside?

The feeble resistance put up by the defenders is all the more surprising in the light of the apparent strength of their position and the ease with which earlier attacks had been repulsed. Previous criticisms of the Welfare State had lacked conviction partly because they concentrated on specific services or aspects of delivery, rather than developing a coherent critique which linked the broad issues raised by collective provision of welfare by the State with the particular experience of individuals. But, more important still, these criticisms did not engage with the concerns of the major political parties; still less did they awake resonances in the arena of public opinion.

Of the earlier criticisms of State welfare, potentially the most formidable was the fundamental ideological challenge presented by Hayek. *The Road to Serfdom* (1944) was unquestionably an effective polemic, although subsequent claims on the right that it has never been refuted are a rewriting of history: if Keynes was apparently willing to concede the case, there was no shortage of others prepared to confront Hayek on his own ground (Herman Finer (1946), Barbara Wootton (1945) and Evan Durbin (1949)). The core of Hayek's argument lay in the assertion that Government intervention through planning led inevitably to totalitarianism; restated in the milder form advanced by John Jewkes, the road's inevitable descent was not to serfdom but ineffectiveness (1948). The experience of the Attlee Government provided a fair amount of evidence for the second proposition, but very little for the first: grumblings about a tyranny of petty form-filling and bureaucratic pen-pushers fell a long way short of the Gestapo rule that Winston Churchill had portrayed, in a rash moment during the 1945 election campaign, as an inevitable consequence of Labour victory. Attlee's cutting response to him on that occasion was widely felt, by supporters and opponents alike, to have put paid to that particular line of attack (R.A. Butler 1971, p. 125).

After an interlude in the United States, where his concern was chiefly with economic theory, Hayek himself returned to the charge in the 1960s, with a series of closely argued examinations of the applications of liberal theory to twentieth-century legal and constitutional issues (Bosanquet, 1983). In particular, Hayek attempted to define conditions under which State intervention could occur which would not damage his fundamental requirements of liberty and individual autonomy. The line that Hayek has laid down in these and subsequent writings does not exclude State action. 'I am the last to deny', he has said, 'that increased wealth and the increased density of population have enlarged the number of collective needs which Government can and should satisfy' (Hayek, 1978, p. 111). However, the services provided should not be a State monopoly, they must not have a concealed redistributive purpose and they should be designed to satisfy the collective wants of the community as a whole, not of separate groups within it. The Welfare State failed this test because it sacrificed the general principles of liberalism to the desire to achieve its aims as rapidly as possible. This turned 'the whole apparatus into a great machinery for the redistribution of incomes, led to a progressive growth of the government-controlled sector of the economy and to steady dwindling of the part of the economy in which Liberal principles still prevail' (p. 145).

At the same time, Hayek expressed concern about the implications of the democratic system of government and the scope that it offered for abuse of these principles, through illegitimate exploitation of the powers of the State (taxation, for example) and the reasons offered for their use, in particular the chimera, as he sees it, of social justice.

Hayek's repudiation of one of the fundamental (if largely unexamined) principles of the Welfare State made little impact at the time at which it was first advanced. The success of Butler's New Conservatism in the 1950s had anaesthetised serious criticism on the right and reduced the ranks of those who still offered it to a rump of caricature Tory backbenchers, of whom Sir Waldron Smithers was the archetype. Thus the ideas which Hayek was attempting to introduce into the political debate lacked a point of entry to the system. The Liberal Party's flirtation with libertarian ideas ended with their sudden electoral revival in the early 1960s; the Institute of Economic Affairs, whose role as communicator and interpreter of policies was later to be of considerable importance, had at this stage little direct influence. Harris and Seldon later complained that both major parties had carried on 'oblivious to individual preferences, hearing only the voices of unrepresentative spokesmen for pressure groups and ideological interests' (Harris and Seldon, 1977, p. 43). The solitary substantial political figure who was prepared to give expression to these views was Enoch Powell.

One of the few consistent elements in Powell's career has been his continued concern with ideas and their applications in politics. His early background as a member of Butler's team of 'Rabians' (as they were unkindly christened by their critics) in the Conservative Research Department and his membership of the One Nation Group of younger Conservative MPs brought him into the area of social policy. The pamphlet that he produced, jointly with Iain Macleod, on needs and means in welfare shows the relentless application of logical principles up to (and in some cases beyond) the furthest point at which they can legitimately be applied – which was to become one of his political trademarks. Logic, in this case, required choices, between going the whole hog with Beveridge and pushing up support to a level which fully guaranteed subsistence for all, or changing to a safety net system which identified for receipt of assistance only those in real want. The postwar system failed, the authors argued (under the heading 'The postwar crisis in the social services') because it satisfied neither objective (Macleod and Powell, 1954).

Powell himself eventually obtained office, though not as rapidly as his co-author Macleod, who vaulted straight into the Ministry of Health as a direct result of a single speech, in which he confronted and defeated that formidable debator, Aneurin Bevan, on his own ground. As a junior minister at the Ministry of Housing, Powell was responsible for introducing the Rent Act, which embodied a substantial element of decontrol of private tenancies; and as a junior minister at the Treasury he resigned, with the Chancellor, Peter Thorneycroft, on the issue of cutting public expenditure. Yet any appearance of consistency is dissipated, first by his spending record when he in turn became Minister of Health and his concurrent defence of welfare as a system of 'vested rights or expectations' (CPC, 1961) and then by his call to battle once out of office against State intervention, delivered as a contributor to one of the IEA's early symposiums, *The Rebirth of Britain*. In this, he argued that 'a welfare state can also be a capitalist state; other things being equal, a state which is capitalist can provide more welfare than one that is not', but it does so through the market, 'impartial and impersonal, treating like things all alike, which is the essence of justice' (Institute of Economic Affairs, 1964, p. 266).

By the late 1960s, Powell was pursuing an increasingly eccentric path, counselling civil disobedience to businessmen faced by demands from government for information about their activities; breaking sharply away from postwar assumptions in Anglo-American defence policies and in the interstices exploring the niceties of theological debate. Eventually, he settled upon race as the theme for his major confrontation with the leadership of his party, achieving immense short-term notoriety but in the longer run decisively blocking any prospect of regaining office. Excluded in 1970 from the Government of Edward Heath, by 1974 he had left the Conservative Party altogether, and the free market tendency within it had lost its potentially most effective spokesman.

Thus before 1974, the conjunction of events had not yet occurred that would permit a thoroughgoing critique of the concept of State welfare to find expression through the Conservative Party. On the left, events followed a broadly parallel path. The sudden effusion of critical ideas that burst out in 1968, largely in imitation of more substantial outbreaks in Europe and across the Atlantic, had given momentary pause to the conventional left in Britain, but the immediate effects rapidly dissipated themselves. There were those who heeded the advice of the hero of the 1968 barricades, Rudi Dutschke, that the long march to power lay through institutions: but for some while the only institutions that took much traffic were academic ones. Among the left's priorities for further theoretical analysis, the issue of welfare took a relatively low place; but concern about the role of the State under capitalism eventually helped to crystallise a set of ideas about the place of welfare. The most influential of the studies that helped to precipitate this process was John O'Connor's *The Fiscal Crisis of the State* (1973). In it, O'Connor argued that the State was facing a double crisis, precipitated by contradictions between its role of providing the circumstances for capital accumulation and its other function of legitimating the processes by which it could take place. The pressure generated by working-class demands, whose satisfaction is an essential element in legitimation, was steadily undermining the capacity of the State to deliver on the conditions essential to accumulation, since costly welfare provision was prominent among those demands. Or, put another way, as Claus Offé presented the issue, the contradiction is that 'while capitalism cannot coexist *with*, neither can it exist *without* the welfare state' (Offé, 1984, p. 153).

This formulation posed dilemmas which those theorists seeking to evolve a political economy of welfare found difficult to resolve. While they were not prepared to take the claims made on behalf of the postwar version of the Welfare State at face value, still less to accept that any significant progress had been made towards equality, viewed in strict class terms, they had nevertheless to concede that the Welfare State clearly represented a form of accomplishment. Not merely had it served as a focus for working-class political action; it was also evidently genuinely popular. In such circumstances, it was difficult to conceive of the postwar structure merely as capitalism's solution, through its creature the State, to problems of labour supply. Nor was it entirely easy to explain why prominent capitalists had begun to express strong reservations about further expansions in welfare spending.

The refinement of the Marxist analysis which took place over the following decade resolved some of these conceptual difficulties, helped by the influence of new ideas from Continental neo-Marxism, and latterly from the growing group of feminist critics of social policy. Of more immediate practical significance was the influence that these ideas began to gain among those employed in the much-expanded public sector of welfare. The experience of workers in Government-sponsored initiatives in addressing poverty set up at the end of the 1960s and in particular on the Community Development Projects (CDPs), was one key example. Frustrated in their original purpose of promoting solutions through community development and identifying as one major source of their difficulties limitations imposed both on resources and the range of their activities by local government bureaucracies, the CDP teams broadened their approach to adopt a broadly Marxist perspective. This identified the problems of the inner areas as lying at the level of the national economy, and the remedies at the same point – or, more sweepingly still, in the international economic sphere. Disenchanted with this approach, and sceptical of its applicability to immediate issues of inner-city poverty, the Labour Government responded by winding up the experiment (Higgins et al., 1984).

The experience of CDP was only the most dramatic illustration of this process of permeation of new critical ideas on welfare, which began to involve an increasing number of younger workers in the public sector, and found expression among public sector unions, and eventually in local government itself through local Labour parties. These ideas, which had until the early 1970s been largely the property of fringe groups, now put down roots and began to exert a growing influence within the Labour Party nationally. While still resisted by the party's leadership during the earlier part of Labour's period in office, some policies based on these views – in particular new concepts of locally initiated economic planning – began to emerge in the late 1970s, during the latter half of the party's time in government.

As in the case of the ideological challenge from the right, these new currents of opinion required a dislocation in the existing structures of belief and the policies based upon them in order to flow into the mainstream of debate. This dislocation was provided by the successive economic crises of the early and middle 1970s, the problems experienced by successive governments in attempting to deal with them and the patent fallibility of many of the devices that were deployed in making these attempts.

AFTER KEYNES?

As in the general area of political philosophy, so in the specific field of economic policy, the new approach adopted by the Conservative Party in the immediate postwar period under the influence of R.A. Butler effectively squeezed out dissent. The apparent success of the policies adopted in the 1950s, not least in the electoral sphere, crowned by Butler's euphoric vision of doubling the nation's standard of living within twenty-five years, disarmed criticism within the party, which only began to revive when the amended version of these policies adopted by Harold Macmillan at the beginning of the 1960s failed to produce the desired effects.

In a situation in which the market for fresh approaches to economic policy had reopened and to express scepticism about the automatic effectiveness of the mechanisms of demand management was no longer heretical, the ideas developed by Milton Friedman proved to be a powerful competitor. Deployed with what one of his later critics has described as an 'amalgam of economic analysis and moral invective', the version of monetarism that Friedman advocated appeared to offer governments a new approach to managing the economy. This would greatly reduce the amount of State intervention but would also guarantee satisfactory results in certain critical respects, in particular control of inflation. The philosopher's stone that would secure this outcome was control of the money supply; and the means to secure this rested in the hands of the State, through its jurisdiction over the central banking machinery. Achieve it, and 'as night follows day', at a set interval, inflation rates would be reduced. Add to that the sweeping away of artificial restrictions in the labour market, and in particular the monopolistic practices of trade unions, connived at by successive governments, and unemployment, too, would fall to its natural level.

These seductively straightforward macro–economic doctrines still lacked convincing empirical proof, despite Friedman's immense labours on the historical data. Like other economists of the opposite persuasion, Friedman and his colleagues from Chicago eventually found opportunities to experiment with the introduction of their policies in developing countries; but penetration of the political system of an advanced economy proved a tougher nut to crack. That monetarism succeeded in doing so, and challenging and ultimately dethroning the reigning orthodoxy, was due in no small measure to the activities of the Institute of Economic Affairs.

The IEA had been founded in 1956, as 'an intellectually congenial "family forum"' for those who dissented from the reigning orthodoxies but could find no place in any political party. The Institute's initial emphasis lay mainly in attempts to apply the principles of neo-classical economics to particular fields of policy, beginning with pensions and housing. Their studies of the health service provoked acrimonious debate with Richard Titmuss and his LSE colleagues; a series of studies of alternative methods of financing and delivering health care demonstrated to the satisfaction of the Institute, if not all its critics, that without price constraints people would always demand as consumers more medical care than they would willingly finance as taxpayers.

The Institute's general assault on what it characterised as the 'go–stop' economic policies of the postwar period began from the same theoretical base, and led to publications attacking both the pursuit of the objective of full employment to the exclusion of other goals, and in particular of the containment of inflation, and to a critique of the use of pay and incomes policies as a means of containing the effects of the rises in wages on inflation. In 1970, the IEA provided Milton Friedman with a platform for the presentation of his position, in their annual Wincott Lecture. Published as *The Counter-revolution in Monetary Theory*, this essay encapsulates the monetarist approach in a phrase when inflation is described as 'always and everywhere a monetary phenomenon' (Friedman, 1970).

Among Friedman's audience at this lecture had been James Callaghan, the former Chancellor. Six years later, as Labour Prime Minister, Callaghan found himself telling the Labour party conference 'in all candour', that the notion that 'you could just spend your way out of recession and increase employment by cutting taxes and boosting government expenditure' no longer existed, because 'it only worked by injecting a bigger dose of inflation into the economy followed by a higher level of unemployment. That is the history of the last twenty years' (Keegan, 1984, p. 89). The collapse of international confidence after three years of mounting economic stress, with inflation and unemployment rising in tandem, in defiance of all the received wisdom, had provoked a major sterling crisis. Britain was rescued from this crisis by the International Monetary Fund (IMF), on terms that involved pledges by the Chancellor, Denis Healey, to secure 'a continuing and substantial reduction in the share of resources required for the public sector' and restraint in public sector borrowing, to curb growth in the money supply (Riddell, 1983, p. 59). The introduction of these measures, more than any one single act, finally knocked the props away from under the postwar certainties. Not merely did it specifically exclude any possibility of applying classic Keynesian remedies; it also explicitly revoked the compact upon which the settlement had been founded. Beveridge's belief that the situation of the poor could be defended in all circumstances through full employment, subsistence level benefits available without means test and good quality services was already a thing of shreds and patches; the deal made in 1976 finally removed it from the active political agenda.

The policies adopted in 1976 were succesful in their own terms. They achieved in 1977–8 a drastic reduction in inflation in tandem with some real fall in unemployment; and James Callaghan was able to secure the support of the trade unions for wage restraint in support of these policies. But these achievements could not disguise the fact that a further basic shift had taken place. Public expenditure, regarded throughout most of the postwar period as a benign instrument for securing the goals of social policy and the final guarantor against the return of economic depressions had changed sides: from being an essential part of the solution it had now become part of the problem. As the IEA put it with pardonable smugness, 'by 1976 the evidence of experience suggested that the middle way was neither stable nor tolerable' (Harris and Seldon, 1977, p. 112).

The crucial difference between the situation in the late 1970s and earlier episodes of questioning of economic priorities was that fully articulated alternative theories now existed, in a form that could be accepted as legitimate within the political arena, and with advocates drawn from among the senior members of both the two main parties. On the Conservative side, Sir Keith Joseph had developed the monetarist approach into a comprehensive critique of postwar economic policy, set out in a series of major speeches drawing upon material assembled by his own Centre for Policy Studies. On the Labour side, the ideas of the left had been developed and codified, most notably in Stuart Holland's study, *The Socialist Challenge*, which argued that in the light of the weakness of Britain in the world economy, the State needed to develop new instruments for intervention in the domestic economy which would enable direction to be exercised in a more effective and flexible style than in previous attempts at planning (Holland, 1975). These views found a ready advocate in Tony Benn, who had been a member of the Cabinet which approved the response to the IMF, but was exploiting his rapidly expanding base in the party at large to articulate a set of ideas about economic strategies that deviated radically from those of the Government.

The new approaches to economic policy which were developed in the course of the 1970s all involved radical changes in approach to the role of the State, although the different versions had diametrically opposed notions of what that role should be. A recasting of the State's function was also a key factor in the alternative approaches to social policy which were being formulated at the same period, though with a greater degree of hesitancy, and with the usual emphasis on all sides on the primacy of economic goals among overall policy objectives. Much of the new thinking in this area derived from a reaction against the form in which State action had been cast, the scale on which it had been undertaken and the capacity of the machinery devised to meet the needs of individuals and communities.

The politics of welfare

WHATEVER'S BEST ADMINISTERED . . .

At the core of the progressive disillusionment of those politicians who had put their shirts on structural reform and their hearts into the successive overhauls of the machinery of government introduced in turn by the Wilson and Heath administrations lay disappointment with the performance of the new institutions that had been created. The most extreme cases have already been cited: Sir Keith Joseph, architect of the reform of the National Health Service, and Tony Benn, as Minister of Technology, had both been active exponents of the doctrines of efficient State intervention through restructuring. In the later 1970s, they both turned to other approaches. But other politicians whose responses had been less drastic had become equally, if less dramatically, disillusioned.

Some of this disillusionment emerged subsequently, by way of memoir and lecture, in the form of a generalised disenchantment with the civil service which indicted both its instinctive conservatism on policy issues and its lack of capacity to manage in situations of rapid change. Rather bewilderingly, this accusation was sometimes combined with the suggestion that the civil service had become altogether too powerful. A more sophisticated version of the same concern pointed to the clumsiness of the machinery of government as a device for identifying and pursuing selected priorities over a substantial period of time. Operating in a partisan political environment, ministers had become locked into a process in which the key criteria were too often short-term party advantage, the only map the manifesto (prepared in different circumstances for quite other purposes) and the key devices for assessing policies electoral success, or the even more ephemeral opinion poll.

Some of these problems had been foreseen. The Plowden Committee on the control of public expenditure, set up at the end of the 1950s, had recommended that a five-year survey of public expenditure should be prepared annually in order to relate spending plans systematically to the anticipated rate of economic growth. This became the Public Expenditure Survey Committee (PESC). But the opportunity to use this device to reconcile the competing claims of economic and social policy was, as Rodney Lowe comments, 'largely missed' (1993, p. 111). The procedures that did emerge became largely another means for the Treasury to hobble spending departments' freedom of action; a process which, as the 1970s went on, developed from annual skirmishing through protracted guerilla warfare to the mighty pitched battles of the second half of the decade. Early attempts to introduce programme planning and policy review to Whitehall as an extension and to some extent a counterweight to this process fell on stony ground (Heclo and Wildavsky, 1974). The Central Policy Review Staff (CPRS), introduced by Edward Heath as a device for providing the Prime Minister and through him the Cabinet with a capacity for longer-term planning, quickly found that ministers were prevented by virtue of the way in which their tasks were defined from operating on such a basis. The CPRS fell instead to working to commission on specific issues with an obvious political application.

These issues assumed particular force in the area of social policy, where problems of defining priorities and achieving a degree of interdepartmental collaboration loomed especially large. Just before the end of the 1964–70 Labour Government, a sub-committee of the Labour Party's National Executive put the case for systematic planning machinery, centrally located under a senior minister. Nothing came of this initiative; nor did the thorough overhaul of the civil service proposed in the Fulton Committee's review (1966–8) bring any substantial changes in this – or indeed any other – area. The ambitiously conceived Joint Approach to Social Policy (JASP) floated by the Central Policy Review Staff during the next Wilson Government yielded nothing more than a series of preliminary studies. The problem was clear enough: the machinery of government, still basically unaltered from the form that it had assumed after the First World War, had very little flexibility when it came to dealing with social issues. Lowe's verdict is severe. In welfare policy, he concludes

> the civil service lacked the expertise and the vision to resolve those critical issues which both political parties had failed to confront in opposition. It also lacked the management expertise and drive to establish beyond doubt the efficacy of state intervention. (1993, pp. 87–8)

These failings were painfully exposed in the 1970s, when new problems began to break surface in increasing numbers and severity just as economic policies had ceased to deliver sufficient resources to cope with them.

Similar difficulties afflicted the relationship between central government and local authorities. The form of this relationship had already been substantially modified over the postwar period as a result of the development of new policies, especially in the field of welfare, which had resulted in a vast expansion of the area of responsibility of local government and the functions it was called upon to perform. The major structural reforms that had been introduced by the Heath Government after the Redcliffe-Maud Inquiry into local government (1966–9), were an attempt to equip the new, larger authorities that had been created with the capacity to perform these tasks with greater efficiency. In creating these larger units and providing guidance on forms of organisation and management and new techniques of policy analysis, central government held out the prospect of closer involvement in the evolution and execution of social policy. In practice the opposite occurred; financial stringency led from the mid-1970s onwards to ever-closer control from the centre, ostensibly from the Department of Environment but in practice from the Treasury.

When the concept of partnership was explicitly put to the test, in the inner-cities policy of Peter Shore, with its six joint committees in selected major cities, linking central and local government and health authorities in the production of common programmes for action, the outcome reflected Westminster's priorities, not those of town halls. Thus when political power changed hands at national level, so did priorities for each individual area. To the reproaches of local politicians, the customary answer was that central government, paying the piper through the rate support grant, had decided to play a new tune. In this instance it was 'The Party's Over' (Tony Crosland's pronouncement to local authorities in 1975 as Environment Secretary). Additional salt was rubbed in the wounds of those who felt that the relationship between centre and periphery was not intended to be quite so one-sided, even in a unitary state, by the spectacular rise of the Manpower Services Commission (MSC). This quango, which was set up in 1974, escaped by virtue of the high political visibility of the problem of unemployment with which it was concerned almost entirely – under both Conservative and Labour administrations – from the full impact of financial restraints. Furthermore, the Commission was encouraged to operate (with ample resources) in areas which had traditionally been local government's responsibility – principally the field of education.

The impact of the deterioration in the economic situation helped to expose these tensions, which were exacerbated by the failures of the new structures to function effectively on their own terms. Corporate management, in which great hopes had been invested, first in the local government reforms and subsequently in the Joseph reorganisation of the NHS, failed to make the adaptation to the new constrained environment. Many of the tools with which corporate managers had been equipped – the programme-budgeting techniques adapted from American experience

– also failed to survive transplantation. Research and intelligence, hailed as the key new local government skill, dwindled into a mere adjunct to the processes of administration or, recklessly politicised, became one of the numerous devices employed by councils in the great game of evading or deflecting the pressures for cuts.

Prominent among the grounds for disillusionment with the machinery of government expressed by politicians at all levels and from all parties was the sense that the new structures were insufficiently responsive to the needs of their constituents. As a result, the issue of democratic accountability began once more to become prominent in debates about the direction of welfare policies. The key obstacles, as perceived by critics, lay in three characteristics of the machinery of State welfare: the question of scale, especially after the creation of new local authorities and the appearance of the super-departments in Whitehall, especially the Department of Health and Social Security and the Department of Environment; the expansion of bureaucracy and the role of professionalism. None of these issues was precisely novel; but the new circumstances of the 1970s caused them to be reviewed from a sharply critical perspective.

Under such scrutiny, the economies of scale and improvements in the integration of policies that had actually been achieved through the creation of larger units were questioned; and the competence and skills of the bureaucracy in the new environment thrown into doubt. The values of professionalism and in particular the attitudes and performance of the newer professional groups that accounted for a large element in the expansion of the social services were also subjected to critical review. Not all this criticism was negative, either in intention or effect: in many instances, it helped to identify possible lines for remedial action. Concern with the issue of scale helped to underline the potentiality of experiments in local neighbourhood action and the creation of institutions on the ground in inner-city areas, rather than relying upon prefabricated structures parachuted in from above. The re-establishment towards the end of the 1970s of a local perspective after the disillusioning effects of the CDP experience, with its bleakly negative message about the irrelevance of local action, had a good deal to do with the new left's belated discovery of local politics and their rapid and successful penetration of inner-city Labour parties.

This concern for local action marched with a renewed interest in client involvement in service delivery and provision for expression of consumer preference – the latter a common concern on left and right, although the prescribed means of satisfying such preferences differed sharply between the two. Renewed pressure was brought to bear from the right for such proposals as education vouchers; the expansion of the private sector in health; and purchase of council houses by tenants, justified in terms of increasing the range of choices. Limited experiments by some local authorities under Conservative control helped to prepare the ground for what was to follow if power changed hands nationally.

Finally, the increased scepticism about the values and performance of professionals in the social services led to a sharp change of mood on the role of the voluntary sector. Exiled to the margins of the welfare system after the postwar expansion in the responsibilities and resources of the State, the voluntary sector's capacity for innovation and flexible response (though sometimes improved in the telling) began to seem more relevant as the certainties of the 1960s faded. Richard Crossman, the first Secretary of State for Social Services, delivered himself of an important apologia on behalf of his party in his Sidney Ball lecture: 'I am now convinced that the Labour Party's opposition to philanthropy and altruism and its determined belief in economic self-interest as the driving dynamic of society has done it grievous harm' (Halsey, 1976, p. 278). The Wolfenden Committee's subsequent review of the voluntary sector identified a number of functions that could be effectively discharged through voluntary action at local and national level. The case was greatly strengthened by a rapid spontaneous expansion of voluntary action, involving both existing organisations, often in fresh or greatly modified guise and new bodies, representing a whole range of interests and client groups.

Even such substantial modifications in State action as those being advocated by the late 1970s would not have gone far enough for some critics. Root and branch scepticism about the intentions of the state and its self-interest in intervening in the field of welfare, common on the left in the early 1970s, had an even longer pedigree on the right. Public choice theorists are not in principle greatly interested in 'mere shifts in policy', since State bureaucracies are themselves by definition corrupted by the role they perform and the manner in which they discharge it. James Buchanan, whose views on this issue were vigorously propagated by the IEA in the 1970s, has painted a chilling picture of the self-interested bureaucrat, managing his bureau to maximise his budget, subject continuously to the expansionary demands of the ubiquitous pressure groups. Another economist who has applied economic methodology to bureaucratic decision-taking, William Niskanen (also an

IEA author), has provided a more detailed catalogue of the bureaucrat's likely motivation: 'salary, perquisites of office, public reputation, power, patronage, output of the bureau, ease of making changes and ease of managing the bureau' (quoted in Heald, 1983, p. 112). The position of critics on the left is more ambiguous; a thoughtful review of the issues facing those who distrust the State's intentions but feel the obligation (in Louis MacNeice's phrase) to 'defend the bad against the worse' is provided in the London–Edinburgh Weekend Return Group's *In and Against the State*. Summarising the position of those employed in the public sector at the end of the 1970s, they write:

> Of course we must defend our jobs and our services. But there is a great danger that in defending ourselves, we will see only one side of the State and forget the other. In our haste to defend our benefits and our jobs, it is easy to lose sight of the oppressive relations in which they enmesh us. In the struggle against the capitalists' attack on the capitalist State, it may seem tactically necessary to paint an unambiguously good picture of the State, to present the Welfare State as a great achievement of the working class, even as a step towards socialism. That is very dangerous. (1980, p. 74)

Both positions are based on an unspoken premise: that drastic change is justified, because it is in the true interests of those for whom the services are intended. In the case of the right, this premise is hedged around with qualifications: new proposals for constitutional safeguards which will ensure that the new role of the State is kept within bounds – for example, an obligation to balance the budget or referenda on all substantial new spending proposals. But despite such caution about the possible consequences of unbridled democracy the assumption is nonetheless that the exercise of free choice will inevitably lead away from State monopoly provision. However, the evidence on this point was a good deal less clear-cut than the IEA asserted.

ATTITUDES TO WELFARE

A crucial element in the change of climate in the second half of the 1970s was the perception that popular attitudes towards State welfare were shifting. Early studies had demonstrated how rapidly the services provided had been taken to the nation's heart. The NHS, in particular, quickly achieved a popularity which not even a rich and varied folklore about delays in doctors' surgeries and arrangements for operations could dim.

As already indicated, the general acceptance on all sides of politics of this popularity played a substantial role in determining the direction of policies advocated by oppositions and adopted by governments. The cry of 'welfare state in danger' was generally seen as potentially almost as electorally effective as the threat of mass unemployment (Crosland, 1956; Macmillan, 1969). Election studies appeared to reinforce that perception; approving references to the Welfare State cut across social class boundaries and united those of different political allegiances (Butler and Stokes, 1971, p. 418).

From the beginning of the 1970s, that perception began to change. Concern about the quality of welfare – not merely the type of service being provided and its accessiblity to consumers but the effectiveness of individual services in meeting their declared objectives – had always been present, although often in muted form. Now it was joined by another anxiety, about the cost of welfare and the burden of taxation implied by maintaining services at their current level. In addition, a more diffuse feeling about the recipients of welfare was making itself felt, centring around the perennial question of the undeserving poor, reappearing in late twentieth-century form as 'scroungers'.

From 1970 onwards, questions asked by the commercial opinion polling organisations began to show an increased level of antipathy towards high levels of public expenditure. Recurrent surveys on the general issue of the public's preferences as between reducing taxation, on the one hand, and spending more on social services on the other, showed up to the late 1970s a rising majority in favour of tax cuts (Jowell and Airey, 1984, p. 76). However, as Bosanquet suggests, these data do not make the connection between the two sufficiently explicit to allow more than a very general expression of choice to be given, so they should be treated with caution, whichever conclusion they suggest.

One of the key factors at work seems to have been the impact of mass unemployment and the vast increase in the numbers of claimants that it produced. This not merely helped to make the issue visible but also triggered off strong reactions among those not prepared to accept being unemployed as grounds for state support at more than a bare minimum level. David Donnison, the last chairman of the Supplementary Benefits Commission, reported that some of the commonest items in his postbag were letters from the working poor, protesting at the over-generous level of benefits (1982). In 1976 a widely reported survey undertaken for the EEC (see Table 3.1) showed that the British, uniquely among the inhabitants of all the European countries included in the survey, chose to

Table 3.1 Public views on the causes of poverty by country (%)

	B	DK	D	F	IRL	I	L	NL	UK	EC (1)
Because there is much injustice in our society	17	14	23	35	19	40	16	11	16	26
Because of laziness and lack of willpower	22	11	23	16	30	20	31	12	43	25
Because they have been unlucky	21	17	18	18	25	14	20	20	10	16
Its an inevitable part of progress in the modern world	15	28	10	18	16	10	6	16	17	14
None of these	9	8	8	7	4	4	6	11	4	6
Don't know	16	22	18	6	6	12	21	30	10	13
Total	100	100	100	100	100	100	100	100	100	100

Note: In the Community as a whole, level of education and income also introduce noticeable differences in the answers. The better-educated , the better-off and the leaders most often blame social injustice and the poorer income groups, the less well educated and the non-leaders tend to suggest that the victims themselves are to blame.

(1) = weighted average.

Source: EUROSTAT, *The Perception of Poverty in Europe* (European Commission, 1977).

blame the poor for their own poverty, rather than putting it down to economic or social circumstances or sheer bad luck (Mack and Lansley, 1985, p. 206). This hostility was expressed despite the fact that the existence of poverty had been accepted as a reality by a substantial majority of those questioned in Peter Townsend's massive survey of poverty, conducted at the beginning of the decade (Townsend, 1979).

Attitudes were far from undifferentiated, however. An extensive study of attitudes towards the health service conducted for the Royal Commission on the National Health Service in 1978 showed that there were still high levels of satisfaction both with the NHS as a whole and with particular aspects of the service. Similar levels of approval were reported for education; and expenditure on pensions retained general public support. By contrast, a high level of concern about social security and hostility towards claimants is a common feature of attitude surveys. Golding and Middleton, whose *Images of Welfare* helpfully brings together a good deal of evidence from the late 1970s, report that the majority of their own sample felt that benefits were too generous and too easy to obtain. Furthermore, six out of ten respondents felt that 'people living on social security can manage quite well nowadays' (Golding and Middleton, 1982, p. 162). The authors attribute much of this hostility to a series of campaigns in the press directed against 'scrounging' and employing a variety of well-tried journalists' techniques: anecdotes, cartoons, straight-from-the-shoulder exposés; editorial appeals to common sense and common experience; and the full-blown campaign, of which the finest flower was the 'Costa del Dole' episode of 1976–7, in which almost all the popular press played a part in projecting a caricature of claimants using benefit as holiday money (p. 106). The direct effect of such campaigns is difficult to pin down; but the impact on the political environment, judged by the use made of this material by MPs both in the House and outside, and ministers' reactions to it, seems to have been considerable.

A different form of response to public concern about the performance of the Welfare State has been to argue that it reflects an unsatisfied demand for an alternative. In a sequence of surveys, the IEA have claimed to have established the existence of a substantial minority in the population that would be prepared to accept a system under which individuals would be able to make their own choices, through the market, in a range of different services now provided by the State. The capacity to choose would be facilitated by reductions in taxes, rates and National Insurance payments, made possible by stringent means-testing and the introduction of voucher schemes (Harris and Seldon, 1979). Whatever the ultimate significance of their results – and the interpretation placed upon them by the Institute has subsequently been challenged – the IEA have at the minimum succeeded in contributing to the debate a set of alternative possibilities apparently validated by statements of consumer preference.

A more limited, but in political terms more immediately relevant means of charting the movement of opinion lies in the ballot box. By this test, the tide began to flow very fast after 1976 against the political representatives of 'collectivism'. The acute electoral unpopularity of the Labour Government led to a number of spectacular by-election losses which in turn forced the Government into an uneasy pact with the Liberal Party to ensure its continued survival. This period of unpopularity coincided with a brief but dramatic increase in support for the extremist National Front, whose crude racism briefly found a response among younger white working-class men. This episode ended almost as suddenly as it had begun. But while it lasted, the grotesque echoes of pre-war fascism that it set off appeared to provide still further evidence that the politics of the middle way had lost its broad constituency and that there was a pressing need for sharply defined alternatives within the democratic mainstream. Of even greater importance for the longer term was the continued evidence of substantial deprivation suffered by members of ethnic minority groups – no longer 'immigrants' but by now settled communities whose British-born children were beginning to pass through the educational system and out onto the job market in substantial numbers. The sequence of studies undertaken by the Policy Studies Institute from the mid-1960s on (see Smith, 1974) illustrated both the persistence of disadvantage and the tenacity of its main cause: racial discrimination. The Labour Government's response – substantially strengthened anti-discrimination legislation and the revamping of the agencies set up to promote racial equality – was widely perceived as inadequate and provoked fears that failure to satisfy legitimate grievances would bring about alienation from the political system.

CRISIS OF THE STATE?

Less dramatic than the street brawls set off by the National Front and its opponents on the far left, but ultimately more threatening to the survival of the postwar settlement was the steady erosion of support for consensus politics among the opinion formers, and in particular the specialist economic journalists who had done much in the postwar period to popularise Keynesian ideas and keep successive governments on the path of interventionist virtue. In the course of the 1970s, several of the most prominent of these journalists formally recanted, prominent among them Sam Brittan and Peter Jay. Both of them were contributors to a polemic published in the United States under the title *The Future that Doesn't Work: Social Democracy's Failures in Britain* (1977): a warning to wanton American intellectuals of the dangers of following the British example. As author of the crucial paragraphs in James Callaghan's speech on the fallacies of public expenditure to the Labour party conference of 1976, Jay had already formally abandoned his previous position. Under the rather unattractive title 'Englanditis', he now argued that democracy was swallowing its own tail: the irresistible pressure of demands generated by the active participation of various interests in the democratic process was preventing government from taking the steps necessary to rescue the economy, without which the demands themselves – and in particular redemption of the pledge to maintain full employment – could not be satisfied (Tyrrell, 1977, p. 181).

Brittan's analysis, subsequently developed and extended in a series of books, was more complex. Like Jay, he attributed much of the immediate pressure on government to a decline in self-imposed restraints within the political system. However, he went on to identify the fundamental difficulty as the misapplication of the concept of equality and the attempt to enforce it by public intervention in an essentially private sphere – setting the relative level of incomes (Tyrrell, p. 141). Brittan's main theme in this and subsequent writing, however, was the weakness of democracy as an instrument for making choices in constrained conditions. This theme was developed, with particular emphasis on welfare policy, in his attack upon the 'Wenceslaus myth' – the idea that services free at the point of delivery are ultimately cost-free in a broader sense, because they fall upon an abstraction, the community, rather than upon the flesh and blood individual benefiting from the service (Brittan, 1983, ch. 1).

The argument stemming from a particular emphasis on democracy had a broader application in the economic sphere. In the mid-1970s, general concern began to be expressed about the implications of the proportion of the GDP being taken for public expenditure. The suggestion was twofold: first, that support for the public sector was becoming an intolerable burden on the economy and a distortion of expenditure priorities; and, second, that it was corrupting the decision-making processes by creating such a large number of separate vested interests that disinterested policy decisions would no longer be possible. The first of these theses was persuasively advanced by the economists Bacon and Eltis, whose theory that the growth of the public sector was 'crowding out' profitable private sector activity was briefly highly influential. It was reinforced by figures produced by the Treasury, which appeared to show that in 1975–6 60 per cent of GNP had been devoted to public expenditure (Heald, 1983, p. 14). This moved Roy Jenkins, who had left active politics in Britain to become chairman of the EEC Commissioners, to comment that in such circumstances it was impossible 'to maintain the values of a plural society with adequate freedom of choice. We are here close to one of the frontiers of social democracy' (Heald, 1983 p. 13). Unfortunately, it later emerged that the Treasury had double-counted and the true figure, when it was eventually established, was very much lower. Finally, and on a less exalted plane, concern about the level of public expenditure was linked to notions that high rates of personal taxation, particularly at the top end of the scale, inhibit individual enterprise.

The importance of such views and in particular those expressed by former Keynesians like Brittan and Jay, and in the field of social policy by John Vaizey (who had been in the 1950s one of the chief architects of the Fabian approach to educational policy) was that they created new openings. As William Keegan subsequently put it:

> Monetarism was still a minority cult, but because Jay and Brittan were in such important posts in the press, it was receiving publicity and approval out of all proportion to its standing in the economics profession and in the Bank of England and Whitehall. (Keegan, 1984, p. 45)

Several of the themes identified by these critics were also being developed within the Conservative Party. The period between the election of Margaret Thatcher to the Conservative leadership in 1975 and the Conservative election success of 1979 has been subsequently compared to Butler's period at the Conservative Research Department during the party's earlier period in opposition, in 1945–51. The comparison is not precisely apt, since in the 1970s this period in opposition was devoted to the reverse of the process that Butler had adopted. Instead of moving towards their opponents' position, the party now moved decisively away from it.

Once Edward Heath had been defeated in a contest among Conservative members for the party's leadership, late in 1975 – an event that subsequently became known as the 'peasants' revolt' – the new leadership set about developing a new approach that would represent a clear break with the past. The dominant intellectual influence in this process was Sir Keith Joseph. Even before the Conservatives had lost the second election of 1974, he had begun to mark out the terrain in a series of speeches in which he proclaimed his reconversion to Conservatism and to free market principles (prompting the sour comment from Enoch Powell that he had not previously realised that it was possible to undergo a post-mortem repentance). The first and most striking of these was delivered at Preston, in September 1974. In it, Sir Keith observed that 'it is the methods that successive Governments have used to reduce unemployment – namely expanding aggregate demand by deficit financing – which has created inflation, and without really helping the unemployed either' (Keegan, 1984, pp. 51–2).

This speech laid the foundations for the new policies, which were developed through two sources: the private think-tank that Sir Keith had himself founded, the Centre for Policy Studies and the more orthodox machinery of Conservative Central Office. The two streams mingled at times somewhat uneasily: the radicalism of the CPS under its joint directors, Alfred Sherman and Hugh Thomas, was determinedly iconoclastic; the Central Office and its Research Department rather more concerned to preserve some ideas and policies from the Heath regime. The point of confluence between the two was Sir Keith himself, who had been given the responsibility by his new leader for coordinating policy development. The new policies were subjected as they emerged to systematic scrutiny by Sir Geoffrey Howe, the Shadow Chancellor, and his team to establish their public spending implications and the extent to which they could be reconciled with the policies of stringent limits on public spending that the Conservatives expected to introduce once in office.

The first public statement of the new line appeared in a general statement of principles, *The Right Approach* (1976). But the closest equivalent of Butler's *Industrial Charter* was *The Right Approach to the Economy* (1977), which represented the formal assimilation of Friedman's ideas on macro-economic policy into the main body of Conservative thinking. The authors stated: 'We shall aim to continue the rate of growth of money supply, in line with firm monetary targets', since 'it is certainly the case that if the management of money is handled wrongly, everything goes wrong' (Keegan, 1984, p. 100). In some respects, this document was less radical than the general direction of the background work upon which it was based implied. For example, on the question of trade union legislation, it took a distinctly cautious line, strongly influenced by the fate of Edward Heath's Industrial Relations Act five years earlier. Nicholas Ridley subsequently commented acidly that James Prior, who had responsibility for this policy 'had no intention of carrying out any serious reforms of trade union law, despite the fact that the trade unions were clearly holding the nation to ransom' (Ridley, 1992, p. 14). Ridley himself was responsible for one of the most innovatory ideas – which was also among the most threatening to the *status quo*: privatisation. He had floated the concept without success under the Heath leadership and was now asked by Keith Joseph to chair a study group to explore it further. However, the group's detailed proposals, though cleared by the Shadow Cabinet, eventually appeared only in the most general terms in the party's manifesto for the 1979 election.

But ultimately the economic arguments were the means to a still more ambitious end – Keith Joseph's insistence that the party must move away once and for all from its previous position, as he characterised it, 'stranded on the middle ground'. This meant an escape not only from the legacy of the postwar consensus but from the party's own role in bringing it about and sustaining it – what Norman Tebbit later called 'the weak complacent Conservatism of the 60s and early 70s' (Tebbit, 1988, p. 267). Sir Keith did not shirk responsibility for his own part in all this. The dust-jacket of his review of the implications of the idea of equality proclaimed that he 'has become increasingly aware of the unintended ill consequences of many well intentioned reforms, including his own'. In the book itself, published (jointly with Jonathan Sumption) under the title *Equality*, in 1979, he took issue in uncompromising terms with the central principles of egalitarianism, arguing that 'equality will not relieve destitution but spread it equally. Equal societies are not contented ones but wretched societies based on the frustration of ordinary human instincts' (p. 103). This repudiation of the basis upon which many of the Welfare State policies were founded had self-evident implications for social policy, should the Conservatives succeed in winning the forthcoming election. Some of this thinking was reflected in the confidential 'Stepping Stones' exercise undertaken under Sir Keith's aegis at the Centre for Policy Studies in parallel with official preparations for the election manifesto (Young, 1990, p. 115).

For the meanwhile, the economic issues took first place. As in the case of Butler's Industrial Charter, the finer detail on the journey along the Right Road eluded the Conservative party conference to which it was introduced. But Margaret Thatcher's presentation of the case in terms of the sovereignty of the market, the elimination of redundant State intervention and above all the reduction of personal taxation found a ready response. In making it she began to reach out beyond a purely party audience to tap a vein of beliefs about self-reliance and individual initiative that had been for some while past politically homeless, but had never wholly disappeared.

Margaret Thatcher's capacity to communicate with a wider public was a new factor in the situation, remarked upon by all commentators, both friendly and hostile, as she began to grow in confidence as Leader of the Opposition. She had not been the first choice of the small group within the party who were resolved after 1974 to rid it of Heath's leadership. Her record as Secretary of State for Education had been unremarkable. As a minister in a spending department she had pressed strongly for expansion in her budget and had been glad to employ increases in expenditure as an index of success (Heclo and Wildavsky, 1981, p. 136).

She had played no public part in party debates about Heath's changes of direction. Her conversion to free market ends and monetarist means, if indeed it was one (it is represented on her behalf that she had always held such views, but had not felt the need to expound upon them) was not primarily intellectual. As Nicholas Ridley puts it, 'she didn't find it difficult to articulate her beliefs and the policies she wanted to pursue. She knew them already, almost as of instinct' (1992, p. 17). Although she participated with some enthusiasm in the meetings of the Conservative Philosophy Group established after the fall of Edward Heath, it was for strictly pragmatic reasons. 'We must have an ideology' she declared at an early meeting. 'The other side have got an ideology they can test their policies against. We must have one as well.' The convenor of the group, Jonathan Aitken, remembers her as being 'constantly on the look out for new phrases. Borrowing or stealing or otherwise taking over other people's language was as regular a quest of Mrs Thatcher's as was the plundering of their ideas' (H. Young, 1990, p. 406).

Conviction had always been Margaret Thatcher's trademark; but what she had to offer was in no sense based on complex analysis. Essentially, it consisted of the permutation of a limited set of views, repeatedly restated with very little variation but delivered with great force and brio: the moral superiority of individual enterprise and the demoralising effects of State intervention; the value of independence and the importance of not living beyond one's means; the importance of discipline and of a proper balance of rewards and penalties; the value of cohesion, within the family, the community and the nation. Sometimes variety was achieved by garnishing these themes with historical references – the 'Victorian values' to which increasing emphasis came to be given. A close adviser, Sir Alan Walters, believes that these historical parallels are of particular importance to Mrs Thatcher; he commented that she sees Victorian society as one in which 'people did do a great deal of voluntary work for the community and people were very upright and honest' (Young and Sloman, 1986, p. 85). There is frequent use of the metaphor of the household, most elaborately in a speech at the Lord Mayor's Banquet in 1981 when she observed that 'some say I preach merely the homilies of housekeeping or the parables of the parlour. But I do not repent. Those parables would have saved many a financier from failure and many a country from crisis' (Riddell, 1984, p. 7). In this instance, the artful alliteration betrays the speechwriters' hidden hand; but in other instances, speaking less formally, the same parallel is pressed insistently home. Finally, the style itself was distinctive; a combination of audacity amounting almost to rashness, that John Hoskyns, later to become one of her policy advisers, found irresistibly attractive (Young and Sloman, p. 65); and a caution at times shading into hesitancy in coming to terms with politically contentious issues. Nigel Lawson, a close collaborator who eventually fell out spectacularly with her (and is therefore not precisely an unbiased witness) has been particularly scathing about this quality, which came to have important consequences in her approach to social policy. In addition, she showed a willingness on occasion to become the mouthpiece for populist sentiment, as on law and order and a notorious aside about immigration, delivered during an important by-election campaign (*Times*, 31.1.78).

If all this speaks to and for any social class, it is the suburban and provincial middle class. But her achievement was to broaden the basis of this appeal, to form the basis of a national programme. Although her intellectual contribution to the definition and development of policy was not great, her personality and enthusiasm were essential to its cohesion and maintenance. Hence, although she was neither architect nor developer of the new policies, as their most enthusiastic promoter it is not altogether unjust that they should be indelibly marked with her name.

Summing up all these developments in a subsequent comment on the counterrevolution in his party, Nigel Lawson (who had had his own Keynesian period as a city journalist in the 1960s) pronounced the epitaph of the 'philosophy of social democracy, with its profound faith in the efficacy of government action, particularly in the economic sphere, and its deep commitment to the notion of "equality"' (IEA, 1981, p. 10). Now the spell had at last been broken, and the Keynesian limb of the postwar settlement could accordingly be discarded. On the Beveridge leg the Conservative position was less clear-cut. Keith Joseph's attempt to reintroduce the issue of population and the implications of selective fertility rates, which unless checked by family planning measures, would produce a permanent underclass, had ended in personal disaster. The hostile response to his speech on this subject had been a major factor in deciding him against running for the party leadership. But the themes of shifting the role of the State from large-scale activity to selective interventions and a greater emphasis on individual enterprise, which were to form the backbone of the new approach to economic policy, clearly had important applications in social policy too. Coupled with the theme of consumer choice in health and education, assiduously promoted by the IEA, it formed the basis of a prospectus with some obvious attractions for the more prosperous voter.

But to achieve electoral success the net would have to be cast more widely. The departure from the consensus would be electorally hazardous if it failed to carry with it some, at least, of the principal beneficiaries of the postwar settlement in the skilled working class. Their progressive disillusionment with many aspects of the condition of Britain in the 1970s provided the essential opening. The inability of Keynesian demand management techniques to protect standards of living in the face of the international economic recession, the mounting level of conflict within society and the apparent exploitation of the Welfare State by the undeserving poor – all these presented specific electoral opportunities. Margaret Thatcher spoke to these anxieties: her particular achievement consisted of convincing many working-class voters that inflation was a greater danger than unemployment and that steps to deal with it could be combined with reductions in taxation and would not involve the kind of pay policy skilled manual workers had found so irksome under both Wilson and Heath.

For other audiences, the prospectus could be presented in different terms. The adoption of monetarism as a technique for expanding the wealth-creating base of the economy and thereby escaping from the blind alley into which Keynesian techniques appeared to have run was an approach that attracted a surprisingly wide range of influential people outside the ranks of the economists and economic journalists – what Peter Jackson calls 'the physiocratic notion of the need to create wealth' (1985, p. 28). The social policy propositions, being less coherent, attracted less attention outside the circle of true believers. But the elimination of waste and duplication, greater efficiency through targeting of resources, deregulation and, above all, the stress on the importance of the family in the community – could all be made to appear attractive. The gap in the range of provision likely to be caused by the reductions in level and extent of statutory services implied by substantial cuts in public expenditure could, the Conservatives argued, be plugged by a greater emphasis on the role of the family and encouraging voluntary sector activity.

However, as in 1951, so in 1979; the party was less well prepared for the problems that were to face it in the social policy arena than it was for the economic issues – at least in part because the primacy of economic policy priorities was taken as beyond argument. Between Keith Joseph's elegant restatement of the libertarian case against equality and Lord Hailsham's version of the dangers of 'elective dictatorship' (as he termed it when out of office) through abuse of democratic procedures, at one level, and Rhodes Boyson's popularisation (or vulgarisation) of the IEA's ideas on phasing out statutory welfare, on quite a different plane, a gap remained where new policies would need to be devised.

As the Opposition's position gained in coherence, so the Government lapsed further into expediency. Since Labour's social policies had always depended on 'cashing the dividend of economic growth', its disappearance left a vacuum that was never satisfactorily filled. After the IMF intervention, Labour was always struggling; although some significant innovations were achieved in both economic and social policy. On the economic side, a set of devices for achieving more effective control over public expenditure (notably cash limits on spending) were introduced; in social policy, attempts were made to introduce long-term planning devices linking the identification of policy priorities to resource allocation. In some of these instances, the Government was anticipating the line subsequently to be taken by their successors; but to present the Callaghan regime as the first monetarist administration is a distortion of the record. Denis Healey's 'pink monetarism' was, as Peter Riddell observes, an improvisation: 'the response of a clever and flexible man to the breakdown of the postwar consensus on economic management and to external pressures' (Riddell, 1984, p. 60). Later, out of office, Healey referred scathingly to his opponents' 'sado-monetarism', explaining that he had published monetary targets 'largely to placate the financial markets. But I never accepted Friedman's theories. Nor did I ever meet any private or central banker who took them seriously' (Healey, 1990, p. 491).

Despite the relatively successful economic performance of the period of the Lab–Lib Pact (1977–8), the Labour Government came under increasing pressure from its own supporters as the failure to make any significant progress towards the egalitarian goals proclaimed on entering office became increasingly evident. The Government's conduct of affairs subsided into a holding operation; and the Prime Minister was aptly compared to a sea captain who could only keep his elderly ship afloat by sailing it slowly round in circles while madly pumping out the water pouring through every seam.

Eventually the pressures on the rotten timbers became too great. The dependence of the Government on powerful interest groups was dramatically illustrated when Callaghan and his Chancellor presumed too far upon the success of their arrangement with the trade unions – the 'social contract' – and attempted to impose a pay norm of 5 per cent. The resulting 'winter of discontent', in which the public sector unions broke ranks in an attempt to secure substantial pay rises for their lower-paid workers, added a set of powerful images, faithfully conveyed by press and television – closed wards, rubbish in the streets, the dead unburied - to reinforce the already potent theme of Britain as an ungovernable country. By the time that defeat in the Commons made an election inevitable, the position of ministers could be reduced to the comfortable repetition of reassurances to the effect that things would eventually improve if no drastic changes were made. In this spirit, strangely reminiscent of Stanley Baldwin and 'safety first', the Labour Government faced the country in May 1979. As it had done fifty years earlier, the electorate rejected the safer option. But this time it had chosen a far more drastic experiment. As J.K. Galbraith subsequently put it: 'Britain has, in effect, volunteered to be the Friedmanite guinea pig' (Keegan, 1984, p. 1).

4

THE RIGHT APPROACH?

Nothing is harder than the admission of failure in the political arena.

Nigel Lawson, *The New Conservatism*, 1980.

Among the many severe strictures levelled by Lord Hailsham at the state of British democracy in his Dimbleby Lecture of 1976 was a cutting attack on the misuse of the theory of the mandate, based upon an election manifesto, as the source of authority. 'Before the Election', he wrote, 'the advertisement is written rather in the style of an advertisement for patent medicines; after the Election, it is treated as a pronouncement from Sinai, with every jot and tittle of that unreal and often unreasonable document treated as Holy Writ' (*Listener*, 21.10.76).

The Government which he joined in 1979 has been no exception to this general rule (Hailsham's Law?). But despite some subsequent claims, the authors of the Conservative party manifesto of 1979 avoided making many specific commitments. It is now clear that this was a deliberate tactic; and that one of the main reasons for adopting it was the leader's own caution. Despite the long and intensive labours of the party's study groups in opposition, her concern about the risk of giving hostages to fortune, and indeed about the acceptability to the electorate of some of the more far-reaching proposals, which had proved controversial within her own party and Shadow Cabinet, duly prevailed. 'Not for the first time' Hugo Young comments, 'Thatcher the tactician got the better of Thatcher the ideologue' (1990, p. 128).

Such caution was understandable enough, since by adopting an overall approach which broke away so decisively from the general direction of policy over the whole postwar period the party was moving into largely uncharted territory. For if the detail of the journey now planned was left in decent obscurity, the general direction that was being signposted was clear enough: the objective now being proclaimed to the electorate was nothing less than a complete change in the climate of national life, through cutting back on the role of the State and thereby decisively altering 'the balance of power in favour of the people'. So were the means: taking a grip on inflation through controlling the money supply, reducing public expenditure and the power of the trade unions; the reassertion of the rule of law; and, key to the whole project, self-reliance, to be fostered by 'action to restore incentives so that hard work pays, success is rewarded and genuine new jobs are created in an expanding economy' (Jackson, 1985, p. 37).

The emphasis within the programme derived from these priorities lay overwhelmingly on the side of economic policy. Not only were social policy objectives to be subordinated to the general goals set out for the economy; the various programmes that made up the Welfare State were presented as being themselves in many respects part of the problems that the Government would have to resolve. To the extent that objectives were defined for these programmes, they were accordingly cast mainly in economic terms. As Sir Geoffrey Howe (who served as Chancellor for the whole of the Government's first term) subsequently put it:

> There are powerful reasons why we must be ready to consider how far private provision and individual choice can supplement, or in some cases possibly replace, the role of Government in health, social security and education. Most of these reasons are economic. (Riddell, 1984, p. 139)

It might therefore be assumed that any analysis of the Government's performance during its first term in office (1979–83) should be based on its achievements in the field of economic policy, to which it attached both in rhetoric and in practice such an overriding significance. But such an analysis, though necessary, is not sufficient to provide a fully balanced account of the objectives that the Thatcher administration was attempting to secure. For the new Prime Minister herself, and the political evangelists of her inner circle, the economic objectives were themselves only means to still broader ends; and those ends were essentially political. Mrs Thatcher's own dislike of the concept of consensus and all that went with it rapidly became proverbial; she expressed it in its purest form in an interview given shortly after coming to power, when she observed that 'to me, consensus seems to be the process of abandoning all beliefs, principles, values and policies' (Kaldor, 1983, p. 15).

This general antipathy took particular shape in Mrs Thatcher's determination to break up the tripartite structure of collaboration between government and the two sides of industry, on which that consensus, in its later form, had rested. Her hostility to the detailed policies that this system had produced, and in particular the form that they had taken during the second half of the Heath administration needs no elaborate gloss; although it had not been evident at the time to those who had sat alongside her in Heath's Cabinet, like Francis Pym and Jim Prior (Young and Sloman, 1986, p. 27). What was in many ways more striking was the form that this hostility took upon assuming office, and in particular her attitudes and those of her inner circle towards those who had been responsible for implementing past policies.

This antipathy found particularly sharp expression in the new Government's dealings with the civil service. This should not have been surprising; after all, senior civil servants had acted throughout the postwar period as 'architects of and advocates of, and continuing administrators of consensus policies'. The words are Tony Benn's (Young and Sloman, p. 81); but the sentiments chime in precisely with those of Margaret Thatcher. Nevertheless, there seems to have been a widespread assumption within Whitehall that the new Government, like its predecessors, would pass rapidly through their ideological phase into the safety of the mainstream, where the civil service could reassume their traditional role of tactful guidance and discreet steering of events (H. Young, 1990, p. 157). The notion that the Government intended to implement their full programme and, more radical still, that the civil service were to be held accountable for past failures took longer to sink in. The enthusiasm with which the Thatcher administration pursued its objectives, both through the blunt instrument of drastic reductions in civil service numbers and the stiletto of exclusion of all but the trusted few from the centres of policy-making was deeply wounding, in particular coming as it did from a Conservative Government. After all, its reconciliation with the bureaucracy had been ceremonially sealed under Macmillan, and reached its apogee in the last stages of the Heath regime, when the Secretary to the Cabinet, Sir William Armstrong, appeared in public alongside the Prime Minister as equal partner in the management of the crisis.

Of the remaining constituent elements in the consensus, the position of industry was less problematic. The task here, as it appeared to the new

Government, was more educational than disciplinary, a matter of weaning industrialists away from the notion that State aid was an essential element in the environment in which they functioned. In strict free market dogma, there could be no such thing as an industrial policy based upon direct Government intervention; but it was recognised very early on that the process of breaking the engrained habits of dependency would be a lengthy business. Nevertheless, in the course of their opening period of office, manufacturing industry was duly exposed by the Government's new economic policies to an icy blast of competition, the shock of which often proved fatal. As for the trade unions, as the third parties in the corporate trinity, the question was merely when, rather than whether, their expulsion from the centres of power should be promulgated.

Thus the outcome of the new approach was intended to be not merely economic revival but the creation of an entirely novel constellation of forces, supported by a permanent shift in the centre of gravity within the political system. As Margaret Thatcher subsequently put it, invoking *vox populi* in the shape of a nameless constituent, the task as conceived in 1979 was to 'get the centre back to the middle because the centre has gone so far to the left' (*Times*, 28.3.86). It followed that in much of what was attempted it was the style as much as the content that was crucial in determining both successes and failures. This was a government which, as Keith Middlemas puts it 'knew (in the Russian phrase) not only who was guilty but what was to be done' (*New Statesman*, 17.6.83)

Even so, when it came to the point of translating policy into action, the Government found themselves facing not just the problems of implementation encountered by all incoming administrations, but further difficulties compounded by the nature of the changes that they were attempting to introduce. The approach that had been agreed upon in opposition required a rapid and decisive change in the direction of policies at the centre, combined with the assumption of greater responsibility at the periphery. This was to be achieved through action by statutory agencies and in the case of social policy by voluntary bodies and crucially, in both rhetoric and practice, by individuals. The conundrum that this approach threw up is more easily expressed than resolved: how can minimalist policies be effectively implemented? The introduction of sweeping new forms of State control over the scale and content of large tracts of activity in the public sector had somehow to be reconciled with a 'hands off' approach consistent with the promotion of efficiency and effectiveness (the sacred duo of the increasingly influential management consultants) in both public and private sectors. The radicalism of the concept – a State that both tightens its control and reduces the scope of its activities – was never to be translated wholly satisfactorily into practice.

Nevertheless, the situation should have been greatly simplified by the clarity and authority with which the Government laid down its basic economic objectives at the outset. The reduction of the rate of inflation was identified from the start as the central objective of policy; and the control of the money supply and reduction of public expenditure as the means by which it was to be achieved. All this was clearly set out in Sir Geoffrey Howe's letter to the Commons' Treasury and Civil Service Committee and embodied in the Medium Term Financial Strategy (MTFS), which formed part of the 1980 Budget. Of this document, Nigel Lawson, then Financial Secretary to the Treasury, wrote at the time:

> The distinctive feature of our medium term financial strategy, which differentiates it from the so-called national plans of other times and other places, is that it is confined to charting a course for those variables – notably the quantity of money – which are and must be within the power of government to control. By contrast, governments cannot create economic growth. (Lawson, 1980, p. 16)

Accordingly, specific targets covering a timespan of five years were set; the introduction of these measures (and the omission of others that had been regarded as equally, if not more, significant by previous administrations) should have provided the essential context in which progress towards the essential objectives in all policy areas could be secured and evaluated. However, in practice the complexities of the differing relationships and interlocking practices of different agencies in both public and private sectors distorted this clarity of purpose and blunted the cutting edge of the Government's initial approach.

Within central government itself, where the administration had the greatest capacity to impose their new policy priorities, the impact of the change of direction was most immediate. No gloss needed to be set on the new policies and compliance was largely, though not entirely, a matter of ministerial (or more precisely prime ministerial) direction. The line of approach adopted very quickly made itself felt; the Prime Minister, acting in tandem with her Chancellor and a small elite group of Treasury ministers and trusted officials, together with her own personal policy advisers, hammered out the major policy decisions and the means of implementation. This was achieved either by directly employing the Treasury's mechanisms for control of public expenditure or by instructions issued through the Cabinet Office, strategically located at the centre of the machinery of government under the Prime Minister's direct control. In this process, the Cabinet, in which supporters of the new departure were at first balanced by a substantial contingent from the *ancien régime*, played a subordinate role: 'I could not waste time in having arguments', the Prime Minister had told one interviewer before coming into office, and by all accounts she tried to be as good as her word. Parliament's consent was substantially guaranteed by the margin of the Government's majority in the Commons; although the Lords began very early in the first term to show a disconcerting readiness to take their constitutional role as a revising chamber seriously.

Within Whitehall, spending departments, and in particular those with major responsibilities in the social policy field – and substantial budgets – could be expected to put up the traditional resistance to cuts and employ in the process all the traditional devices of delay, obfuscation and waving the bloody stump of judiciously selected and politically painful cuts. However, firm Treasury control over the public expenditure process, supplemented by the imposition of discipline in Cabinet through the so-called 'Star Chamber', presided over by the Prime Minister's deputy, William Whitelaw, appeared to provide the means to secure compliance. Nevertheless, implementation took a puzzlingly long while to achieve, even when apparently underwritten by the despatch of selected members of the Prime Minister's praetorian guard of favoured civil servants to take charge of key spending ministries. The cumulative effects of this style of management eventually led disgruntled former members of the Cabinet to complain vigorously of the insensitivities of 'Treasury-driven social policies' (Pym, 1985).

Solutions became even harder to secure in those areas of policy where the levers of power did not fall directly under the hands of ministers. In particular, the role of local government posed a series of increasingly vexing difficulties. During the latter stages of the Labour administration, the Treasury had devised a series of mechanisms – the introduction of cash limits and the tightening up of the public expenditure survey (PESC) procedures – to keep a closer check on departmental spending. These measures were coupled with the introduction of a forum (the Joint Consultative Committee) within which the direction of government policy could at least be debated, by representatives of the local authority associations with the Chancellor and his officials. However, central government's position on the paramount importance of national goals was formally excluded from debate, as the evidence given by the Department of the Environment to the Layfield Inquiry on local government finance made clear. Local authority representatives used these opportunities to point out that needs in most major service areas were rapidly increasing, and that the consequential burden of additional responsibilities laid upon local authorities in legislation was also expanding. Despite this, local government had actually achieved reductions in the proportion of public expenditure consumed (although it was less often pointed out that this was the result of substantial cuts in capital programmes, as opposed to current expenditure).

Many of the same issues also arose in the case of the National Health Service. Here, the Government's undivided control over resources made their position considerably stronger than in those areas of social policy where local authorities are responsible for the delivery of services. However, much of the initial rhetoric stressed the importance of local decision-taking; and the Secretary of State was even found to be denying the existence of a national service and talking instead of a loose coalition of local services (Klein in Jackson, 1985, pp. 189ff.). After the reorganisation of 1982, which eliminated an area tier in the NHS, the Government attempted to devolve many of the resource allocation decisions: the distributing of funds to the regional level and their detailed allocation to the districts. Nevertheless, the complications arising from the complex interplay between the responsibilities exercised by the health authorities and the power of the professional interests and the public sector unions led gradually to the reassertion of stronger central control over both resource allocation and the content of policy.

Thus the complexity of the various structures through which the Government's basic objectives had to find their way before being translated into action distorted to a greater or lesser degree the purposes that they were attempting to achieve and helped to compromise the outcomes. A particular difficulty lay in securing viable social policies which would be consistent with the broad goals that had initially been laid down. Reduction of State involvement in the design, control and delivery of services; encouragement of the hiving off of functions to the private sector and liberalisation of the terms upon which they should be provided; abandonment or drastic curtailing of central mechanisms for planning and monitoring policy changes; decentralisation of responsibility and encouragement of individual initiative; a central role for the informal sector and in particular the family; the elimination of waste and inefficiency – all these had figured prominently among the manifesto commitments. Yet their reconciliation proved in practice to be a great deal more complex and implementation, in the form of workable policies, more difficult to achieve than the Government had predicted. As a result, despite the initial impact achieved by the Government's actions, the measurable outcomes in social policy terms during the first term generally reflected the Government's intentions less closely than had been hoped – or indeed expected, by both advocates and critics. This held true both in economic terms and more specifically in the context of welfare programmes. To explain how this situation, which provoked considerable discontent among the Government's ideologically committed supporters, came about, a more detailed account of events over the four-year span of the first Thatcher Government is required.

PROMISE AND PERFORMANCE: THE THATCHER GOVERNMENT'S FIRST TERM

The keystone of the Conservative Government's financial and economic policies over their first term in office was inserted with the introduction of the Medium Term Financial Strategy (MTFS), in March 1980. In terms of the function it performs in the Government's approach to the economy, this document has been compared with the National Plan of the Wilson Government; but it could hardly have been more different, either in content or in outcome, as Nigel Lawson made clear in pointing up the contrast between them (1980, p. 14). In place of the complexity of the National Plan, with planning targets based on detailed forecasts and set, industry by industry, across the whole economy, the MTFS sets out what appears to be a simple and straightforward basis for achieving what one critical analyst calls an 'acceptable level of growth at a tolerable rate of inflation' (Jackson, 1985, pp. 38–9). In its presentation and in accompanying policy statements, great stress was laid upon the firmness of the Government's commitment to achieving the targets established in the strategy. The intention, from the outset, has been to provide a policy environment in which the element of uncertainty is eliminated as far as government actions can secure it.

Given the extent of commitment and the apparent simplicity of the general design, an appraisal of the success or failure of policy should be straightforward. Unfortunately, there are difficulties attached to both the major measures employed as indicators of success in the application of the Government's policies: namely, the growth in the money supply and the size of the Public Sector Borrowing Requirement (PSBR). In respect of the money supply, the choice of a 'broad' measure (£M3) (not merely all notes and coins but all sterling balances held in the public or private sectors in the UK), was determined as much by the ready availability of data series as for its explanatory value. Similarly, the use of the PSBR as an indicator attracted criticism, both on the ground that the real significance of the level of Government borrowing was open to question and because it has proved in practice extremely difficult to control with any degree of precision. This uncertainty has led one commentator to the conclusion that 'the unadjusted PSBR is a meaningless target for economic policy' (Jackson, p. 35). Thus the apparent clarity of the picture presented in the MTFS conceals hidden complexities which substantially modify the conclusions that can be drawn from any assessment of performance using the targets which it contains.

From the Government's perspective, this may be just as well, since the fallibility of the forecasts contained in the MTFS and rolled forward from year to year show up clearly when the record is examined. In no year during their first term in office did either the money supply or the borrowing requirement fall anywhere near within the range of forecasts made (Jackson, p. 48).

The selection of measures was, of course, determined by policy priorities rather than the other way about. In due course, the unsatisfactory nature of the indicators chosen – or, rather, of their behaviour – was recognised by modifications which first discarded £M3 in favour of a 'narrower' measure, £M0 (cash in circulation and in banks' tills, and balances at the Bank of England) and eventually moved to the point where (in the words of the Governor of the Bank of England) the Government decided that 'we would do better to dispense with monetary targetary altogether' (*Independent*, 23.10.86) and substituted other methods of imposing control.

The role of the PSBR was also problematic, linked as it was to deep-seated beliefs on the part of some members of the Government, and in particular the Prime Minister, about the importance of reducing dependence on borrowing to the maximum extent possible, on the analogy of the household budget to which she was so passionately wedded. Of equal significance, in the first stage of the Government's period in office, were two indicators which were not incorporated in the strategy: the level of pay settlements and the exchange rate of the pound.

The first was excluded because it was a matter of faith in the new administration that increases in pay were not associated with inflation. This belief was intimately connected with the commitment that had been entered into during the election campaign, not to introduce an incomes policy, which in turn stemmed from the unhappy experience of successive governments with such policies, and in particular the statutory version introduced by Edward Heath. The exchange rate, at least in the first phase of the Government's period of office, was regarded as a matter to be determined by market forces rather than a subject for direct intervention. Here again, traumatic memories of costly past struggles in defence of sterling played their part in shaping the new policies. Finally, no target was set for the rate of unemployment, although the Government did provide forecasts of likely trends. This was justified on the ground that the level of unemployment was an outcome of other developments within the economy, and not a suitable focus for separate initiatives. Here, too, the Government's new approach reflected the sharp change of direction advocated by Keith Joseph as a result of his reviews of policy in opposition. His conclusion, that 'full employment is not in the gift of governments and should not be promised' represented one of the most thoroughgoing of all departures from past policy; it abrogated the informal compact embodied in the famous pledge to maintain full employment contained in the Coalition Government's White Paper of 1944 which had provided one of the foundation stones of the postwar settlement. It also represented a sharp departure from Margaret Thatcher's own position in opposition, when she had vigorously attacked James Callaghan for allowing unemployment to rise to 1.3 million, commenting that 'we'd have been drummed out of office if we'd had this level of unemployment' (H. Young, 1990, p. 140) – a line perpetuated in Saatchi and Saatchi's 'Labour isn't working' poster for the Conservatives' 1979 election campaign.

In practice, the Government quickly found itself in difficulty in all the three areas not explicitly incorporated in the MTFS. The Prime Minister's undertaking to accept public sector pay rises already in the pipeline as a result of awards made under the previous Government (the so-called 'Clegg awards') contributed, a new conventional wisdom about the irrelevance of pay rises notwithstanding, to the burst of inflation that followed the first budget of the new administration. The rapid strengthening of the pound against both European currencies and the dollar cut sharply into the profitability of British exports; and the resumed rise in unemployment which began immediately upon the

Conservative Government's election and continued unchecked throughout their first term brought with it a whole range of problems which had been neither anticipated nor provided against.

Indeed, measured either by the indicators included in the MTFS or by those excluded from it, the record of the Government's first two years in office was little short of disastrous. Sir Geoffrey Howe's first budget combined immediate implementation of the Government's pledges to reduce taxation, both standard rate (from 33 per cent to 30 per cent) and at the top end of the range (from 83 per cent to 60 per cent) with a sharp increase in VAT, to a new unified rate of 15 per cent. Despite the confident line adopted in the Chancellor's statement to the Commons Committee (HC450, quoted in Jackson, p. 37), inflation proceeded to rise rapidly from the inherited rate of just over 10 per cent and eventually reached a peak of 21 per cent; outside estimates ascribed at least 3 per cent of this rise to the steps he had taken. Despite the imposition of exceptionally high interest rates, the money supply targets showed no signs of accommodating themselves to the Government's forecasts. Meanwhile, the exchange rate moved rapidly upwards, as interest rates and the pound's status as an oil-backed currency attracted foreign investment. The combination proved fatal for large segments of manufacturing industry; the effect of the spate of closures and job losses brought the West Midlands, the archetypical manufacturing region and still one of the most prosperous regions in the country in the 1960s, down to the status of a depressed area.

A crucial test came with the 1981 Budget. The Prime Minister and the Chancellor, after discussion with close advisers but without consulting their Cabinet colleagues, took a policy decision not to slacken the tight fiscal policies or attempt a reflation, however modest. Instead, the squeeze was tightened by increases in personal tax, petrol and other indirect taxes. This was despite official forecasts that output would decline by a further 1 per cent and unemployment would rise in the following year to over 3 million. This decision flew in the face of the reservations that were being strongly expressed both inside and outside government. The intellectual basis of the Government's approach had been strongly challenged by a group of 364 economists, including a number of past Treasury advisers, who urged the Government to reflate before irreversible damage was done not just to the economy but to the nation's social and political stability (*Times*, 30.3.81). At a different level, the problems of manufacturing industry had brought about a rebellion by the CBI, whose chairman, Sir Terence Beckett, promised the

Government a 'bareknuckled fight' on the problems his membership were experiencing with high interest rates and an overvalued pound.

These criticisms helped to precipitate what amounted to an open revolt in Cabinet. The principal wets, Prior, Peter Walker and Sir Ian Gilmour had hesitated to press their objections to the Budget to the point of resignation. But in July 1981, at the last meeting of the Cabinet before the summer recess a number of ministers attempted without success to force a reversal in the direction of policy, in the face of the Chancellor's stubborn determination to soldier on, with projected further cuts of £5 billion on the drawing board. The Cabinet meeting

> proved to be an extraordinary occasion, perhaps the most memorable meeting of the cabinet in the whole decade of the Thatcher government. It was certainly a time when outright disagreement, amounting almost to open rebellion, reached a climax never attained before or after. (H. Young, 1990, p. 218)

The Government's problems had been further compounded by an outbreak of civil disorder in a number of multi-racial inner-city areas, notably in Brixton and in the Toxteth area of Liverpool. These episodes lent force to the view that had been widely expressed by the Government's critics, that the fabric of civil society was becoming intolerably strained by persistent high rates of unemployment, particularly in the areas of multiple deprivation in most major urban areas.

Although the Prime Minister and her colleagues resisted this conclusion, preferring to regard the episodes as illustrations of declining standards of morality and lack of respect for law and order, the publication of Lord Scarman's report on the Brixton episode eventually vindicated the critics. His call for more effective Government intervention found some resonances within the Cabinet. Michael Heseltine, Secretary of State for the Environment, circulated a paper to colleagues immediately after the outbreaks with the provocative title 'It took a riot'. As newly styled 'Minister for Merseyside', Heseltine had subsequently embarked on an energetic campaign to attract new resources into Liverpool, linking additional funds from the urban programme with new investment from private industry. This deviation from the Government's general non-interventionist stance did not go unremarked; but it did not arrest the decline in their standing with the public.

Faced with pressures from every direction, the Prime Minister's nerve held. In Cabinet, she poured scorn on the demands by her critics for reflationary measures: did they want another Barber boom, with all the inevitable consequences? And in September 1981, in a Cabinet reshuffle, she summarily dismissed some of her more disaffected ministers. Among those who perished in this purge was Sir Ian Gilmour, whose widely quoted comment about monetarism ('the indefinable in pursuit of the uncontrollable') had not endeared him to the new establishment. Jim Prior was shuffled off to Northern Ireland, despite his ineffectual attempts to resist the move. Willing to wound but afraid to strike, the wets collectively did not come well out of the episode. Walker, who kept his head down, became the great survivor, serving throughout the whole period of the Thatcher administration, saving his dissatisfaction to record in his memoirs. Prior, who at the time of the 1981 Budget 'had come very close to resigning and a year later regretted very much that I hadn't' (Prior, 1986, p. 140) lasted until 1984. Gilmour became one of the Government's most persistent critics on the Tory backbenches and eventually produced in *Dancing with Dogma* (1992) the most scathing critique of the whole Thatcher episode produced by a practising politician of any party. Yet even he is reduced to casting around for excuses before concluding that: 'unquestionably, I should have resigned on the 1981 budget or, failing that, manufactured a resignation issue shortly afterwards' (1992, p. 42).

Margaret Thatcher was rewarded for her resolution by a quite unexpected stroke of good luck, in the shape of the Argentine invasion of the Falklands. Although her good fortune came at first heavily camouflaged, when the Foreign Office's failure to foresee that the Argentines would resort to armed force led to the resignation of the Foreign Secretary and all his team, her conduct of the successful campaign to recover the islands greatly enhanced her standing with the electorate. The largely rhetorical ultra-patriotism of her platform performances now found a real focus in the unlikely setting of the South Atlantic.

Having outfought her immediate opponents (literally so, in the case of the Argentine General Galtieri), Mrs Thatcher could afford to adopt a more pragmatic style. Industrial policy, which until 1981 had been the responsibility of Sir Keith Joseph, so wracked with doubt about the implications of intervention that he was apparently moved on one occasion to oppose in Cabinet a paper from his own department, was entrusted to Patrick Jenkin. British Leyland, the last of the British-owned volume car producers, were bailed out with a substantial injection of new funds. An ambitious programme of support for the 'sunrise' industries was developed, with a particular emphasis on new jobs to be created in information technology.

In executing this manoeuvre – an adjustment in course rather than a U-turn – the Government was much assisted by the lifting of immediate political pressures. The newly created Social Democratic Party (SDP), formed as a result of the defection of several prominent members of the Labour Party, had concluded an electoral alliance with the Liberals, and immediately began to make sweeping inroads into the support for both major parties. As a result, the Government suffered a series of damaging by-election defeats, notably when Shirley Williams won the previously safe Conservative seat at Crosby. However, after the Falklands episode, the Alliance wave subsided almost as rapidly as it had arisen; but not to the benefit of the Labour Party, which remained riven by the internal conflicts that had helped to precipitate the SDP secession. The introduction of legislation to circumscribe the legal immunities of trade unions and limit secondary action during strikes had exposed the essential powerlessness of the TUC leadership during a severe recession. Brushing aside their objections – and sidestepping the threat of action by the miners to avert pit closures – the Government had been able to concentrate on bringing its own employees in the civil service unions to heel. This task was carried through with gusto: a long and potentially damaging strike was faced down with minimum concessions, and the elaborate structure of pay bargaining within the civil service, based on the concept of comparability with the private sector, was swept aside. The Government had a pay policy, and an extremely tight one, even if it applied only in the public sector.

All these developments had a direct impact on social policy. By far the most significant were the consequences of the attempts to reduce public expenditure, expressed as a proportion of GDP. Not only had this been one of the main objectives identified in the manifesto; it had been restated in unequivocal terms immediately after the Government had come into office, with the assertion that 'public expenditure is at the heart of Britain's present economic difficulties' (HM Government, 1979). As an essential element in this process, a further rapid reduction in the level of local authority spending was identified as an immediate priority, and initial target figures of cuts in expenditure of 3 per cent in 1979–80 and 5 per cent in the following year were set in circulars issued by the Department of the Environment to local authorities. However, the imposition of such cuts depended upon the existence of effective means of translating target figures into outcomes; and the existing system of local government finance, with its complex mixture of locally and centrally raised funding, did not furnish that means. Successive Secretaries of State for the Environment were accordingly charged with the task of bringing local government expenditure under control; and two separate rounds of enabling legislation, in 1980 and 1982, were laboriously pushed through Parliament in the face of protests not confined to the Labour-controlled local authorities.

The resulting system (if it could be so described) was immensely complex. It rested on an evaluation of need carried out centrally, area by area and service by service, which would enable ministers to set a limit on the expenditure of individual authorities; spending above this limit would be penalised by the withdrawal of grant. In practice, these controls proved more effective at a crude aggregate level than they were at the level of individual authorities. While the proportion of the Rate Support Grant met from central funds was progressively reduced, from 61 per cent in 1979–80 to 52.8 per cent in 1983–4 and further drastic reductions were achieved in capital spending, some high-spending authorities persistently escaped the net. Meanwhile, the complementary goals of increased efficiency in service delivery and securing reductions in manpower levels were to be achieved by the creation of new machinery for central surveillance set up by the Audit Commission under the 1982 Act, which was to play an increasingly significant role through the rest of the decade and through the Joint Manpower Watch system.

But the fundamental concern on both sides of the argument was over finance. For the local authorities, the issue was of constitutional propriety and the capacity of elected local bodies to spend in accordance with the expressed wishes of their electorates. On the central government side, increasing frustration at the daunting practical problems involved in bringing local authority expenditure under control led to the reopening of the issue of replacing the rates system by some new method of raising revenue locally. This had been the subject of a pledge by Margaret Thatcher, when (briefly) Opposition Environment spokesman in 1974; but it had been allowed to lapse after the Layfield Committee's abortive report in the late 1970s. Tentative attempts were now made to revive the issue in a Green Paper (Cm 8449, Dec 1981). However, this document concluded that none of the three main alternatives to a rating system – a local sales tax, a local income tax or a poll tax – would work satisfactorily. After a period of consultation, the issue was allowed to lapse, for the time being. Meanwhile, both sides were agreed that the new procedures that had been introduced represented a sharp departure in principle from all previous practice: 'for the first time the Government has gone beyond a concern with the totality of local government spending to a concern with the expenditure of individual authorities' (Meadows in Jackson, 1985, p. 164). The rationale for this innovation was clearly set out in a speech by the then Chief Secretary to the Treasury, Leon Brittan, to the Society of Local Authority Chief Executives (SOLACE) in September 1982, in which he referred to 'the Government's overriding duty to intervene, both in pursuit of national economic policies and in order to safeguard the interests of local industry' (Meadows, p. 166). Or, as Nigel Lawson subsequently expressed it, the Government was being forced into acting through 'the collapse of the traditional understanding that, irrespective of the colour of the Party in power at local level, a local authority would conduct its affairs in more or less conformity with the economic policy of the Government of the day' (Lawson, 1992, p. 565).

Yet only in the field of housing among the whole range of services for which local government is principally responsible did substantial reductions in expenditure emerge from the elaborate processes which had been set in motion. The singling out of housing had much to do with the Government's long-standing ambition to break up the great municipal housing empires; this was to be achieved in part by introducing a right to buy for council tenants and in part by cutting resources for new construction allocated through the Housing Investment Programme (HIP) system introduced by the Labour Government. This had the additional merit, from the Government's perspective, of substantially reducing the activities of the local authority Direct Labour Organisations (DLOs), a particular *bête noire* of theirs, representing as they did municipal enterprise rather than the use of competitive tendering in the market.

By 1983, substantial cuts had been achieved in housing; but in other fields also marked down for reductions the pattern was very different. Personal social services had been one of these; but the residual autonomy of local authorities had allowed them to deflect the Government's intentions. In fact, the picture over the whole term is of a small increase in this sector; but this is misleading, since pressures created by demographic and social changes would under normal circumstances have produced far more substantial increases – as, for example, in expenditure on care of the elderly. Rather than attempt to challenge local government directly, central government initially preferred instead to promote alternative approaches, stressing the merits of entrusting care in this field to voluntary organisations or informal carers, in particular the family. Such an approach built upon initiatives already taken by the previous administration to encourage care in the community ('Good Neighbour' schemes) and the use of informal neighbourhood networks. Local authority Social Services Departments, in this concept, were to perform a supporting and enabling role rather than directly providing services. This alternative was presented in its most developed form in a full dress (in every sense) speech by the Prime Minister to the Women's Royal Voluntary Service (WRVS) in 1981. In this speech, she emphasised the importance of the contribution of the voluntary sector, and went on to declare that:

> I believe that the volunteer movement is at the heart of all our social welfare provision. That the statutory services are the supportive ones, underpinning where necessary, filling the gaps and helping the helpers.
> (quoted in Ungerson, 1985, p. 214)

Similar speeches by other ministers, notably Patrick Jenkin when Secretary of State for Social Services, praised the flexibility, adaptiveness and capacity for innovation in the voluntary sector, in contrast to the inflexibility of the bureaucracy. Though initially flattering, these sentiments quickly became a source of embarrassment to voluntary bodies faced with the need to collaborate with local authorities and health authorities within their own areas. The difficulties that began to arise as a result were compounded by the introduction of a number of new schemes, under which local voluntary agencies were funded directly by central government, often without any form of consultation with statutory agencies. Such initiatives cut across the efforts of the local authority associations and the National Council for Voluntary Organisations (NCVO) to establish a set of workable ground rules for collaboration between the two sectors (Association of County Councils and NCVO, 1981).

The area in which this problem of the impact of central government interventions in local situations most frequently arose was also that of Government's main policy failure: unemployment. The rise in unemployment that had continued unabated from the moment when the Conservatives took office did not merely pose an electoral threat to the Government, as concern about high levels figured more and more prominently in public opinion polls among the issues causing concern; it also began to have drastic consequences for the Government's attempts to control public expenditure. The most immediately visible impact was on expenditure on social security, where the number of unemployed claimants rose from under 600,000 in 1979 to 1.7 million in 1983. But the rise in unemployment also had consequences across the whole range of social policy programmes: in housing (where the increase in the rate of defaulting on mortgage payments threw a shadow over the Government's attempts to promote a wider social basis for home occupation), more contentiously in health and in the personal social services. By 1983, it was estimated that the net cost in public expenditure terms of each individual unemployed person was in the region of £7,000 (Sinfield and Fraser, 1985).

The Government's major contribution in this field, and the main focus for positive intervention during the first term, lay in the activities of the Manpower Services Commission (MSC), which fell precisely at the intersection between economic and social policies and had substantial implications for both. The MSC was in many senses the epitome of the early 1970s, the era in which it was first conceived. Staffed by civil servants, but hived off from the Department of Employment, the Commission was accountable only indirectly to Parliament through the Secretary of State, and run by a tripartite governing body composed of representatives of both sides of industry and local government. The chairman of the Commission when the Conservatives came to power, Sir Richard O'Brien, was himself a personification of the middle way. He succeeded in carrying his diverse group of colleagues through a difficult period of transition when, from being an agency whose main function had been to increase the levels of skill in the workforce (and only incidentally to deal with the consequences of 'frictional' unemployment) the Commission found itself having to cope with the situation that confronted it after 1979, of a seemingly endless increase in the numbers of young people leaving school with no realistic prospect of jobs. In addition, there were the rapidly growing rates of unemployment among older workers produced by the collapse of manufacturing industry, which by the early 1980s had reduced even formerly prosperous regions like the West Midlands to depressed areas. Together, these developments posed a formidable set of problems.

In addressing these linked difficulties, the MSC did not lack resources. One indication of the level of expenditure that the Government was prepared to commit in this sector can be obtained by comparing the respective budgets of the Commission and the Department of Industry: in 1979 they were approximately equal; whereas by 1983 the MSC was receiving approximately three times as much. With these funds, the Commission attempted to address the problems of youth unemployment, in a succession of schemes with confusing acronyms and broadly similar objectives. The extent of success achieved was debatable; unkind critics talked of merely 'shuffling places in the dole queue'. Nor was the Commission's position always helped by the attitude of the Treasury, despite their permissive attitude on funding. As it became clear that unemployment represented an area of potentially acute electoral vulnerability, Treasury ministers and the Prime Minister's own advisers attempted to devise their own schemes that would address the problem and yet remain consistent with the proclaimed objectives of Government policy. In at least one instance (the Community Programme) the outcome was sufficiently similar to schemes already being operated by the MSC to raise sharp questions about the effectiveness of communications within Whitehall.

Some success could be claimed for the Commission's programmes, if only in the limited sense that the various schemes for the young unemployed, though restricted both in duration and in the amount of training received did keep a substantial number of young people temporarily out of the unemployment statistics. But the inability of the MSC to deal satisfactorily with the problems of long-term unemployment among older workers represented a crucial area of weakness. The Community Programme, designed for this group, which was given increased emphasis after the enforced departure of Sir Richard O'Brien and his replacement as chairman by the ideologically sounder David Young, was in practice often little more than a 'makework' scheme. Substantial investment of public money in this area, though it brought some practical benefits for those voluntary bodies and institutions of further and higher education that have taken part in schemes, yielded only dubiously adequate results for individual participants. However, the MSC, one of the few survivors among the quangos created in the 1970s, had at least been able to demonstrate in practice some virtues in public enterprise, in the Government's own terms: flexibility, rapidity of response and high turnover.

PATTERNS OF PUBLIC EXPENDITURE

The impact of increased unemployment across the whole field of social policy expenditure, coupled with the effects of implementing the

Government's pledges on law and order and the commitment made to NATO allies to increase the defence budget by 3 per cent annually left very little room for manoeuvre on the reduction of public expenditure, once early hopes of substantial efficiency savings began to fade, and local authority resistance put reductions in locally managed services in question.

In the autumn of 1982, Sir Geoffrey Howe, having tried in vain earlier in the year to persuade his Cabinet colleagues that a further round of reductions in public expenditure was necessary, caused two documents to be circulated to his fellow-ministers for discussion at a meeting on 9 September. The first of these was an analysis produced by the Treasury, with the support of an interdepartmental working party, indicating what the consequences of a failure to reduce public expenditure would be under two separate sets of conditions: a 'low growth' and a 'normal growth' scenario. The second was a short paper prepared independently by the Central Policy Review Staff (CPRS) and identifying four areas of public expenditure where substantial cuts might be made. The two together were intended to make the case for a six-month study of options for a new public spending strategy (H. Young, 1990, p. 300).

One of the unanticipated by-products of the Prime Minister's management style was the creation of a vigorous underground resistance movement within Whitehall, one of whose tactics was to expose the inner workings of Government to public view through leaks to the press. Many of those who practised this form of opposition were civil servants; in one or two notorious cases the culprit was identified, prosecuted under the Official Secrets Act and in one case jailed. But increasingly dissident ministers turned to using the same weapon, when they could find no alternative way of obstructing the progress of policies of which they disapproved. The CPRS report provided one of those occasions; as Mrs Thatcher glumly concluded on first seeing this paper 'it would certainly be leaked and give a totally false impression' (Thatcher, 1993, p. 276). She was right: a copy duly appeared in *The Economist*. This particular leak (by most accounts the work of Peter Walker) was one of the more effective coups of the first term, although its final outcome was probably not the one intended. Public exposure of the CPRS's very sweeping and imperfectly digested proposals did indeed cause considerable embarrassment to the Government; but the inability of the Think-Tank to keep proper control over the material it produced was eventually cited as one of the principal reasons for its abolition, shortly after the beginning of Mrs Thatcher's second term.

In one sense, this was far from just; the CPRS's proposals, naive though they were, did represent an attempt to introduce into internal discussion some of those radical ideas whose absence the administration's supporters on the free market right were finding increasingly irksome – even if the way in which they had been selected owed more to 'Treasury-inspired arithmetic' (Nigel Lawson's phrase). The four areas of spending selected – health, defence, higher education and social security – did include, in the first two items, a couple of the sacred cows whose status the Cabinet had previously left undisturbed. But in the event the uncompromising character of the proposals – transfer of the NHS to an insurance base, the withdrawal of public funding support for higher education – was their undoing. Ministers combined to express their disapproval; and subsequent verdicts have been even harsher. Lawson, describing the episode as a 'cabinet riot' and Geoffrey Howe's part in it as 'maladroit' sums up the episode as an undeserved victory for the wets, who succeeded in using it to push cuts in welfare expenditure off the Government's agenda (1992, p. 304). Certainly, the political embarrassment caused was too great for the report to be left on the record uncorrected; and the Prime Minister herself made it clear that it did not represent Government policy. Her speech at that autumn's Conservative party conference set the tone for her colleagues ('the National Health Service is safe with us') and for the pre-election period that followed, with its talk of defence of standards in the public sector, extending even to urging local authorities to engage in more capital expenditure.

The Government's rhetoric provided them with a breathing space – and incidentally exposed the extent to which they were not yet prepared to explore radical options on welfare in public. But it did not convince their critics. In fact, exploration of alternative strategies did continue in private; another series of leaks during the general election campaign in 1983 exposed the activities of the 'family policy group', a committee convened by the Prime Minister's personal adviser, the journalist Ferdinand Mount, with the brief of collecting proposals that would help to restore the family to a central role in social policy. A series of options were produced by ministers, ranging from the ever-present concern to arrest the alleged weakening of self-reliance through the benefits system to teaching children to manage their pocket money more efficiently. Strategic thinking in rather greater depth was also taking place in the Cabinet committee (codenamed MISC 14) charged with responsibility for developing policies for the longer term. Some of this thinking was also shortly to break surface. Most important, the Treasury paper of 1982, which had been lost to sight in the row over the CPRS presentation, was still on the table. The question it posed, of the feasibility of maintaining current rates of public expenditure, with their apparent implications for high rates of taxation and non-achievement of real growth in the economy, remained a matter of acute concern for the Prime Minister and her inner circle.

The questions that had been raised looked sharper still against the background of the overall record of the first term. The deep depression of the early 1980s was now past; but the objectives set out in the MTFS were far from having been met, with the single (if conspicuous) exception of the inflation rate, whch fell from a high of 21.9 per cent in May 1980 to 3.7 per cent in May 1983. But targets for monetary growth had been missed by a wide margin, the tax burden had risen from 34 per cent of GDP in 1979 to almost 40 per cent and GDP over the whole period had fallen by more than 3 per cent. Reflecting subsequently on this first period of management of the economy, Nigel Lawson concluded that the MTFS, although 'not fulfilled in any literal sense' had had a salutory purgative effect which satisfied its fundamental aims, albeit in ways that had not been anticipated (Lawson, 1992, pp. 71–2). Success, in this rather special sense, was deployed to justify relaxing the squeeze on Government expenditure in the period running up to the 1983 election.

Nevertheless, the outcomes in terms of patterns of actual expenditure in welfare programmes, measured against the broad objectives laid down in 1979, were not impressive. The 1979 commitments to promote self-reliance, build up the informal sector of care, eliminate waste in bureaucracy and above all to reduce absolute levels of public spending; all these should in principle have been reflected in the record but were not. The reasons why no significant changes in broad expenditure patterns were achieved are complex. Some are general: local government fought a long and partly effective rearguard action, transcending party loyalties, to retain some degree of local discretion, which was employed to defend some services against cuts. The scope for some of the more spectacular changes in policy direction, and in particular the privatisation campaign that had made its debut in industrial policy during the Government's first term, was less great in social policy, with one conspicuous exception (housing). The campaign to secure savings within the bureaucracy was initiated in Whitehall through the efficiency scrutinies conducted by teams directed by Sir Derek Rayner, who had been brought in from Marks and Spencer for the purpose. These

produced reductions in staffing levels that affected certain key areas of
social policy, notably social security, where the resulting pressures on
local offices provoked a series of strikes, particularly in the West
Midlands (Coetzee in Ward, 1985, p. 41).

However, the approach adopted for the Rayner scrutinies which
eventually developed into a full-scale attempt to introduce a new style
into Government, under the title of Financial Management Initiative
(FMI), made less impact (for reasons already explained) within locally
controlled services. Some areas were beyond the capacity of the
Government – at least as it then conceived its responsibilities – to
control; in others, the impacts were measured not in terms of absolute
reductions in expenditure or staffing levels but in a steady decline in the
quality of the service provided or in a failure to keep pace with new
demands.

But the most important reason why the level and distribution of public
expenditure in welfare did not reflect the broad principles laid down by
the Conservatives in opposition was a lack of confidence on the
Government's own part about both means and ends. This was not a
question of the strength and coherence of the opposition provoked by the
steps taken during the first term; rather the contrary. Energetic efforts
were made, notably by the public sector unions, to mount mass
campaigns against the Government's proposals; but although these
achieved local successes, the general impact was muted. Towards the end
of the first term, a clearer form of opposition began to emerge within
local government, where some Labour-controlled local authorities had
begun to evolve a new approach to the provision of public services, based
on a decentralised model, with emphasis on the involvement of clients
and local community groups. This model found its most effective form in
Sheffield (Blunkett and Green, 1983); but its most visible political
expression was in the Greater London Council, which had been
controlled by Labour since 1981. Under Ken Livingstone, who had been
elected to the leadership in an internal putsch, the GLC acted as a focus
for these new approaches and a funding agency for local experiments of
almost infinite diversity. By the end of the Government's first term, the
alternative presented by this form of municipal socialism had become
more than a mere irritant, and steps were accordingly to be taken to end
it.

But these were essentially little local difficulties (to adapt Harold
Macmillan's phrase); within the national political arena, coherent
opposition to the Government's position on social policy was not

forthcoming. Under Michael Foot's leadership, the Labour Party remained ineffective and divided, demoralised by the Government's unanticipated recovery of popularity after the Falklands War, on which Labour's own line had been lame and incoherent and dogged by continuing conflict between left and right. The Alliance threat had failed to materialise; the SDP, from being the wave of the future had come to be widely perceived as naive, opportunistic and lacking in consistency. In Ralf Dahrendorf's cruel phrase, the party seemed to be mainly interested in securing a 'better yesterday'; and the stream of policy documents that began to emerge from the SDP's headquarters did little to correct that impression. Early in 1983, these weaknesses were exposed in a disastrous by-election campaign in Darlington. Electorally most significant of all, the division within the opposition between the Alliance and the Labour Party gave the Government a tactical advantage whose importance became increasingly evident as the election approached.

Yet the Government's hesitations on social policy continued. Partly, this was a question of public attitudes; despite the IEA's devoted labours, assumptions about the popularity of the Welfare State, especially the Health Service, remained an element in the situation whose electoral implications could not be neglected. Conventional wisdom had long had it that laying impious hands on the postwar structure of welfare would spell disaster; but conventional wisdom had held the same about permitting mass unemployment to return, and had been proved wrong. Or at least had been proved wrong so far; the evidence of mounting public concern about the continued rise in unemployment represented the area of potential vulnerability most troublesome for the Government's tacticians. If viable alternative policies offering a reasonable prospect of reductions in unemployment could be put convincingly to the electorate, the Government might even be in serious difficulty.

Viable alternative policies on welfare were another matter. The Government's decision not to promote an immediate public debate around the theme of radical changes in welfare provision was not prompted by fear of engaging in debate with the defenders of the Welfare State. Once, the access enjoyed by the radical Fabians like Peter Townsend to the press and television and the vigour of the pressure groups that they had helped to create would have made this a risky course of action. Earlier governments had on several occasions to give this lobby best. Now, as members of this group were themselves masochistically eager to point out, their position had come under increasingly effective assault from both ends of the spectrum of opinion and could be maintained only by making concessions damaging to the intellectual coherence of their own case (Dean, *Guardian*, 18.4.83). Nor did the alternative positions defined by Marxist critics of welfare, now being put into wider circulation through the journal *Critical Social Policy* pose a particular threat. To the extent that these criticisms were perceived as having any significance, their generally hostile line on State services was regarded among critics of the right, also intent on 'breaking the spell' of the Welfare State, as useful supporting evidence for their own position. In essence, the dilemma was tactical: could the Government, concerned to make certain of the second term to which such significance was being attached, afford to adopt radical positions on welfare, which were of doubtful electoral appeal, would certainly prove difficult to implement and were of unproved effectiveness?

The record of the first term across a diverse range of services clearly provides the answer. In health, fundamental changes were avoided; and by the end of the first term the pendulum had swung back from the modest degree of decentralisation promoted at the outset to the familiar style of managerial centralism. Despite some expansion in private insurance schemes, the role of private medicine remained marginal: a symbolic alternative rather than a real option for a significant proportion of the population. The initial radicalism displayed in education, with the introduction of the Assisted Places Scheme to support pupils from the state sector at independent schools and threats to abolish the largest of all the education authorities, the Inner London Education Authority (ILEA), tailed off into debate about how to use demographic trends to secure some expenditure cuts. In housing, far more substantial cuts were achieved; in addition, this was the only area of social policy in which a major ideological shift was implemented. The sale of council housing produced a substantial movement from public to private sector provision: it was both demonstrably popular and electorally highly advantageous, as subsequent events were to show.

Finally, in the largest of all the areas of Government expenditure, social security, the nature of demand and the increases brought about by pressures generated elsewhere confined the Government to making its reductions at the margin: delaying upratings, trimming entitlement and launching with much sound and fury campaigns against abuse of the system. The amounts withheld in these ways were substantial (they were estimated by the House of Commons Library at £4.3 billion between 1980–1 and 1983–4 (*Times*, 25.6.84)); but the complexities of the system itself and the interactions between different departmental policies had inhibited attempts at more fundamental changes. This was well illustrated in the case of housing benefit, hurriedly introduced as a simplifying and cost-cutting measure, only to prove in practice complex and expensive. That some changes would prove necessary, however, had become a matter of conviction, strongly urged upon the Government by economic advisers both formal and informal. The interdependence that they assumed between levels of benefits, taxes and employment guaranteed that the issue of social security would find a place in the agenda for the second term.

However, for the moment these difficult problems were set on one side, as the Government concentrated on securing victory at the polls with the minimum exposure of potentially controversial issues. Their success at the general election of 1983, by an overwhelming margin in terms of parliamentary seats, but with a reduced proportion of the votes, might be taken as sufficient in itself to validate the policies that had been pursued in the first term. All general elections are in one sense referenda on the record of the party in power; 1983 was no exception. Yet there is no mistaking the flavour of disappointment in the analyses of the record in social policy provided even by otherwise sympathetic critics. As Peter Riddell of the *Financial Times* concluded in his comprehensive review, *The Thatcher Government*: in 1983, Thatcherism meant 'primarily bold rhetoric, a new style and a determination to persist with a difficult economic policy. It has not yet meant a shift in the frontiers of the public sector or changes in the welfare state comparable with those of the late 1940s' (1984, p. 20). But even if in its approach over the course of the first term, the Government had more often than not failed with flying colours, the Welfare State had merely been reprieved, not acquitted.

5

PRICKING THE WELFARE BALLOONS?

I am asked about our policy. It is to control public spending and bring
down expenditure.

Norman Fowler, Secretary of State for Social Services, Hansard, 22.4.85.

The point is that even the Good Samaritan had to have the money to help,
otherwise he too would have had to pass on the other side.

Margaret Thatcher, speech to Conservative Political Centre, 10.10. 68,
in Wapshott and Brock, 1983.

One of the striking features of the 1983 general election was that a
government which prided itself on setting clear objectives and pursuing
them with conviction chose to present itself to the electorate with a
manifesto almost totally devoid of substantial content. The best that Mrs
Thatcher could subsequently claim was that 'much of the manifesto
promised "more of the same", not the most inspiring of cries, although
there was no doubt that a lot more was needed' (Thatcher, 1993, p. 305).
This approach was widely remarked upon, both by critics and
supporters; and gave rise to much speculation about the possibility of a
'hidden agenda', containing contentious items that would be concealed
from the electorate until after polling day. Some substance was lent to
these rumours by the leaking to the press shortly before the election of a
number of Cabinet papers, principally those dealing with family policy.
Speculation was intensified by the known fact that the Conservative
Party had organised a number of informal commissions to examine issues
that might be pursued in the course of a second term.

The truth was that there was no secret second manifesto. The decision
to present the case for the Government in bland and non-specific terms

was a deliberate matter of tactics. As Jim Prior, then one of its senior members, later explained it,

> Margaret, for all her radical rhetoric, and despite her dominance in the party after the Falklands, was fighting on an ultra-cautious manifesto. She had been frightened by the reception given to the Think Tank documents suggesting radical reforms to the Welfare State. (Prior, 1986)

However, the lingering impression left by the adoption of this approach was that there was something to conceal. Francis Pym, who was dropped from the Cabinet immediately after the election, commented subsequently that the tone adopted by the Government had 'encouraged the belief that it did not care about people' (Pym, 1985, p. 33). Nor was this impression dissipated by the major interview that Mrs Thatcher gave to *The Times* immediately before the election, when she firmly refused to express sympathy with the unemployed, saying

> I cannot express responsibility for those that strike themselves out of jobs, who insist on having overmanning or restrictive practices, who refuse to accept new technology, or who have not got good management, or who don't design products that other people want to have. (*Times*, 5.5.83)

The uneasy mixture of hardness and hesitancy conveyed by this approach throws some doubt on the widespread belief that the Prime Minister had come to incarnate a new, and ideologically coherent perspective in British politics. Those who have argued in this sense – paradoxically, most of them, like Stuart Hall and Andrew Gamble, among her fiercest critics – suggest that she had succeeded in welding together two disparate strands, a new 'social market' consensus on the economy and an authoritarian populist consensus on race, law and order and the family. Andrew Gamble goes on to argue that although there are important tensions between the two, 'it is precisely what makes Thatcherism an indispensible construct for analysing recent British politics that so far they have been successfully reconciled through the political strategy and practice of the present Conservative leadership' (*Marxism Today*, June 1984).

An alternative view is that the Government's political successes turned more narrowly on the personality of the Prime Minister herself: she had achieved an almost hypnotic effect by endless repetition of a few very basic themes – responsibility, independence, individual freedom – in a style which she herself has labelled 'conviction politics'. This interpretation gains force from the failure of even the most assiduous biographers to identify, with the solitary exception of her Conservative Political Centre speech of 1968 ('What's Wrong With Politics?') any evidence of adherence to the broad philosophy of the New Right before her election to the Conservative party leadership in 1975. Her steady, but undramatic ascent through the political hierarchy to the Cabinet was achieved almost entirely by competent handling of briefs whose contents had been determined elsewhere. Of her commitment to the ideas to which she was exposed on gaining the leadership there can be no doubt; but there is also evidence to suggest that the influence of the more flamboyant of the ideologues, like the former Communist Alfred Sherman, was fading even before the end of the Government's first term.

This interpretation suggests that the failure to be challenging and specific in the 1983 manifesto was a reflection of another of Mrs Thatcher's characteristics, less often remarked upon: her caution. Some of the intractable issues that had defied solution in the course of the first term had been deferred; there might be a good case for not advertising these failures too publicly. This argument would have had particular force in relation to some of the major objectives set in 1979. Then, Mrs Thatcher had chosen to encapsulate her case in a call for less taxes and more law and order. It would clearly be difficult to explain precisely why a government which had been in office for four years had in the event presided over increases both in tax levels and in recorded crime, especially since it would be impossible not to make some attempt to explain the failure that was potentially most damaging of all, the unchecked increase in unemployment, which had now risen past 3 million and showed little sign of levelling off.

In ordinary circumstances, the inability to explain these failures would in itself have been enough to compromise the Government's chances of re-election. But 1983 was not an ordinary year, politically. The Labour Party under Michael Foot's leadership had found it impossible to define coherent positions over a whole range of issues, in both domestic and foreign policy. Deprived of the automatic bonus of support that high levels of unemployment were supposed to confer, and finding that the cry of 'Welfare State in danger' evoked only an uncertain reply, the Labour Party eventually gave birth, with much strain and stress, to a manifesto that one member of the Shadow Cabinet subsequently described as 'the longest suicide note in recent history'. As for the Alliance, after the disappointment of Darlington, the opinion polls, reinforced by local government election results, suggested that the electorate's brief flirtation with three-party politics was beginning to draw to a close.

In such circumstances, the result of the election seemed to be almost a foregone conclusion; and impressions did not deceive. While the Labour Party lashed itself into a self-defeating frenzy, the Prime Minister, her appearance at press conferences and in the country carefully stage managed by an astute team of advisers, scarcely had to break sweat. The second term, which had always been seen by Conservative strategists as essential in order to secure all the objectives that had been defined in opposition was safely secured, and without giving any hostages to fortune. The blank cheque had been endorsed; though the problem of how to fill in the figures still remained.

Victory at the general election satisfied an essential precondition by removing the political obstacles to radical new initiatives. The comprehensive defeat suffered by the Labour Party precipitated the expected internal debates. Even to those who had anticipated defeat, the extent of the disaster came as a severe shock. Not merely had Labour been pushed down to its bedrock support; only the geographical concentration of its remaining supporters prevented disaster from becoming cataclysm. As Eric Hobsbawm observed, 'the Labour vote remains largely working class, but the working class has ceased to be largely Labour' (Hobsbawm, 1983). An especially disturbing feature was that there was clear evidence from post-election polls that the electorate had had considerable sympathy with the basic concerns expressed by the party in the course of the campaign, especially about employment, but no confidence in its capacity to deal with them. Nevertheless, the party succeeded in managing the transition caused by Michael Foot's inevitable resignation as Leader with more skill than had been demonstrated at the time of the Deputy Leadership elections three years earlier. Neil Kinnock, greatly assisted by the absence from the contest of a convincing candidate to his left as a result of Tony Benn's loss of his seat in Parliament, won the election comfortably and settled in to the daunting job of providing an opposition to a Government with a parliamentary majority of 144.

For the Alliance, the tactical dilemmas had sharpened. Having run the Labour Party close for second place in the popular vote, and replaced them as the main opposition party through the South outside London, they were left with a mere handful of seats – only six, in the case of the SDP. With such a meagre reward to show for a quarter of the votes cast nationally, the partners were reduced to crying foul at an electoral system that could produce such a manifestly unfair result. However, immediately after the election, the elevation of William Whitelaw to the peerage gave the Alliance an unexpected opportunity to show that they were no spent force, by running his Conservative successor to an agonisingly close finish at the resulting by-election. And David Owen, who succeeded Roy Jenkins as leader of the SDP with the minimum of fuss, quickly proved to be an effective parliamentary performer.

Nevertheless, the only substantial obstacles to the Government's freedom of action in the new Parliament proved to be those of managing a large majority (a problem of which Francis Pym had vainly warned before his summary dismissal), and the emergence of the House of Lords in its full glory as the custodian of popular rights through its constitutional revising role. This was a function that their Lordships were to exercise frequently at the expense of Government legislation, with every sign of relish at doing so.

Since economic policy remained at the centre of the Government's preoccupations, the main burden of laying down the new lines for policy in the immediate post-election period rested on the new Chancellor, Nigel Lawson. One major diffculty that faced him from the outset was the problem of unredeemed pledges from the first term. In each successive Public Expenditure White Paper, Sir Geoffrey Howe, his predecessor, had declared his intention of reducing public expenditure as a proportion of GDP. On each occasion, it had risen. This steady increase represented a major impediment to delivering on other pledges, principally those to achieve reductions in the level of public borrowing and in the amount of tax paid by individuals.

In attempting to address these issues, Lawson had not merely the advantage of a clear run in Parliament, but the authority of the Prime Minister to adopt a new and more rigorous approach to the issue of public expenditure and in particular expenditure on welfare. But his scope for manoeuvre was still limited. Growth in the economy remained sluggish, and manufacturing industry in particular was still performing below the level of 1979. Higher taxation was ruled out on political grounds. Lawson could therefore not expect any substantial increase in the resources available to government, apart from windfall gains from an extension of the privatisation programme. If further reductions were to be achieved, there was only one direction to go. Wapshott and Brock, in their analysis of the first term, conclude that Sir Geoffrey Howe 'had by now reduced public expenditure by as much as possible without changing the foundations of public expenditure itself: the extent of the welfare state' (1983, p. 211). On his arrival at the Treasury, Lawson found that a further attempt was in hand to dramatise the dangers of established levels of departmental spending by publishing estimates of likely future requirements. However, he preferred to attack the problem by a different route, on the grounds that 'public exposure of the various departments' spending aspirations would give the figures a legitimacy that would make savings harder, not easier to achieve' (1992, p. 304).

Lawson therefore chose to begin by setting out the intellectual foundations of his new approach. The line that would be adopted was set out in stages: the principal public landmarks in the process were the Treasury's Green Paper, *The Next Ten Years: Public Expenditure and Taxation into the 1990s* (March 1984) and the Mais Lecture, delivered by the Chancellor in June 1984. In the lecture, Lawson distinguished, as is customary, between micro- and macro-economic goals of policy, but offered a new definition of each. Instead of standing as a key goal of macro-economic policy, as it had since the Coalition Government's White Paper of 1944, the objective of securing and sustaining full employment was relegated to a subsidiary role of micro-policy, to be replaced by control of inflation (*Sunday Times*, 24.6.84). The broader implications of the policy choices that derive from this change of approach are spelt out in the Green Paper, which emphasised that 'the growth rate will also depend on how successfully public expenditure is controlled so that the burden of taxation can be reduced and incentives improved' (para 49). And earlier in the same year, in a private memorandum to the Prime Minister, Lawson underlined the importance of the 'tax reform strategy' that he intended to adopt as Chancellor, which would couple tax reductions with a set of new initiatives designed to simplify the system and improve incentives to individuals and industry (1992, pp. 334–6).

The performance of the economy as it emerged from the deep trough of the 1979–81 recession was by then sufficiently encouraging to permit a cautious degree of optimism. It also allowed Lawson to aim some pointed shafts at the 364 economists and their round robin of 1981 calling for a radical change of approach. But the Green Paper is stern in its warnings about the penalties of backsliding: 'spending decisions taken issue by issue have steadily raised the burden of taxation without regard to what taxpayers will tolerate or to the consequences for incentives and growth. This process cannot be allowed to continue indefinitely' (para 47).

Such an approach left a substantial number of subsidiary issues untouched, chief among them the question of employment. Regardless of whether it figured as a macro- or a micro-objective, it was now politically essential, even with a substantial majority and a full term in prospect, to be seen to take this issue seriously. Having rejected the option of reflation to create 'real' jobs, the Government's alternative approach was a substantial investment of public funds through the continually expanding activities of the Manpower Services Commission. Another form of direct investment by the State, also necessary as much in political as in economic terms, was in new technology. The use of State subventions to create new jobs by attempting to secure a greater share of a rapidly expanding international market led the Government into direct competition with other countries, principally Japan but also France, where high technology industries have received greater support from their governments (Richardson and Moon in Deakin, 1986).

At a different level, a further item of unfinished business on the economic policy agenda was the position of the trade unions. Despite the substantial changes in the legal position of unions brought about by legislation in the first term, the Government's desire to move towards a situation in which the labour market could function more freely implied further steps in the direction of limiting the unions' freedom of action.

The effective implementation of Government policies, once devised, raised a different set of unresolved issues. The debates in the first term about efficient translation of policy into action by the civil service, and the measures introduced to secure it, had left a residue of bad feeling on both sides. Sir John Hoskyns, who served as an adviser in Downing Street during the first term, left a record of his disillusionment in a series of combative speeches and articles, in which he excoriated what he saw as the defeatism of the civil service, culminating in the half-serious suggestion that all civil servants over 50 should be summarily dismissed (*Times*, 22.11.83). Passive resistance within the service, which had steadily stiffened over the first term, found expression in industrial action, notably over the decision in January 1984 to bar workers at the Government Communications Headquarters at Cheltenham from union membership, and also in an increasing stream of leaks which not even the fate of the Think-Tank (CPRS), summarily abolished for continuous leakages, could staunch.

The other major problem of implementation, clearly evident from experience in the first term, was the ability of agencies responsible for implementing policies at local level – principally (but not exclusively) the local authorities – to frustrate Government objectives. The financial controls imposed in the first term having proved insufficient, another round of action appeared inevitable, with the abolition of the GLC and the metropolitan counties, one of the few specific manifesto commitments, serving the function of encouraging the others to come into line. Local government reform, however, quickly proved that it had lost nothing of the trench warfare quality that had made it the Passchendaele of the Government's first term and the able resistance put up by the GLC, in particular, guaranteed a high level of ministerial casualties.

These obstacles notwithstanding, it remained evident that the issue of Welfare State expenditure would be tackled, as a substantive, if not the major second term priority. That raised the question of selection within the range of Welfare State programmes. Since the presenting issue was the cost of welfare, it followed that the choice would be largely determined by the respective sizes of the different programmes and their rates of growth. A second important factor would be the degree of control that the Government would be able to exercise over the size of a selected programme, and the extent to which the levers of change fell directly under ministers' hands.

A third (and crucial) element in any choice would be ideological. To choose to pick off a peripheral programme merely because it was convenient and relatively uncontroversial would be unlikely to satisfy the Government's supporters on the New Right. They had been urgently pressing from the first day in power for a systematic attack on the 'flagships of collectivism', notably the NHS and State education, and had become increasingly dissatisfied by the Government's failure to launch it. A promising area for intervention, which would meet at least some of these anxieties, would be one which satisfied the Government's economic policy imperatives: measures that would eliminate or at least check the demoralising effect of over-dependence that the Government's supporters attributed to most welfare programmes, and thereby help to stimulate individual enterprise. Such an approach would also relate closely to the struggle for hearts and minds so energetically waged by the IEA and the newer, competing New Right think-tanks that had sprung into being in the 1970s, notably the Adam Smith Institute. Welfare reforms which demonstrated conclusively the superior merits of private choice over public provision would clearly be preferable to those that merely helped to reduce burdens of public expenditure, laudable though this might be.

Finally, it would be desirable for the chosen area of reform to be one in which large public bureaucracies were closely involved. The need to cut these organisations down to size had been one of the main elements in the Government's campaign rhetoric in 1979 and subsequently. Such an approach could also be seen as an element in the process of depressing the pretentions of the bureaucracies (who had arrogated to themselves the role of defenders of public services) and of the unions that flourished in such environments.

The selection of social security satisfied most, if not all of these objectives. As both the largest, and fastest growing sector of welfare expenditure, it was a natural target for a Treasury committed to a new, major, cost-cutting exercise and dissatisfied with the chipping away at individual benefits that characterised policy in the first term.

However, it is characteristic of all social security expenditure that it cannot be kept effectively in check solely by interventions by ministers to keep down the level of benefits. In the jargon, much of it is 'demand-led'. Demographic pressures, in the case of pensions, or overspill from the effects of failures in other policy areas, in the case of unemployment benefit, inflate the level of expenditure in ways over which the Secretary of State for Social Services can exercise no direct control. This aspect of spending on social security is aptly caught in David Howell's image of the 'balloons' of public expenditure, in his influential article in *Political Quarterly* (1984). It is therefore difficult to guarantee in advance that a specific level of savings can be secured over a set timescale. This is a substantial disincentive in terms of Treasury forward planning, unless the weight of political commitment that can be brought to bear is so overwhelmingly strong as to engage the whole machinery of Government in the enterprise.

This ambitious undertaking might have been easier to pull off in an area where intervention chimed in well with the ideological priorities of the Government and its supporters outside Parliament. For social security expenditure touches the core of the ideological debate in two places: first, in the assumed impact of benefits on incentives to work; and, second, in terms of entitlement. Do those who have apparently chosen not to work deserve to be supported by the State? Both these themes had been amply exposed over the previous decade by critics on the New Right and their sympathisers (Minford, 1984). An intervention designed to cut such expenditure could expect to secure ample backing from these quarters.

At the same time, the benefits field could be plausibly represented as one in which the complexities of the current system and the bureaucratic quality of administration justify a new intervention which might simplify and humanise the basis on which the system functions. The example of the poverty trap, sprung when a fixed cut-off point is applied for entitlement to benefits which will penalise those just below that point for earning more, is a case in point. It has been universally condemned as an example of rigidity and complexity in operation. In the light of past criticisms along these lines from critics ranging from claimants' groups, and younger neo-Marxist critics through the traditional defenders of the Welfare State to the New Right, it should in theory have been possible to secure a broadly based consensus for review, leading to reforms, if not for cuts.

One other helpful feature of the situation, viewed from the Government's perspective, was that, despite these criticisms of the shortcomings of the existing system, no effective pressure group speaking for the collective interests of all those affected had yet emerged. There are effective lobbies for specific groups of claimants; and the Child Poverty Action Group could point to past successes in persuading Governments of both major parties to modify their policies. However, a government contemplating intervention in this field could be reasonably confident that, with the important and conspicuous exception of pensioners, there is no automatic fund of public goodwill towards any particular group which critics of proposals for cuts in expenditure can call upon in attempting to frustrate them. Indeed, despite some signs of softening of attitudes towards claimants – especially the unemployed – over the first term, the evidence of public reaction to episodes like the 'Oxfraud' case (Franey, 1983), in which a bogus social security office was set up to entrap those putting forward false claims, strongly implied that an intervention portrayed as eliminating waste and fraud would be likely to secure widespread approval. This presented a sharp contrast to the other 'flagship' areas of welfare, and in particular the National Health Service. There, proposals for drastic changes or reductions in expenditure could expect to encounter formidable opposition from a range of pressure groups, trade unions and interested professionals, with the certainty of strong support from the general public (Taylor-Gooby, 1985). Nor had the attempts of the trade unions representing staff responsible for administering the benefits system had any significant success in enlisting sympathy or support for the difficulties that their members have experienced in operating the system at a time of greatly increased use and reductions in staff numbers.

Thus, while the selection of social security expenditure as a major potential source of savings in public expenditure did not satisfy all the conditions that might have made it an ideal target for action early in the Government's second term, it came close enough to meeting them to provide a tactically and strategically suitable case for action.

A NEW BEVERIDGE?

Given that it was clear from the beginning of the Conservative Government's second term that their main economic objectives could not be met without significant cuts in social spending; and with an obvious target already in the Treasury's sights, in the form of the social security programme, it is surprising, at first sight, that Nigel Lawson, the new Chancellor, should have chosen to make what appeared to be an immediate clumsy grab at a few short-term reductions in public spending. Lawson's emergency round of additional cuts, introduced two months after the election, in July 1983, set off an immediate chorus of knowing remarks about the emergence of the alleged 'hidden manifesto'. But Lawson's move also met a more important longer-term objective, by serving notice both to political colleagues and Whitehall Departments that, this time, the Treasury was not prepared to let the case for substantial reductions be smothered by arguments of political expediency. Short-term embarrassment was a small price to pay, especially with the Opposition divided and politically almost impotent, for securing such a public declaration of intent. As Lawson told his party conference in October 1983, in his first speech as Chancellor, it was essential to establish the goal of cutting public expenditure before embarking on the longer-term agenda of tax cuts. In order to do so, it would be necessary to confront the whole range of arguments for higher public spending, including

> the ageing of the population, the development of costly technologies, the lobbying of vested interests, the innate desirability of many of the forms of public expenditure, the inherent desire of all bureaucracies to expand their empires, and the failure to recognise that what is provided free still has to be paid for. (Lawson, 1992, p. 306)

In this enterprise, the Chancellor could count on powerful support - within the Cabinet from the Prime Minister, and outside it from the bulk of the press, and in particular *The Times*. Over the next two years, *The Times* helped to establish the basis for public debate in a long series of editorials, sometimes hectoring, sometimes sycophantic. In addition, it provided a platform for a series of articles by major protagonists in what the paper had christened the '2001 debate', covering both technical and political aspects of social policy. In addition, together with *The Sunday Times* and *Financial Times*, it served as a ready recepticle for the stream of leaks that punctuated the debate as it developed and conflicts began to erupt between ministers and their respective departments.

The motto under which *The Times* chose to launch their campaign was 'No Tinkering': if the second term was not to be wasted, the Government (to which *The Times* had given virtually uncritical support throughout the first term) would have to strike out boldly for root and branch reform. As part of this enterprise, *The Times* castigated the minor adjustments made to public expenditure levels before the start of the 1984–5 round, observing of the health cuts that: 'This is not the time to tinker. Mr Fowler, with his one per cent, looks like a man who is tinkering' (26 September 1983). And to further the process, it played host to an extensive restatement of the Treasury's case, complete with the full version of Sir Geoffrey Howe's 1982 analysis, and carefully distanced from contaminating association with the prematurely leaked think-tank report. Bilateral discussions between the Treasury and the spending departments once the public expenditure round had begun led in turn to another public row, supported by selective statements of the case from both sides, precipitated by the particularly disastrous mishandling of an attempt to cut back on expenditure on housing benefit, long regarded by the Treasury as a blatant example of a programme that had been allowed to get out of control. It was becoming evident that the Secretary of State for Social Services, as the minister reponsible for much the largest element in social expenditure, was being forced into a corner.

The method that Norman Fowler chose for extracting himself was ingenious, and in the short term effective. In a speech at Brent on 22 November, he boldly challenged the gloomy views that the Chancellor had been expressing about the future burden of welfare expenditure; in particular, he refuted the proposition that not only Nigel Lawson but the Prime Minister herself had advanced about problems arising from 'constant pressure of the ageing population', pointing out that the longer-term demographic trend was in fact favourable. Having neatly made the point about the lack of an informed context for decision-taking, he went on to call for a 'rational appraisal' of social policy options, leading to a debate that would be 'responsible, realistic and open' (*Times*, 23.11.83). Warmly praised next day in the inevitable *Times* editorial, Fowler proceeded to marshal his strategy. The issue of pensions had been on the boil for some time; and the Secretary of State had already established an inquiry, which he was chairing himself. He now proposed to add to this operation a further three investigations: one, with an independent chair, into the question of housing benefit, which had just caused such political difficulty, and two further examinations of different aspects of the benefits system – one into supplementary benefit and one into benefits for children and young people. Each of these would be chaired by a junior minister in his own department, supported by two selected assessors. Central to his approach was the concept of a public examination of the issues; the lesson that he had drawn from the abortive exercise of 1982 was that lasting reforms could not be achieved by a *coup d'état* behind the closed doors of the Cabinet room. At the same time, Fowler wanted to broaden the objectives of Government policy; although he supported Nigel Lawson's general approach, he argued that 'the reduction of taxation was not our only objective. We had other social policy commitments and we also needed to keep to those' (Fowler, 1991, p. 202).

Urged on in a further New Year exhortation in *The Times* editorial columns ('what is needed is not so much facts as clearer political priorities' (5 January 1984)), the Cabinet decided to let Norman Fowler have his way. But it was made very clear that the Treasury expected that in consideration of immunity from the stringencies of the current expenditure round, the outcome of the inquiries would be to produce substantial savings in future years on the social security budget. Against this background, the Secretary of State unveiled in the Commons on 2 April his package of reviews and studies.

In presenting the initiative, Fowler was at pains to stress the connections between the different studies, and to glide discreetly over the disparate nature of the arrangements for the individual investigations and the uneven coverage that would be achieved of the total field of social security. One point that he was particularly anxious to emphasise was the openness of the exercise: there would be public hearings and some form of publication before legislation was introduced. In order to achieve as much consistency as possible between the individual studies and the investigation of the problems of the disabled that was also being initiated, a central coordinating unit was to be established within the DHSS. The timetable for the whole exercise was brisk: completion within a year, in order to provide ample time for legislation within the lifespan of the Parliament recently elected. And, under pressure, the Secretary of State admitted that, as in every recent exercise in this field, there was to be a 'nil cost' constraint. As he told the lobby in a briefing after the announcement: 'if there are savings in any particular area, then the Government would basically have the alternative of putting the money into another benefit area or conceivably of deciding that it would like to reduce taxation.' The nod in the direction of the Chancellor, whose marker had been firmly put down in the Public Expenditure Green Paper (HM Treasury, 1984) published with the Budget a month before, was unmistakable.

Despite the suspicions provoked by the final element in the statement, the general disposition was to give the Secretary of State the benefit of the doubt, and to accept his good intentions at their face value. But Norman Fowler had gone further than simply declaring a desire to clarify a complex and costly area of social policy. He had ended his statement in the House by declaring that: 'the various reviews and studies I have set in hand constitute the most substantial examination of the social security system since the Beveridge Report forty years ago.'

In order to complete such an ambitious undertaking in such a short space of time, Mr Fowler would have to face up to and overcome the potential opposition of a wide range of interested parties. Of these, the most formidable and determined was undoubtedly the Treasury. 'Like every Secretary of State who has ever been in charge of social security' Fowler subsequently commented, 'I was under pressure from the Treasury' (1991, p. 206).

But not merely had the Chancellor's intention of extracting substantial savings from the exercise been made crystal clear; the Treasury also enjoyed what amounted to a right of veto on the content of the exercise itself, if it was to be genuinely comprehensive, in the form of their control over taxation policy. As numerous critics had already been anxious to point out, no fundamental review of social security could possibly overlook the implications of the problems created by interactions between the tax and benefits systems, in the form of the 'poverty trap' and work disincentives. Yet the slow tempo of computerisation at the Inland Revenue had already ruled out any comprehensive solution based on the applications of new information technology. And on the question of taxation policy, Lawson, in his own words, 'felt obliged to baulk Norman right from the start' (1992, p. 596). Even a revised offer of a joint study group was firmly refused. Lawson's objection, as he later put it, was 'not simply an obscurantist defence of my own turf' but 'based on a careful assessment of the issues involved'. The most that he would concede was a promise to provide that assessment for public discussion in the form of a separate Treasury

Green Paper on the subject. Fowler's subsequent comment was that 'by excluding taxation we missed an undoubted opportunity' (1991, 209). Scarcely less problematic was the position of other ministers. The Prime Minister herself was fully committed to the concept of the reviews, but also had her own strongly held views about the outcome that she would like to see. She had already told the *New York Times* shortly before the announcement about the reviews that the growing cost of social security was a 'time bomb', the consequences of which should be brought to the attention of the British people without further delay (Cairncross, 1985). On content, she was at the outset deeply sceptical about the value of a universal child benefit, and briefed staff in her policy unit at Downing Street to try to ensure that proposals for drastic cuts appeared in the final report. Other ministers had welcomed the reviews, partly as a means of relieving the immediate pressure on other spending departments, but mainly as a means of providing unspecified but substantial savings at a later date that would resolve the political dilemmas the Government still faced. In such a situation, as *The Economist* observed, there was a danger of the reviews 'becoming the New North Sea: a source of dream money for all' (24 November 1984).

Other interests within the machinery of government also presented potential problems for the Secretary of State. Over nearly forty years, the structure devised by Beveridge had acquired its loyal adherents, some blind – or nearly so – to its increasingly obvious faults. The founding concept of an insurance-based system with its own funding, viewed with impatience or scepticism by many critics, was a case in point; harried by the Select Committee on Social Services on the essential meaninglessness of the concept, the under secretary in charge was eventually goaded into a simple statement of faith: 'I am a social insurance man' (Dilnot, Kay and Morris, 1984, p. 33). The Select Committee itself, which had patiently scrutinised the policies of successive Secretaries of State over the preceeding Parliament, also had views of its own on the issue, and the capacity to express them in a form that the Government could hardly refrain from noting. At a different level, the civil service unions, already locked in a series of long-drawn-out battles with DHSS management, had a clear interest in trying to influence the outcome of a review which could hardly fail to deal with issues of staffing, management and the implications of the introduction of new technology.

Potentially, at least, the pressure groups, the turnip-bogles of the New Right theorists, presented less of a problem. The Child Poverty Action Group, with the scalp of the Callaghan Government, acquired in the row about introducing child benefit, as rather dated proof of its capacity to change the direction of policy on social security possessed the ability to reach and influence the media; a whole series of specialised groups representing client groups or organisations likely to be affected by a review, would also make their voices heard in due season. The public sector trade unions could, if necessary, provide the resources and the rank and file. But much would depend on the capacity of the lobbies to construct a convincing and coherent case that went beyond a simple attempt to defend the indefensible *status quo*; and on the willingness of the public to listen to their arguments, once deployed. Similarly, the array of right-wing think-tanks, which had placed so much emphasis on the importance of individual choice and had not been slow to criticise the Government for failing to come to grips with welfare issues, could scarcely be expected to refrain from taking their own case to the public, once the opportunity was presented.

The question of public reaction remained the most probiematic of all. Norman Fowler's insistence on an open review, complete with sessions in which evidence was given in public, had been based on the premise that reform within strict cost constraints could be sold on the open market; yet public opinion, as measured by opinion surveys, had by 1984 swung decisively against restrictions on public expenditure, even when the incentive of tax cuts was offered as a rationale. In such circumstances, a justification for further cuts in benefits cast in terms of the burden on the public – or even upon private individuals – would clearly need to be carefully argued if it was to be convincing. The inclusion of an opinion poll among the investigations to be conducted for the reviews signalled that the Secretary of State was taking the importance of winning the public debate very seriously.

The conditions for a debate of the kind that Norman Fowler wished to promote therefore appeared to exist; even if the timescale was cramped, the terms of reference of the individual inquiries often unduly restrictive and the built-in obstacles to securing support for the kind of reforms that his reviews were likely to throw up formidable. The period after the announcement in the Commons tended to confirm this view: a Grand Inquest upon the Welfare State in which views from all points of the spectrum of opinion would be heard appeared to be getting under way.

The first in a series of substantial contributions to appear was a statement by the Liverpool monetarist Patrick Minford, in the form of a special appendix to the IEA journal *Economic Affairs*, entitled, 'State expenditure: a study in waste' (1984). The essence of Minford's approach was simplification through the use of negative income tax to provide a minimum income for all, set as low as possible (a 'true' minimum (p. xiii)) but supplemented by generous child benefits for families. By providing a single simplified cash benefit, Minford's scheme would, he argued, 'return the Welfare State to the people', by giving them simultaneously basic security and choice. In addition, it would provide an incentive for younger workers to take low-paid jobs. National Insurance contributions would be abolished; together with the vast state bureaucracies in the DHSS and Department of Education, made redundant by the wholesale privatising of all welfare services.

This arresting opening bid in the debate at least had the merit of simplicity; although critics were not slow to point to some of the obvious inflexibilities and naiveties of such an approach. Minford's squib was followed by two major descriptive studies of the benefits system as it was currently operating. Geoffrey Beltram's contribution was of particular significance, both because he had himself held a senior position within the DHSS and because he was able to show that the objectives of the previous reform introduced in 1980 had not been realised. 'In theory' (he wrote) 'discretion has given way to entitlement. In practice, the persistence of quasi-discretionary decisions covering a wide range of alternative payments, undermines the concept of entitlement' (*New Society*, 16.8.84). A substantial study of the supplementary benefits system by the Policy Studies Institute, published in the same month, confirmed Beltram's findings. PSI investigators established that both staff and claimants found it difficult to find their way round the system; that payments to which claimants were entitled were not being made; and that hardship was common, especially among families on the lower rate of benefit. In addition, in a section of the report not initially published by the DHSS, who had commissioned it, evidence of prejudiced attitudes among some DHSS officers towards claimants was found. Taken together, these two studies powerfully reinforced the case for reform.

Over the course of the summer of 1984, a whole series of additional reports put in their appearance, now mostly cast in the form of evidence to the reviews and containing proposals for amendments to the system. So rapid was the flow and so complex the variety of arguments being presented, that some form of 'consumers' guide' was semi-seriously suggested: a 'Green Paper Chase' not unlike the period after the publication of the original Beveridge Report appeared to be under way.

The products of this period ranged from the advocates of a simplified, 'big bang' approach (although none of them quite matched the heroic simplicity of Minford) to those who advocated a version of Beveridge's approach, adapted to changed circumstances and better financed. The former tended to place their faith in devices like negative income tax, and rely heavily on means-testing in order to target benefits to those most in need; the latter to opt for universal benefits paid of right, using the insurance principle both as a means of establishing entitlement and as a symbolic expression of common citizenship.

By far the most developed and intellectually sophisticated statement of the first case was contained in the report published by the Institute of Fiscal Studies (IFS), *The Reform of Social Security* (Dilnot, Kay and Morris, 1984). The IFS argued for a more precisely targeted scheme based on a dual system of tax and benefit credits. The authors were contemptuous of the lack of substance in the contributory system, observing that 'there is really nothing left of the contributory principle in national insurance but 10,000 civil servants administering contribution records, and a good deal of intellectual lumber. It is time to consider whether we need either' (p. 30). Their alternative required extensive means-testing of benefits both to the elderly and to those in work and withdrawal of universal assistance to families with children. Initial reaction suggested that the intellectual attractions of what was clearly a thoroughly developed set of proposals were not matched by any great degree of political sophistication.

Proposals from the National Council for Voluntary Organisations (NCVO) fell somewhere between the two basic categories. Their document (*Social Security after Beveridge; What Next?* see Ashby, 1984) opened strikingly with a powerful call for an altogether more comprehensive inquiry which would place social security in its policy context, as Beveridge had done in his Report. For the immediate future, the NCVO argued for moving towards a 'basic income guarantee', which would replace the insurance-based benefits and supplementary benefit, but would be reinforced by substantial increases in child benefit. Like every other set of proposals, the NCVO's document stressed the importance of dealing effectively with the poverty trap; but placed particular emphasis on improving the situation of women.

The last of the three major sets of proposals was prepared by the National Consumer Council *Of Benefit to All* (1984). This was the clearest of all the statements of the 'New Beveridge' position, arguing for effective insurance-based provision against all major contingencies, with substantially increased child benefit. In the NCC's proposals, means-testing was as far as possible to be eliminated; the cost of higher levels of benefit would be met by abolition of the married man's tax allowance.

Some, at least, of the conditions for a comprehensive debate accordingly seemed satisfied; vigorous and informed advocacy of a wide range of alternatives had ensured that the main issues were now in the public arena. The public hearings on the two investigations that had been entrusted to ministers, those on supplementary benefit and benefits for children and young people, which began towards the end of the summer, seemed an ideal occasion to extend the debate. However, the general impression left by these hearings was of a different sort of exercise in progress: a thin ideological skin covering a preoccupation with technical and above all economic concerns. The evidence of hostility towards the continuation of child benefit that emerged from the questioning by ministers at some of these hearings was sufficiently disturbing for the Child Poverty Action Group to launch a full-scale – and apparently effective – lobby of the Prime Minister at the Conservative party conference in the autumn.

Appearances were not deceptive: behind the scene, the Treasury was already preparing to ensure that it was not deprived of the promised fruits of the exercise. When, immediately after Christmas 1984, Norman Fowler took a selected group of civil servants and advisers away to consider the shape and contents of the Green Paper, it was evident that some substantial offering would have to be made on the altar of economies in public expenditure. As it emerged, when the special Cabinet sub-committee charged with overseeing the final form of the proposals met at the beginning of February 1985, the order of cut that the Treasury initially had in view was £4 billion. The proposal that Norman Fowler, after exhaustive discussion within the group preparing the Green Paper, was prepared to make would provide savings of a far more substantial size: the difficulty was that these savings would be deferred well into the next century.

What Fowler was now proposing was the abolition of the State Earnings Related Pensions Scheme (SERPS). This scheme had been established by bipartisan negotiation in 1975, after two earlier rival schemes had in turn been frustrated when the party that introduced them lost power before they could be implemented. The agreement that had then been reached – to which Norman Fowler had himself been a party – was based on a common recognition that the area of pensions policy, with its exceptionally long lead time, was particularly unsuited to the kind of short-term partisan changes that had characterised some

other social policy topics. The scheme itself, which only began to be
phased in at the end of the 1970s, was an ambitious attempt to
supplement the basic state pension by reference to an individual's best
twenty years of earnings. A major difficulty, as its critics saw it, was that
the main cost of the scheme was deferred, and would fall upon a
population, early in the twenty-first century, in which the ratio of those
in employment to those out of it would be much less favourable.

In many ways, SERPS was a logical political target for a Conservative
Government led by Margaret Thatcher. That it was the product of inter-
party consensus was in itself almost enough to damn it. The
arrangements for funding, on a 'pay-as-you-go' basis, rather than the
prudent Beveridgian approach of building up a fund before paying out –
a principle which must have met with an approving echo in Grantham,
even if it was never realised in practice – had an unhappy flavour of the
free-spending 1960s about them. To argue for substituting private
provision for a State scheme chimed in happily with the preoccupations
of the New Right pressure groups: the IEA, in particular, had been
concerned with pensions issues from the very beginning of its activities.
The main political difficulty lay in the fact that the scheme had barely
begun operation, and any savings would correspondingly be deferred
well into the next century. This could be represented as prudent
statesmanship; but such fine words buttered no financial parsnips for the
Treasury. As one commentator subsequently put it, the proposal only
made political sense if the Tories could be certain of remaining in power
for the rest of the century. Not even Margaret Thatcher, despite her
brand-new parliamentary landslide majority, could offer such a
guarantee.

The discussions in the Cabinet sub-committee were accordingly sharp
and accompanied by the now familiar round of leaks and repudiations.
Alerted by these, the lobbies began to prepare their special cases against
the day of publication. But behind the scenes the conflict had become
even sharper than the leaks implied. First, the Treasury reiterated, in a
minute from the Chief Secretary to the Prime Minister, who was
chairing the sub-committee, its demand for substantial savings from the
exercise – now, a minimum of £2 billion. A personal meeting between
Fowler and the Prime Minister was necessary before this condition could
be lifted. Then Nigel Lawson belatedly discovered – according to his
account, through the failure of his own officials to alert him – that what
the Cabinet sub-committee (MISC 111) considering the issues was
proposing to substitute for SERPS would be a system of compulsory

private insurance. Two days before the proposals were due to go to full Cabinet, Lawson fired off a minute to MISC 111 stating baldly that he could not accept compulsory private provision at the level envisaged. As he described it subsequently:

> I had never seen Norman so cross. He insisted on cancelling the Cabinet discussion planned for that Thursday, 25 April – even though it was entirely concerned with other items of the social security review over which there was no disagreement between us – and came round to see me at Number 11 on the morning of 24 April. He was furious at what he saw as a last-minute attempt to sabotage his plans, and claimed that I had no right to act in that way. I had considerable sympathy with him. (1992, p. 589)

But not enough to make the Chancellor change his mind. the scheme was modified and eventually agreed by the full Cabinet, where the Chancellor once again attempted to reopen the issue of immediate cuts. However, with the Prime Minister's support, Fowler was able to carry the day, and his amended draft was agreed. Lawson had to be content with reflecting that although he had failed in his bid to secure immediate savings 'the changes Norman made, with my full support, undoubtedly checked the escalation that would otherwise have occurred' (1992, p. 593). For the moment, all references to specific financial saving were removed from the draft, although the global sum expected to be saved on introduction (£750 million) was made public.

Thus, when Norman Fowler came to present his Green Paper (1985a) in June 1985 to the Commons and the wider public that he was so anxious to reach, his proposals reflected a series of compromises between different imperatives – political, economic and administrative – some knowledge of which had already leaked into the public arena. Despite this, the initial response to the Green Paper was puzzled, rather than hostile. As *The Economist* put it, 'a handsome package, but what's inside?' (8.6.85). Great care had been taken with presentation: Fowler's expertise with visual aids had contributed towards his success in Cabinet, and this concern was also reflected in the Green Paper itself and its two supporting volumes of evidence, clearly written, crisply laid out, with copious tables and diagrams in full colour. But the content itself, and the essential strategy, were considerably less clear.

In outline, the main proposals were the abolition of SERPS, the simplification of supplementary benefit by the abolition of many discretionary payments and the creation in their place of a new 'social fund' to provide assistance in emergencies; the introduction of a family credit system to replace Family Income Supplement, paid through the wage packet to the principal earner, and substantial reductions in the numbers of those eligible for housing benefit, linked with a stipulation that all households should meet at least 20 per cent of their rates bill.

Yet the package lacked a strong central theme equivalent, however approximately, to Beveridge's theme, of common citizenship expressed through flat-rate 'social' insurance. The individual elements did not fuse, but rather suggested different emphases. At one level, a strong theme was simplification – the 'consensus' thread, reinforced by the constant repetition of images like the 'labyrinth' of the current system. Here, the presentational emphasis was on the lack of clear guidance for users of the system, reinforced by the endless complications of the current rules and procedures, the creation of anomalies like the poverty trap, and the numbers of staff required to operate the system. The proposals that best fitted this emphasis were the more technical 'smoothing' amendments and the attempt to link tax and benefits in rather rudimentary style, through the new family credit system. Suggestions about the enhanced use of new technology supplemented this broad approach, although they also served to introduce a second theme, the elimination of waste.

The introduction of new technical systems and simplification and better 'targeting' in the distribution of benefits neatly matched a pervasive general emphasis in public administration under the Conservatives: securing efficiency savings. One obvious area of such savings, implied but not stated in the Green Paper, would be in staffing levels. The other main implication of targeting would be reductions in the numbers of those receiving benefit. The Green Paper travelled part of the way down this road, with substantial cuts in housing benefit; but baulked at what had seemed at the outset the easiest of all the fences, the means–testing of child benefit.

The surprisingly strong emphasis placed in the Green Paper on the value of universal child benefit was linked to a third major theme – the position of vulnerable groups. The Green Paper, identifying as crucial a shift in the composition of those in poverty from a predominantly elderly population to one in which families with children feature more and more prominently, laid particular stress on meeting their needs, and identified child benefit as one of the most efficient ways of doing so. But in giving to families, the Green Paper took away from others, notably the under-25s, whose entitlement to benefit was to be severely restricted, regardless of their status, whether as parents or in higher education. The position of women as heads of one-parent families was to be safeguarded, but their position in a two-parent family was defined along traditional lines – payment of the new family credit through the pay packet, ensuring that in most cases it would end in the hands of the male partner.

These apparent inconsistencies reflected a deeper ambiguity about objectives. As critics began to come to grips with the proposals, the implications of a number of the compromises that had been made during the preparation of the Green Paper began to become clearly evident. Ambiguity about the role of the State was one central example. Seizing onto the example of Beveridge as their precedent, the authors of the Green Paper repeatedly underlined the importance of collaboration between State, private enterprise and the individual: what was described as the 'Two Pillars' approach, 'which recognises the importance of state provision . . . but seeks to define its limits' (para 1.11). Yet the relative importance of these 'pillars' changed in a bewilderingly arbitrary way from one policy sector to another, from pensions to child benefit. The contributory principle, butt of so much sarcasm from its critics, would be retained, on the (unproven) ground that it satisfied psychological (if not practical) objectives and reinforced individuals' sense of taking a share of responsibility for their own situation (para 6.8). More drastic still, the insistence that even the poorest should pay some share of rates was defended on the principle of making the system of local administration accountable to those individuals for whom services were being provided. However, discretionary payments, roundly criticised at the time of the 1980 reforms for increasing dependency and obscuring the legal entitlements of potential claimants, were to be reintroduced as the proposed Social Fund, which reminded many critics of the less attractive features of Victorian parish relief.

Part of this muddle, it was persuasively argued, stemmed from the failure to face the need to define the basic objectives that a social security system should seek to meet. The relief of poverty would clearly be central to any definition of objectives, right, left or centre; yet the whole question of the means by which poverty is to be defined – so important in seeking to define ways in which it can most effectively be relieved – was relegated to the margin of debate in the Green Paper in the form of a dry discussion of the technicalities in the Appendices. Arguably, this evasion is rooted in the contextual factor that the Secretary of State and his departmental colleagues were never able to escape, the 'nil cost' constraint. Trapped within this politically defined limit, precluded from exploring issues in the taxation system like mortgage interest relief and the married man's allowance and with the subject matter of the reviews confined strictly to those services designed for the traditional clients of the Welfare State, the Green Paper's direct impact on the relief of poverty was almost certain to be little more than marginal.

Such issues, the Green Paper implied, lay beyond the scope of the social security system, and indeed Welfare State services generally: they were properly the concern of those responsible for the management of the economy. Yet, except in the form of the broadest of general statements to the effect that the cost of social security 'must not be allowed to become a millstone' (para 6.15), no attempt was made in the Green Paper to deal with the interactions between economic and social policy and their implications for the delivery of welfare. In this sense, the Green Paper was Hamlet without the Prince of Denmark – or, as some people might have preferred to describe him, the Prince of Darkness: the Chancellor.

Most of these issues emerged only gradually, as the debate developed. The initial focus of comment was on the absence of any figures to identify who would be gainers from the proposals, and where the losers would be. Heavy pressure on this point, in Parliament and outside, eventually led to an undertaking by the Government to provide figures at the conclusion of the second stage of consultations, with the publication of the White Paper containing the Government's detailed plans for legislation. A deadline of the end of September was set for this phase and comments invited.

'The phoney war is over', proclaimed the National Campaign Against Social Security Cuts, one of several ad hoc lobbying coalitions brought into existence as a result of the reviews. The Government was duly bombarded with a whole array of commentaries of different calibre from a wide variety of organisations and perspectives. The principal focus of most early published responses was the proposal to abolish SERPS; the revelation that neither of the Government's own advisers on the pensions review was happy with the proposals that had emerged greatly strengthened the hand of the critics, which was further reinforced by the evident general reluctance to abandon bipartisanship in such a difficult field. The evident lack of enthusiasm of much of the pensions industry, and the firm line taken against the proposals by the Confederation of British Industries left the Government with few supporters, with the ever loyal exception of *The Times*. And behind the scenes, Nigel Lawson had, as Norman Fowler put it, 'made no secret of the fact that he saw the proposals as financially prohibitive' (1992, p. 592).

The CBI was also among many critics who were unhappy with the concept of the new family credit, paid through the wage packet. Since employers would clearly need to be closely associated with the introduction of the new system, their opposition was of considerable significance. Equally important, the Government's Social Security Advisory Committee (SSAC) devoted a substantial part of their response to arguing the case for modifying the proposals in the light of the potential damage that they would cause to the interests of women.

Other commentaries drew special attention to the consequences of cuts in housing benefit and the implications for pensioner households, in particular. Almost all those who made comments on the proposed social fund and the new provisions for supplementary benefit referred to the low level at which benefit would still be set, especially in the case of the under-25s. Many went on to draw comparisons with the higher rates of equivalent benefits in other EEC countries. Only the Institute of Directors, in their evidence, argued that supplementary benefit rates were being set too high.

In general, the quality and range of the commentaries published was impressive. But the wider debate that both Norman Fowler and his critics were hoping to see was not taking place. Traditional campaigning techniques failed to muster more than token support, despite strong backing from the public sector unions. The public were either not prepared to come to terms with the issues, or reluctant to identify themselves with either the Government or its critics. The DHSS's own poll, taken for the reviews, showed a very low level of awareness among respondents about the organisation of the system and the basis on which benefits are paid; some disposition to criticise the standard of service provided by the DHSS, and a rather lukewarm disposition to look for a service that better matched the requirements of the most needy. Less than half the respondents (45 per cent) had even heard of SERPS, which formed the centrepiece of the Government's original proposals.

In such circumstances, the debate inevitably tended to become a dialogue between specialists, a development reflected in the progressive decline in the level of publicity given to the reviews as the date for the publication of the White Paper summarising the Government's conclusions approached. Some of their critics were disposed to welcome this development. Peter Townsend, in the comments he provided for the Fabian Society's response, argued that there had been a succesful exercise in damage limitation; the Government's proposals, though in many respects deplorable, were less bad than they might have been, given the Government's ideological predispositions – an outcome for which he was inclined to give credit to the civil servants (Silburn, 1985, p. 2). Others regretted the lost opportunity. Richard Berthoud, author of the Policy Studies Institute's study of supplementary benefit, concluded a long review by observing:

> there is no funding crisis, but there is a resource problem; it could have been solved if the analysis had spread wide enough. Mr Fowler has sat his examination and handed in his paper. He is waiting for his grades. If they are disappointing that will be because he has studied only half the syllabus. (1985a, p. 14)

Michael Meacher, Labour's shadow social services spokesman, had earlier attempted to fill the gap by producing his own proposals (1985); but the indicative costs that he rashly placed on them embarrassed his own front bench and gave his opponents a propaganda advantage that they were quick to exploit. The fate of this initiative served as a deterrent to others contemplating similar tactics.

The Government's White Paper, when published in December 1985, proved to contain only one significant concession. Instead of being abolished, SERPS was to be scaled down, as Nigel Lawson had wished. When MISC 111 met again to put the White Paper in final form 'there was little disposition', Lawson tells us, 'to argue with my contention that the misbegotten notion of a compulsory private scheme should be dropped, and we should simply make SERPS a good deal less generous' (1992, p. 592). The situation of the under-25s was also marginally improved; and some relief given on the proposed withdrawal of housing benefits. But in most essential respects, the proposals were largely unchanged. The authors summed up the contextual issues by once again emphasising the paramount importance of securing economic growth:

> social security must not hinder that growth, either in the way the system affects individuals, or in the burden it places on the economy generally. Social security accounts for one third of all public spending. It cannot be ringfenced from the requirements of sensible management of the economy as a whole. (White Paper, para 1.6)

Appearing before the House of Commons Select Committee on Social Services in January 1986, just after the publication of the Social Security Bill based on the White Paper, Norman Fowler contrived to give the impression of a man who had seen through a complex tidying-up operation, defending the specific options he had selected and declining to be drawn into discussion of broader issues. His private judgment was very different. 'As long as I live' he says in his memoirs, 'I will regret having to abandon our plans to give an occupational pension to every worker in the country. It was the worst decision I ever had to take in government' (1991, p. 22). And Richard Berthoud of PSI, writing in *The Times* the same week, answered his own earlier question about the impact of the exercise as a whole. Claims that the reviews represented 'fundamental reform', he concluded, were in his judgment 'grossly exaggerated' (28.1.86).

PASSING THE LEGISLATION

It was probably inevitable that the Second Reading debate on the Social Security Bill should have been an anti-climax, consisting as it did largely of the repetition by the main protagonists of arguments well polished through repetition elsewhere. The main focus of interest was on how far the arguments that had been put together by the extra-parliamentary lobbies and pressure groups would succeed in detaching a significant number of Conservative backbenchers from their political allegiance. In the event, although a number of doubts were expressed, only two members, Jim Lester and Sir Brandon Rhys-Williams, actually went so far as to withhold their support in the division lobbies. However, there was a notable speech of dissent from Francis Pym. Although he did not carry his protest as far as abstention, he took the opportunity to restate the One Nation theme that he had been developing from the back benches in speeches and writing and condemn the legislation as another example of the Government's insensitivity to the importance of this theme of unity rather than division.

The Bill was accordingly despatched to a lengthy period of scrutiny in Standing Committee, with little obvious sign of difficulties to come. And indeed in the long slogging match that followed, the Government, prudently supplied by the Whips with a substantial working majority on the Committee, was rarely in serious danger of defeat. But weak points in the Bill were identified and extensively explored, to the point where the Government were constrained to apply a guillotine at both Committee and Report stage. The use of these procedural devices ensured that despite the fact that 140 amendments had been selected for debate the Bill left the Commons largely unaltered. The only concessions made to critics were on two new pieces of machinery for payment of benefit. The arrangements for paying family credit – originally to be paid through the wage packet, and hence in nine out of ten cases to men – were to be reviewed; and the discretionary character of the Social Fund and its provision for emergencies was to be tempered by the introduction of a form of appeal based on review by an inspectorate, although one still located in the DHSS. But attempts by Sir Brandon Rhys-Williams to secure the index-linking of child benefit failed: such additional changes as were made to the Bill were introduced by the Government, for their own purposes.

In his defence of the use of the guillotine in the Commons, the Leader of the House, John Biffen, had described the legislation as 'a Bill which has aroused such strong feelings in this place and in the public at large', and added that 'the other place [that is, the House of Lords] has shown that it takes seriously its role as a revising chamber, and no doubt it will continue to do so'. In the event, the Lords fully justified the implied compliment. At Second Reading at the beginning of June, the leading Opposition spokesmen laid down a fierce barrage of criticism; Lady Jeger, for the Labour Party, assured the Government that they would not be able 'to quietly hustle the Bill here'. And so it proved. Although constitutional convention rules out any possibility of outright defeat, amendment after detailed scrutiny lies within the Lords' discretion; and on this occasion discretion was thoroughly exercised.

The essential difference between consideration of the Bill in the Lords and previous discussion in the Commons lay not so much in the nature or weight of the arguments advanced, as in the different context in which they were deployed. Two especially important distinctions are, first, the considerably greater scope for cross-party alliances in the Lords, combined with the involvement of non-party peers, who have no equivalent in the Commons and are usually among the most active members of the House, unlike the hereditary peers who make up a large part of any Conservative Government's hypothetically overwhelming majority. Second, argument on the merits of detailed aspects of legislation have far greater impact in a House where party loyalties are much less strong and openmindedness is frequently proclaimed to be the legislator's supreme virtue. Many peers referred during debates to the briefings that had been received from what one of them called 'non-party agencies concerned with human welfare'; and it was evident in the Committee debates that followed how influential many of those briefings had been.

The combination of these different effects was enough to produce three substantial defeats for the Government during the Bill's passage through the Lords and to lead to further defensive concessions from its managers. One defeat – the narrowest of the three – was on the proposal for a minimum contribution towards the payment of rates, which had been justified by the Government on grounds of preserving local authorities' political accountability. Two more decisive setbacks were on income support for those engaged in care in the community and (perhaps most significant of all) on the right of independent appeal from refusal of payment out of the Social Fund. This amendment was coupled with another providing for the procedures for appealing to be the subject of regulations laid down by Parliament, not a matter of administrative discretion for the minister.

Taken together with the concessions made to avoid running the risk of further parliamentary defeats, these amendments represented significant shifts of principle in the content of the Bill; and also, as *The Economist* (no great friend of theirs) observed, 'a testimony to the lobbying power of organisations which represent every conceivable group of the unfortunate and deprived' (28 June 1986). What *The Economist* did not add was that the lobbies had also demonstrated considerable tactical sophistication, in forming alliances and coalitions appropriate to particular issues – as, for example, the Child Poverty Action Group's protracted struggle to change the method of payment of family credit, in which it enlisted both Conservative women's organisations and representatives of small businesses. Finally, the coalitions on the floor of the House across party lines were of decisive importance in securing the passage of amendments. These involved crossbench peers, Bishops, dissident Conservatives, among whom Lady Faithfull (a former local authority children's officer) was particularly active, the Alliance parties and Labour. The relationship between the last two was noticeably closer than in the Lower House; and this added to the Government's difficulties, reducing their whips to extreme measures – ransacking the final reserves of hereditary peers – in order to preserve their working majority.

Faced with these substantial obstacles, and with time before the summer recess rapidly running out, the Government decided against compromising, and on the Bill's return to the Commons used their safe majority there to repair most of the damage done by the Lords. This tactic, news of which was obliterated in the press and on television by coverage of the wedding of the Duke and Duchess of York, ensured the

Bill's passage into law (in only moderately amended form) at the end of July 1986.

Despite the eventual outcome, the Conservative Government had experienced, by the standards of Westminster and Whitehall during the 1980s, some sharp setbacks during the passage of the Social Security Act of 1986. But the 'little Peterkin' question has to be asked: It may have seemed like a famous victory at the time, but does it have any lasting significance?

In order to answer Peterkin sensibly, the outcome of the whole episode, from the Secretary of State's original declaration of intent at the beginning of the reviews to the passage of the legislation in its final form needs to be evaluated against the Government's declared intentions, and set in the context of the wider political debate on welfare policies.

Norman Fowler's bold (not to say rash) claim to have given birth to the 'New Beveridge' has already been reviewed in an earlier part of this chapter. The conclusion suggested there was that in their original form, the reviews and the Green Paper based on them – which was packaged with considerable presentational flair – lacked the intellectual coherence and the strong central focus that characterised Beveridge's Report of 1942. As the wrapping paper was peeled away over the course of consultation and parliamentary scrutiny, what had once seemed a 'handsome package' began to fall apart and become little more than a jumble of inconsistent elements. As this process continued, ministerial defences became increasingly little more than ritual incantations, of which Baroness Trumpington's speech at the second reading in the House of Lords is a typical specimen: 'if social security is to serve the ends for which it is intended, it must be better directed, it must be simpler, it must strengthen rather than weaken incentives' (Hansard, 2.6.86). But the extent to which the legislation would contribute in practice towards achieving these highly general ends was already problematic.

Apart from his unifying theme, of securing an end to want through comprehensive social insurance, Beveridge's Report was also unusual for the boldness with which he intruded (if only rhetorically) into areas which were only by the broadest stretch of the imagination within the terms of reference of his inquiry. The image of the five giants, which when considered merely as a piece of synthetic folklore is enough to make even his most enthusiastic defenders cringe, takes on a different significance when seen as a means of legitimising his introduction of the linked assumptions about unemployment, health and the situation of children (personified in Giants Idleness, Disease, Ignorance and Squalor) as indispensible elements in the Plan for Social Security. At the same time, Beveridge was careful to ensure that his reach did not exceed his grasp. He carefully cultivated his main Treasury contact, Maynard Keynes, in order to arm himself against the inevitable attack on the costs of his scheme. At the same time that he was working to secure his position within Government he was sufficiently concerned about the importance of the public response to his Plan to mount and sustain a most effective campaign through journalism and public speaking to mobilise opinion behind it. Corelli Barnett, the fiercest of his latter-day critics, has been moved to describe him as 'the Field Marshal Montgomery of social welfare' (Barnett, 1986, p. 26). Although the compliment is certainly intended to be double-edged there can be no denying that Beveridge, too, duly won his El Alamein.

In almost all these respects, Fowler was unable, or perhaps unwilling to emulate his predecessor's tactical dexterity. One of the most striking features of his review is its narrowness; and this increased, rather than diminished as the debate continued. The leading theme of 'targeting' failed to capture public imagination; and although the links with economic policy issues were faithfully projected, the form in which they came across, and in particular the significance of the 'nil cost' constraint imposed at the outset only served to enhance the impression of an area of policy where decisions were subordinated to other priorities. In this sense, as Frances Cairncross commented, Norman Fowler was starting in 1931, that archetypal year of economic crisis, not 1942, the turning point of the 'people's war'.

For it is only fair to add that Beveridge had the enormous advantage of working in a situation which gave him, in his own phrase, a 'clear field' (para 8), whereas any attempt at reform of social security now has to contend not only with the detritus of forty years of patchwork, but also with formidable entrenched interests, both inside and outside Government. Furthermore, the Treasury, while it may not have changed its basic position on essentials very much – there is a remarkable consistency between the views expressed by Sir Kingsley Wood as Chancellor in 1943 about the likely future cost of welfare and those of Nigel Lawson in 1983 – has now developed far more sophisticated mechanisms for the management of social expenditure. These make it even harder for any spending minister to embark on radical new departures at a time of economic stringency. And as we now know, Nigel Lawson was ruthless in employing all the devices at the Chancellor's command to impose the Treasury's agenda. In his account of his involvement in the social security review, Lawson justifies his intervention not only on the specific ground of the scale of the social security budget and its 'profound bearing on economic performance' but also on the basis that 'the Treasury is not simply a Finance Ministry. It is also, both in name and in reality, the central Department, with a finger in pretty well every pie that the Government bakes' (Lawson, 1992, p. 586). Lawson himself was a frequent visitor to the social policy kitchens during his period in office as Chancellor.

Yet even granted these additional constraints, the limitations of Fowler's approach when compared (as he invited us to do) with that of Beveridge are very clear. As the debate on his proposals proceeded, it also became more technical: and once reduced to this level, the Government's opponents began to enjoy a substantial tactical advantage. From then on, the debate was being conducted on terrain that the major pressure groups, notably CPAG, knew well; they are adept at expounding and where necessary dramatising the issues in ways that the Government and its supporters, especially the New Right groups, who approach these questions from an altogether different perspective, had not yet learnt to employ. For this narrowing down, and the failure to make connections to related policy areas, the Government had only itself to blame.

As should be clear from the preceding analysis, the crucial failing in the original proposals was that no serious attempt had been made to link the tax and benefits systems. Taxation policy is a Treasury responsibility; and Nigel Lawson had made it very clear to Norman Fowler that he intended to keep it that way – no outsiders admitted when the Treasury does the catering. Lawson justified this refusal on the grounds of the 'fundamental philosophical difference between tax and social security' which (for reasons that he professes not to follow) his colleagues seemed unable to grasp (1992, p. 598). To clarify the situation and set out the Treasury's position in greater detail, a Green Paper on Personal Taxation had been promised. However, it was not until March 1986, when the Social Security Bill had been before the Commons for two months, that this document finally appeared. When it did, it proved to be largely devoted to issues of equity in the taxation system between married couples, a question which had already been the subject of an earlier Green Paper during Sir Geoffrey Howe's Chancellorship.

Lawson's new document (*The Reform of Personal Taxation*, Cm 9756) did contain two brief sections, one on the link between the tax and benefits system and the other on the possible integration of payment of tax and employees' NI contributions. But the first of these concluded, after the most cursory examination, that 'full integration of all benefits with tax is never likely to be either desirable or practicable ' (para 6.25) and offered only the possibility of a few longer-term experiments, identifying (rather unfortunately, since this was one of the few amendments to the Social Security Bill actually made by the Government itself) family credit paid through the pay-packet as an example, pending that ever-distant day 'when computerisation of the Inland Revenue and DHSS is complete' (para 6.23). The second chapter, after a limp restatement of the familiar dogma about the psychological value of the contributory principle, concluded that 'the Government's view is that the benefits of a combined charge would be unlikely to justify the ensuing upheaval' (7.18). So much for the confident declaration of intent in the original White Paper on Social Security, looking forward to 'sensible cooperation' between the social security and tax systems (para 1.5). And as for the debate that had been taking place outside Government about the respective merits of rival models of integrated tax and benefit systems, the Treasury's lordly indifference was more eloquent than any comment. Those who wished to do so, could submit their comments by September 1986 – by which time, the 'New Beveridge' legislation would be safely on the statute book. The Treasury's reluctance to become embroiled in public debate on any but its own terms was palpable. However, it enabled Nigel Lawson to draw the conclusion that his department had 'lucidly demonstated the overwhelming practical case for keeping the two systems apart – a case which, significantly, no-one even attempted to refute' (1992, p. 596)

TOWARDS THE HUSTINGS

As the original ambitions for comprehensive reform of social security diminished to a bundle of unrelated measures tied together in a cost-containment exercise, so the Government's declared intention to adopt a root and branch approach to all aspects of welfare, once to have been a centrepiece of domestic policy in the second term, began to look less convincing. While the focus was still on social security, the largest single item of Government expenditure, and significant reductions in the level of increase in costs were being secured, the argument that the Welfare State was under stringent review could still be sustained, by opponents and advocates alike. But as the second term wore on, the Government's unpopularity began to deepen. The 'political bonus' that the Government had expected to receive as a result of what had been trumpeted as the domestic equivalent of the Falklands War – their success in seeing off Arthur Scargill and the National Union of Mineworkers earlier in 1985 – had not materialised. The inexorable logic of electoral politics began to assert itself. Social policy issues, on which the Government were uncertain of the extent of support that they could call upon – especially where reform implied addressing complex technical issues that would be difficult to put across convincingly – slipped down the agenda. The ratio of strong medicine to soothing syrup in policies began to alter. It was symptomatic of this situation that the area of social policy that was still attracting concentrated ministerial attention at this period should have been the inner cities, where the priorities were still essentially those established by the Labour Government in their 1977 White Paper.

The Government's period in the doldrums lasted through most of 1986, beginning with the Westland helicopter affair in January, which cost Margaret Thatcher the services of two of her senior colleagues, Michael Heseltine and Leon Brittan and much of her own credibility as a firm, decisive leader. Hugo Young's verdict is harsh: 'manipulation, vicious division, hole-in-the-corner dealing: this was the governing mode which Westland put on display' (1990, pp. 454–5). If Neil Kinnock had not made a complete hash of his speech in the subsequent censure debate, she might well not have survived. A period of 'acute weakness' on her part (Lawson's phrase) followed; as he candidly confesses, this was helpful to him in coping with continued difficulties that he was experiencing, mainly in relation to the position of sterling. In a sequence of progressively more fraught meetings over the course of 1985, the Prime Minister had refused to allow him the option of applying for admission to the European Community's Exchange Rate Mechanism (ERM), in part to underpin the shift of policy direction away from a purely monetarist approach – the 'fragility' of which was now very evident (Lawson, 1992, p. 497). After the last of these, on 13 November 1985, at which the Prime Minister formally declined to accept the combined advice of her Chancellor and Foreign Secretary and the Governor of the Bank of England that Britain should enter, Lawson abandoned his efforts and switched to an alternative policy of 'shadowing' the Deutschmark by linking it through a specific (but undeclared) 'target' exchange rate with the pound (Smith, 1992, pp. 104–5). This device was subsequently denounced by Mrs Thatcher, who claimed that she first heard of it from *Financial Times* journalists, as 'Nigel Lawson's personal economic policy' (Thatcher, 1993, p. 701). Gradually, over the course of 1986, the economic situation began to improve. The unemployment figures peaked at 3.2 million in July, enabling the Secretary of State (David Young) to contemplate (without irony) the task of working towards the great prize of bringing the level down below 3 million in time for the election – although the Treasury remained deeply sceptical about the impact of the froth of special schemes he had whipped up (Lawson, 1992, p. 642). Mrs Thatcher, by contrast, described his 'Action for Jobs' initiative as 'the single most effective economic programme we launched in my term in office' (Thatcher, 1993, p. 422). Inflation remained low; and by the third quarter of the year growth had begun to move vigorously upwards, although Lawson did not, as he put it later, foresee 'the full extent of the boom that began to develop' (p. 643).

By the beginning of the 1986–7 public expenditure round, it was becoming clear that the period of extreme stringency was nearing its end. In the Chancellor's Autumn Statement of November 1986 a planning total for expenditure in the next financial year some £5 billion higher than the previous year was announced. The Autumn Statement confirmed the impression left by the Conservative party conference a month earlier – that the Government was switching into electoral mode. That conference, successfully orchestrated by the party chairman, Norman Tebbit, set ministers the task of identifying policy priorities for the next term in government. It also gave Nigel Lawson a starring role as 'economic miracle worker', a part which he was to perform frequently during the brief interlude of what he subsequently called 'my "unassailable" period' (1992, p. 684). In general, the conference was, in Lawson's words 'a turning-point in the Government's fortunes so marked you could sense it at the time' (ibid.). From that point until the election the Government enjoyed an unbroken lead in the opinion polls.

Immediately after the conference, Margaret Thatcher summoned another of her occasional economic 'seminars' at Chequers. At it, she told her Chancellor and Chief Secretary that she was concerned about the underlying state of the economy, with 'the combination of shrinking savings, high consumer spending, booming retail sales, growing current account deficit and the falling pound, [which] smacked of another "Barber boom"'. Lawson's retrospective comment is: 'stop there and Margaret looks impressively prescient. But in fact she was far more wrong than right; and it was hardly surprising that I chose not to alter course as a result of the seminar' (p. 660). Nor did he. Against this background, the Cabinet set out to prepare for a putative 1987 elections. As is customary on these occasions, policy groups were assembled to review policy areas and come forward with proposals for inclusion in the manifesto. Nigel Lawson, who was responsible for work on the future direction of the economy, has subsequently described the work done as 'primarily public relations'; he used his group principally as a further means of reinforcing the internal argument for early entry to the ERM (p. 664). But in one vital respect the 1987 exercise was different. The Prime Minister had

> resolved in early 1987 that she must embark on a reform of the public services. There followed a remarkable series of meetings of groups of cabinet ministers concerned with subjects in which she was taking a 'special interest'. These subjects were housing and education. (Ridley, 1992, p. 86)

The obvious omission was health; but here the Prime Minister 'still feared that the reform of the NHS was too sensitive a topic to expose to the electorate' (ibid.).

Of these two topic areas, the more problematic was education. With his customary modesty, Nigel Lawson claims in his memoirs full credit for initiating this review; however, Margaret Thatcher's own background as a former education minister made it always likely that she would wish to make progress in an area where change had proved frustratingly slow. Keith Joseph's departure from office in May 1986, to be replaced by Kenneth Baker, appeared to Lawson to provide the ideal opportunity: by private arrangement with the Prime Minister, a Treasury paper was produced, setting out the Chancellor's thinking on the future of education policy, the centrepiece of which was to be 'the wresting of the schools from the so-called local education authorities' as 'the essential basis for education reform' (Lawson, 1992, p. 609). This was done in circumstances of strict secrecy, without reference to the Department of Education. The issues raised in this paper were taken forward to the Cabinet committee, on which Lawson and Nicholas Ridley, who subsequently claimed the credit for originating the eventual scheme for schools to opt out of local government control, also sat. Both are agreed on the unusual character of the proceedings, with the minister ostensibly in charge, Kenneth Baker, treated by the Prime Minister with rather less respect than the office boy and his department's proposals regularly shredded by the committee. Despite this treatment, we are told, 'Kenneth remained in unruffled good humour throughout . . . and the outcome was the raft of proposals that appeared in the 1987 Conservative manifesto' (Lawson, 1992, p. 610).

Matters were simpler when it came to the topic which was Nicholas Ridley's own responsibility, housing. This, as he remarks, was 'the area where Margaret Thatcher thought it was easiest to start to dismantle the dependency culture' (1992, pp. 86–7). The success of the policy of selling council housing provided the basis on which to push forward. The new proposals concentrated once again on putting further and drastic limitations on the role of local authorities. This was also the rationale for another proposal with even more sweeping implications: the reform of local government finance – the flat-rate 'community charge' (or poll tax) – already due to be introduced in Scotland in substitution for the rates and now to be extended to the rest of the country.

By the time that all these proposals had been agreed, the improvement in the economic situation was fully established. In best butter-wouldn't-melt style, Nigel Lawson describes the reaction of party colleagues to his Budget – 'our backbenchers thought the 1987 Budget a good election budget, without being blatantly so'; *The Sun* headline was cruder – 'What a Lot You Got' (two pence off the basic rate of income tax, to be precise). At least one of Lawson's political colleagues, Ian Gilmour, was scathing about this 'electoral Keynesianism'; but even he had to admit later that 'the Chancellor had done a superb job on the electoral economy, making the economy look like a Derby winner throughout the election campaign. The question was whether he had, as it were, doped the economy to produce palpably unsustainable growth' (Gilmour, 1992, p. 62).

Fortified by these achievements, the Government set out to the polls in June 1987. In retrospect, the result of the 1987 election seems preordained. The fact that it seemed for a brief interval to be in some doubt is attributable to two factors; first, the slickness of the Labour Party's campaign (admittedly from the low base of the shambles of 1983) and, second, the quite astonishing disarray behind the scenes in the Conservative camp. Of the plethora of rival accounts that we have subsequently had, none reveal any disagreements on issues of substance; all boil down to questions of personality and presentation. Nigel Lawson, as always, has little doubt about the significance of what had occurred: he dates the deterioration of his relationship with the Prime Minister from the election and her perception that he had been given too much credit for what she regarded as her victory (1992, p. 708), though she denies this. However, some substantial issues did also emerge and most of the ones that damaged the Government were in the social policy area. The funding and management of the NHS were once again hotly debated. The consequences of the new policies devised in what David Willetts subsequently called the 'in-flight refuelling' exercises on education and housing and the manifest lack of preparation on the detail of these policies also proved controversial. But these concerns were swamped by the economic issues. Under close scrutiny, Labour's alternative tax and spending plans unravelled and their campaign lost momentum. The Conservatives duly returned to power with a three figure majority in Parliament and a share of the popular vote that was once again slightly reduced.

A WASTED OPPORTUNITY?

At the end of their second term in office, what had the Conservatives achieved in Government, in the social policy arena in particular? Had it been, as Nicholas Ridley was subsequently to conclude, 'the time when a serious effort to effect reform should have been made'? He adds: 'the 1983 to 1987 Parliament has often been described as a wasted opportunity; that was the time when a serious effort to effect reform should have been made. There would have been time to see the results come through' (1992, p. 257). Was the cause of the apparent failure to do so, as Ridley also suggests, that 'the supply side still dominated the agenda although the programme, in fact, became rather thin' (p. 86)?

Government apologists less brutally frank than Ridley have suggested that significant progress was nonetheless made over the period up to 1987, admittedly not to the extent that they would have wished, in at least four different directions. First, measures had been taken to contain the cost of welfare. As we have seen, the Government came into office at a time when the notion that welfare was becoming an insuperable burden had become common currency. One of the initial objectives set by the Government had been the reduction of public expenditure, seen as being 'at the heart of Britain's present economic difficulties' (HM Government, 1979, p. 1). Expenditure on welfare, and in particular on social security had been seen as central to that concern; hence the Treasury's ill-fated attempt in 1982 to get drastic reform of welfare onto the Cabinet agenda and its subsequent passionate desire to secure really significant economies from the Fowler review.

By the mid-1980s the notion that the burden of providing welfare would inevitably grow to the point where it would become insupportable had been the subject of a number of careful reviews, based on comparative evidence. These clearly demonstrated that on current demographic and economic trends the cost of providing services and benefits at levels then applicable was not likely to be beyond the capacity of the country to afford. As the authors of one of these reviews put it: 'the case for zero growth in public expenditure is not based on economic criteria but rather on a political desire to give absolute priority to tax cuts' (Davies and Piachaud in Klein and O'Higgins, 1985, p. 110).

This was in practice precisely what the Government intended. The 1984 Green Paper on Public Expenditure and Taxation, in many respects the key document of the middle period of the Thatcher Government, set out to establish the principle that there must be a break with 'the debilitating pattern of the past in which public spending and taxation took an ever-larger share of our national product' and that 'without firm control over public spending there can be no prospect of bringing the tax burden back to tolerable levels'. And, even if 'the virtuous circle of lower taxes and higher growth' (a favourite Lawson image) were established 'there should be no general presumption that higher public expenditure is inevitable...given the scope for switching from public to private sectors, and for improved efficiency within the public sector' (1984, pp. 20–1).

One presentational problem was that, in Lawson's own words 'during the period 1978–9 to 1983–4, when the Thatcher government was supposedly trying to cut public spending, the ratio of public spending to GDP rose embarrassingly' (1992, p. 316). As a means of coping with this embarrassment, Lawson decided in 1986 to redefine the Government's public expenditure objective as ensuring that General Government Expenditure (GGE) should continue to fall as a proportion of GDP. Thus, as long as the economy continued to expand (as measured by increases in GDP) absolute increases in the level of public expenditure could be tolerated (or, in election years, welcomed). Nevertheless, as he puts it in his memoirs, Lawson:

> had to insist on the reformulation almost over the dead bodies of the Treasury mandarins, who seemed to feel that simply aiming at a falling share of GDP was selling the pass. Critics from the political Right also attacked me for being content merely to cut the public spending ratio rather than the absolute level of spending. They were not living in the real world. (1992, p. 315)

In that real world, the logic ('of course') was that 'public expenditure falling as a share of GDP is the necessary and sufficient condition for tax cuts'. Such cuts, concentrating (as we have seen) at the top end of the range, were duly delivered; and 'the goal of reducing public spending as a share of GDP was, as the Soviet planners used to say, overfulfilled' (pp. 315–16). But one outcome of this redefinition of objectives was that the cost of welfare was contained rather than reduced. The authoritative LSE survey concludes that up to 1987, compared with the record of its predecessor, 'during the Conservative period, the year-on-year changes were less dramatic (increases mostly about 1 per cent) with the significant exceptions of increases of nearly 5 per cent in 1983/4 and of over 4 per cent in 1986/7, both around election years' (Hills, 1991, p. 340).

The second area in which the Government had some claims to have made progress was that of structural reform. Some of these measures were internal to Whitehall: the follow-up to the introduction of the Financial Management Initiative (FMI) and attempts to modify the operating culture of the civil service to bring about a greater emphasis on the importance of effective management. Others extended partly or wholly outside it: the extension of the public audit machinery through the development of the role of the Audit Commission and the National Audit Office (NAO) – subsequently to be described by a former Permanent Secretary as 'what may prove to be the most important administrative reform in the UK since the Second World War' (Stowe, 1992, p. 393).

The significance of these changes was particularly great for local Government, on whom the Government were anxious to impose the closest approximation to market disciplines that could be achieved, including an experimental programme of contracting out of selected services to tender. Similar measures were in the course of being implemented in the health service. But for the moment these reforms were overshadowed by the running battle with the Department of the Environment about expenditure levels, in which the Treasury was a principal mover behind the scenes. This battle was by 1987 about to enter a new phase with the introduction of the poll tax, of which the Treasury did not, however, approve. Abolition of the GLC and metropolitan counties could be reckoned as one political achievement, however narrowly achieved; but the instrument of more drastic change was to be the squeeze on local authority expenditure in the twin pincers of the reduction imposed by successive Chancellors on the proportion of total expenditure to be met by central government and the discipline that the poll tax was intended to impose. As Nicholas Ridley (one of its main authors) subsequently put it 'I found the arguments about accountability very powerful. Under a poll tax, everyone would have to pay something, even if it was very little. Thus everyone would have a financial interest in keeping their council's expenditure to reasonable levels' (1992, p. 124). However, by 1987 the best that could yet be said was that the new machinery was being put in place but its effects had not yet been tested (even on the Scots).

Linked to the measures designed to improve efficiency and effectiveness in the public sector was the explicitly political goal of reducing the power of the public sector unions and the various interest groups active across the field of social policy – what Nicholas Ridley calls the 'articulate representatives of those who benefited from the enterprise culture' (1992, p. 81). Their activities were seen by many of the Government's strategists as a crucial obstacle to reform; and ministers attributed much of the bad publicity that their welfare policies attracted specifically to 'the lobbies in the public service'. However, by the end of the second term there was some confidence, based on experience with the civil service and in education, that their opposition could be faced down, despite the difficulty that 'they could never be subjected to the market disciplines that eventually overcame the power of the trade unions in the public sector – there were no markets' (Ridley, ibid.)

But the most important of all the four areas of achievement to which the Government could refer was not in social policy but in the general area of management of the economy. At the time of the 1987 election the Government's contention was that the perennial problem of securing steady and sustained growth without intervals of 'stop–go' had been resolved. By then, the cautious prediction of the 1984 Green Paper that maintaining a steady annual growth rate at the pre-war level of between 1.5 and 2.5 per cent was feasible already looked certain to be surpassed. These developments had been mirrored by the improvements in the situation of individuals in work; in the four years between 1983 and 1987 average weekly earnings rose by 14 per cent in real terms. The same period also saw a Stock Exchange boom of unprecedented size and duration – the *Financial Times* index quintupled in value (H. Young, 1990, p. 300). The resulting image of competent management that was being established in the economic field was an asset that might prove transferable from the economy to social programmes.

Against these achievements the Government's critics could cite a number of failures. One possible measure of success – greater equality in outcomes – would not have been accepted by the Government and its supporters as a legitimate test of the success of their policies. It had passed out of official currency with the abolition of the Royal Commission on the Distribution of Income and Wealth at the beginning of the Conservatives' period in office. The subsequent period saw a striking reversal of the established postwar trend towards greater equality of income – largely as a result of the tax reforms. These have involved not just cuts in basic rates and drastic lowering of the higher rates but a switch within the system from direct taxation (income tax) to indirect taxes (like VAT). The effect of this, combined with a failure to raise the threshold at which individuals become liable for taxation, was to increase the tax burden on those earning less than half the average wage while dramatically reducing it for those earning more than twice and above. When all taxation is taken into account, by 1988 'the poorest fifth paid out 40 percent of their income in taxation, while the richest fifth paid out only 35 percent' (Gilmour, 1992, p. 125).

The impact of these changes on those in work was therefore substantial. The differential effect was justified on grounds of incentives to better performance through higher rewards for enterprise, the benefits of which would then 'trickle down' to those at the lower end of the system. Among several problems with this thesis was the persistence throughout the first two terms of very high levels of unemployment – for much of the period it stood at over 3 million, even after several readjustments of the definitions employed. The Government's achievement of securing re-election comfortably in the face of this failure might suggest that the electorate attached less significance to this factor than it was traditionally supposed to do – contrary to Margaret Thatcher's dictum in opposition, they did not take the opportunity given to them in 1987 of drumming the Conservatives out of office. This may also have had something to do with the uneven distribution of unemployment during the first half of the 1980s, with the worst impact concentrated in those areas of traditional manufacturing industry that had suffered so severely from the measures introduced at the beginning of the Conservatives' period in office and not affecting London and the South-East to anything like the same degree. Nevertheless, the unemployment remained a significant drag on the economy and a powerful factor in producing the substantial increases in the level of poverty that characterised the first two terms of the Thatcher Government.

Statistics on the extent of poverty over this period have been grudgingly supplied and are open to a variety of interpretations.

Nevertheless, the trend that became established during the first two Conservative terms in office was quite clear. If the level of supplementary benefit is taken as a definition of the lowest income the State can accept as adequate for its citizens, we find that 12 per cent of the population were on or below this level in 1979 and that by 1987 this had risen to 19 per cent. If we take the percentage of the population living in households at below 50 per cent of the National Income, the measure employed by the European Community, this more than doubled between 1981 and 1987, to 19 per cent or 10.5 million people. When after some delay, official statistics on changes in income distribution were produced, they confirmed that between 1979 and 1988–9 'the poorest tenth of the population experienced a fall in their real income of 6% after housing costs, compared to a rise of 30% for the whole of society and a staggering leap of 46% for the top tenth' (Oppenheim, 1993, p. 170).

The public perception of these developments was a further significant element in the situation. As we have seen, concern over continuing high levels of unemployment did not translate into votes at the 1987 election. On that basis, a number of Conservative politicians have been dismissive of the significance of evidence drawn from surveys of public opinion about trends on attitudes towards key issues and in particular the willingness of voters to sanction higher taxes and public expenditure (Ridley, 1992, p. 85; Lawson, 1992, p. 375). Nevertheless, it is striking that attitudes towards the poor and unemployed as measured in the British Social Attitudes Survey (BSAS) should have swung so sharply round in the course of the 1980s. From a willingness to see the poor as at least in part the authors of their own misfortunes, respondents were by the middle and later 1980s far more inclined to see poverty and unemployment as problems that should be addressed by Government, as a matter of high priority (Taylor-Gooby, 1991).

In a much quoted comment after the 1983 election, the political scientist Ivor Crewe concluded that Keynes was dead; but not Beveridge (*Guardian*, 14.6.83). Keynes was to prove harder to kill off than this judgment suggested; his survival – even if in the bastard form of 'electoral Keynesianism' – was one of the less publicised features of economic management in the 1980s. But one of the main problems facing the victorious Conservatives in 1987 was certainly the obvious continued attachment of the British to the traditional Welfare State. Now, with the supply-side reforms in place and the problems of the economy apparently resolved, the Government were at last free to turn their full attention to the reform of welfare.

6

THE THIRD TERM AND BEYOND

O that thou hadst hearkened to my commandments! Then had thy peace
been as a river, and thy righteousness as the waves of the sea.

Isaiah 48:18.

The more a Government professes to be non-interventionist, the more it
has to intervene.

David Young, *The Enterprise Years*, 1990.

THE AGENDA FOR CHANGE

Although there is general agreement across the political spectrum that
the 1987 election marks a watershed in the Conservative Government's
approach to social policy, opinions vary on the reasons for the delay in
addressing these issues systematically and the implications of not tackling
them earlier. Three prominent Conservatives offer different
perspectives. As we have seen, Nicholas Ridley looks back with regret on
the 'wasted opportunity' of the 1983 to 1987 Parliament. Nigel Lawson is
– as usual – more robust: he attributes the delay to the Prime Minister's
nervousness about addressing highly controversial areas – a diagnosis
supported by her unwillingness (quoted by Ridley) to tackle health in the
pre-election reviews. Ian Gilmour is scathing; his explanation is that
when it came to social policy, the Thatcherite wing of the Conservative
Party was so completely blinded by their ideological preconceptions that
they simply did not understand what they were trying to achieve.
'Thatcherism' (he adds) 'scarcely had a social policy; to Thatcherites the

means if not the end were suspect' (1992, p. 107). However, what the Thatcher administration did unquestionably enjoy, at the beginning of their third-term, was unchallenged access to political power and with it the capacity to address the 'flagship' welfare issues that still had the potential to embarrass them, as the general election campaign had shown. The third-term initiatives were not a clean break with the earlier approach. Apart from the review of social security and the subsequent legislation, tentative beginnings had been made (see Chapter 5) in a number of areas. But the post-1987 reforms and the legislation that enacted them do have both novelty and coherence. Although she did not like to hear these proposals described as 'social Thatcherism', Mrs Thatcher herself saw them as providing conclusive refutation of any suggestion that 'we were stale and running out of ideas' (Thatcher, 1993, p. 572). She saw the reforms as 'clear, specific, new and well worked out'; and critics as well as supporters have accepted that this was not mere electoral hyperbole. Glennerster and his colleagues conclude that:

> The last comparable period of legislative activity to affect local government and its social welfare powers was that between 1944 and 1948. Taken together, these acts constitute the most significant break in the incrementalist tradition of social policy making that we have seen since that time. (Glennerster, Power and Travers, 1989)

Julian Le Grand reaches much the same conclusion: 'a major offensive against the basic structures of welfare provision was launched in 1988 and 1989: years that in retrospect will be seen as critical in the history of British social policy' (1990, p. 1). David Willetts' verdict (as a man who was on the spot as a government adviser) is even simpler: 1988, he says, was an '*annus mirabilis*' for social legislation (1992, p. 61).

What was the nature of the miracle that the Government was attempting to work? Stripped of much rhetoric (both pre- and post-event) it might be summarised as a systematic attempt to extend the benefits of privatisation to the welfare system – what might be called 'social privatisation'. With the exception of the special case of housing and a few tentative experiments in contracting out services in health and local government, privatisation (a policy that had developed incrementally rather than springing fully formed from Margaret Thatcher's brow) had until 1987 stopped short at the boundary of the Welfare State. The new policy initiatives outlined in the 1987 manifesto and their successors represented a decision to bring the solvent of market conditions to bear on the problems of the welfare system. Or rather, the problems as Conservative politicians perceived them – and as rehearsed in detail for them in the publications of New Right think-tank publications: the IEA, the Centre for Policy Studies and the increasingly influential Adam Smith Institute.

What was proposed was not, however, fully fledged privatisation – despite what the Government's political opponents were later to allege. The principal difference was that no transfer of ownership of State undertakings into the private sector was attempted. The position of the individual user of reformed services was also quite unlike that of user of privatised utilities – there was to be no equivalent to the shareholders created by those privatisations. Rather, there was an attempt to simulate market conditions – hence description of the whole package as 'quasi' (or some would prefer to say, 'mimic') markets. Some Conservative politicians would want to describe them as 'managed' or 'controlled' markets (D.Young, 1990, p. 267).

The working arrangements under these imitations of market conditions also deviated from the real thing in a number of important respects. As Julian Le Grand puts it, the quasi-markets

> differ from conventional markets in one or more of three ways: not-for-profit organisations competing for public contracts, sometimes in competition with for-profit organisations; consumer purchasing power in the form of vouchers rather than cash; and, in some cases, the consumers represented in the market by agents instead of operating by themselves. (1990, p. 5)

The assumption was that the introduction of these procedures into the delivery of welfare would generate an environment in which competition is the key feature. This would both improve performance (as measured in levels of economy and efficiency) and help to bring customer satisfaction up towards the top of the agenda. However (it has been asserted) the character and culture of the public sector as it has developed over the postwar period had become so inimical to securing these objectives that nothing short of drastic structural change would enable welfare to be delivered in this different style. By their nature, critics like Nicholas Ridley argued, state agencies would always be 'producer-oriented, not consumer-oriented' (1992, p. 82). The State (for these purposes, effectively the local state) should therefore cease to be a monopoly provider of services and become an enabler. This new role involved employing such powers and resources as central government was prepared to allocate to secure the availability of a balanced range of services which collectively offer the customer real choices. Structural change was the necessary condition for a cultural change which would empower managers to take responsibility for their action, both in style and content, and produce a 'passion for excellence', sharpened where necessary by pressure of the duty to satisfy customer requirements.

Changes along these lines can be seen as the means to satisfy a number of objectives, pitched at various different levels. In principle, restoring competition and choice should empower the users of services and enable individuals to take responsibility for their own welfare. In so doing they would cease to be passive clients and become active customers, making informed choices between different forms of provision and expressing any dissatisfaction by taking the opportunities provided to complain or take their custom elsewhere. This change of attitude on the part of recipients should, in turn, address the pervasive problem of dependency, which in the Conservative critique of State welfare is the inevitable outcome of a system which offers no incentive to individuals to tackle their own problems. This problem has come to be exemplified for many Conservative politicians by single parents – once described by Ridley as 'free-riders on the system, directly exploiting the dependency culture' (1992, p. 91). In place of dependency (the 'hand out'), market-based provision should offer incentives to bring individual enterprise to bear on these problems (a 'hand up').

The next agenda item (based on the priorities that had evolved over the first and second terms) was the 'value for money' objective. The argument here was that efficiency and economy could be better achieved through the use of market-based procedures, partly through efficiency gains in management performance (generated by the stimulus of greater responsibility and larger material reward) and partly through structural change, which would enable management to make economies in staffing levels and rates of pay. This in turn would make it possible to dislodge the public sector unions from the position which they have previously occupied in large public bureaucracies – as Ridley puts it, 'it seemed to me vital to bypass the power of the monopoly unions' (1992, p. 82). Breaking large units down into small, semi-independent entities with control over their own recruitment and employment, and locally determined rates of pay and conditions of service would help to erode the veto power of the producer interests. This term encompasses not just the unions as such but the major professional interest groups which have been portrayed as using their control over entry to professions and setting of standards in practice to obstruct the introduction of changes at the point of delivery (the hospital ward, the classroom, the case conference).

In addition, the agenda for change included eliminating or emasculating obstructive intermediate bodies – and in particular local government, with its inconvenient claim to an alternative source of legitimacy through electoral expression of user preferences. As we have seen, that claim has never been accepted by the Government or its supporters, some of whom have gone so far as to assert that local government, as such, has never really existed in this country (Letwin, 1992). But the third-term reforms offered a new avenue for not merely bypassing the obstructions set up by local authorities or punishing their transgressions (as the poll tax was intended to do) but for changing their nature permanently by redefining their responsibilities and placing them under even tighter constraints.

One other possible agenda item, securing equity in the distribution of benefits and services, did not feature prominently on the third-term agenda. It had been a guiding principle of the earlier reforms that equality of outcome was unacceptable as a goal for policy; but even in the much narrower sense of ensuring that variations in quality and access to services fell within acceptable limits the policies of the second term had not made a substantial impact. The best that could be said was that, as Howard Glennerster argues, welfare provision generally had mitigated the profoundly unequal consequences of economic recession (Hills, 1991, p. 350). The third-term agenda, being based on the premise that economic problems were on their way to being permanently resolved, took less account of these issues, on the basis that, as Margaret Thatcher put it in 1988, 'everyone in the nation has benefited from the increased prosperity – everyone' (Gilmour, 1992, p. 110). Or put even more succinctly, in Keith Joseph's dictum, 'a rising tide lifts all boats'.

The implementation of the reforms between 1987 and 1992 rested on the solid foundation of a parliamentary majority large enough to dispense ministers from any requirement to consult with those whose position or views might lead them to dispute the validity of the general analysis set out above. The progression from the social security review (Chapter 5), in which, whatever the constraints that had been set, there was some opportunity for those outside Government to make their views known to the review of the National Health Service – a process which Ian Gilmour has compared to a nineteenth-century aristocrat trying a man caught poaching on his estate in his own drawing room – speaks eloquently both of the removal of any political constraint and the growing confidence of those engaged in the enterprise. In the military metaphors in vogue after the Falklands episode, there was much talk of the capturing of the high ground. As the economic boom gathered pace the objective being contemplated became not merely achieving the manifesto goal of zero inflation but even eventually paying back the national debt.

The parliamentary majority not only made consultation redundant but guaranteed the passage of legislation put before the House. This freedom of action was only slightly constrained by the Lords' continued willingness to listen to professional lobbies whose interests the Government appeared to be about to trangress. This was seen at its most majestic when the judiciary's turn came to confront reform and the Lord Chief Justice was moved to Hayekian hyperbole about the threat posed to Britons' native liberties. Another such episode occurred in 1988 over the higher education provisions of the Education Bill, when the Government succeeded in alienating even its own remaining supporters in academe, many of whom were inconveniently located in the Lords.

Despite the traditional tendency of ministers to confuse the passage of legislation with implementation the enactment of the programme left the main social policy departments with a very substantial task to complete. Rumour has rather unkindly suggested that a degree of planned 'turbulence' in the public services was a deliberate part of the third-term agenda (Wistow in Marsh and Rhodes, 1992, p. 116). If so, that was amply achieved: education and health in particular exhibited all the symptoms of services suffering violent destabilisation, including a vigorous backlash of professional protest. This was not as unhelpful as it might have seemed at first sight, since it enabled ministers to denounce those concerned as 'politically motivated' or in extreme cases 'Marxist' – a term elastic enough to cover the Health Education Council and the Archbishop of Canterbury's Commission on Urban Priority Areas. The extreme case was the response, first from the Scottish guinea pigs and later in the country as a whole, to the introduction of the poll tax. But here the turbulence exceeded all tolerable limits.

There has also been an element of divide and rule in the manner in which the third-term reforms were introduced. The appeal of the new style of governance to managers was clear: not just the status and financial rewards that had been so effective as incentives in the public utility privatisations but the opportunity to assert their authority in areas where they had previously been denied access by the producer lobbies, like health. At the same time, professional groups could be persuaded that reforms meant 'less bureaucracy' – and by extension fewer interfering bureaucrats (as in education). Local users could be offered the incentive of the appearance of more local control, with improved access and closer involvement in crucial resource allocation decisions (in housing). To each of these groups, the case for change, though similar in broad outline, could be presented with a special emphasis for their own particular policy area, and garnished with some visible rewards for participation. But for local government there were few presents left at the bottom of the bran tub – only the wizened walnut of responsibility for implementing the community care reforms.

A common characteristic of all the reforms – despite the lavish use of the rhetoric of empowerment and of the image (attributed to Kenneth Baker) of the redistribution of power 'from the hub to the rim' – was that they were conceived and executed from the top down. The principal means (the spokes, in Baker's image) by which the hub held the rim firmly in place was continued rigid control over resources, supplemented by restriction of access to policy-making and the process of defining issues. Structural change made no impact on the Treasury agenda of strict surveillance over the public finances, which did not abate even during the brief period of the transient British 'economic miracle'. Whether the Department of Social Security or the Benefits Agency managed social security was a matter of no concern to the Treasury when on the perennial hunt for economies. But the civil service, too, had some rewards. As Glennerster and his colleagues argue, the danger that central departments would lose their bureaucratic empires and fail to find a role (to paraphrase Dean Acheson) was avoided by the substantial increase in responsibilities conferred on their ministers by new legislation – most conspicuously, in education. This development had the additional consequence of extending the need for advice from the civil service to the privileged outsiders, thereby providing another point of entry for the think-tanks of the New Right.

Generally, this pattern of increased centralisation – in the sense of the gathering in of executive power, largely at the expense of existing intermediate institutions – has been widely remarked upon. Gilmour says flatly that the Thatcher Government 'did more to amass and centralize power than any other peacetime British government in this century' (1992, p. 178). Ministers' response to these criticisms tended to be along the lines that they had to concentrate power and authority in order to achieve decisive change. This attitude was characterised by Elie Kedourie in an IEA pamphlet on higher education policy as 'one of those antinomian heresies which hold that salvation can only come through

sinning and the greater the turpitude the more certain the salvation'
(1989, p. 44). By this test, there were many sinners in ministerial ranks
during the third term.

Not all the increased responsibilities generated by the reforms have
fallen to traditional departments. One of the other distinctive features of
the changes has been the creation of a whole series of new intermediate
bodies – some freshly devised, others transformations of existing bodies,
ranging from the 'Next Steps' agencies hived off from central government
through the reshaped District Health Authorities to the so-called micro-
quangoes – opted-out schools and trust hospitals. The institution of this
layer of governance, foreshadowed by the invention of Urban
Development Corporations at the beginning of the Conservatives' period
in office, had by the third term begun to take the form of a systematic
replacement of politically accountable bodies by appointed agencies
managed by a 'new magistracy' (in John Stewart's phrase) of ministerial
appointees, explicitly charged to bring business values to their new tasks.

This dismantling or downgrading of a whole tier of intermediate
institutions and the professional groups associated with them and the
substitution of new or drastically modified machinery rested on a basic
assumption – that the capacity to operate a new system successfully
already existed and could be readily drawn upon. This implied not just
the availability of new techniques – information technology and its
potential for improving the accessibility and quality of services
particularly prominent among them – but also additional human
resources. One of the repeated assertions made by ministers over the first
two terms had been that the potential of volunteers and voluntary
associations had not been fully realised in the traditional system of State
welfare. The assumption was that the unique virtues of voluntarism (as
ministers chose to represent them) – flexibility, freedom from
bureaucracy and capacity to innovate – would be at the Government's
disposal, once new policies had been devised that would play to these
strengths. In practice, there were some obstacles to tapping this resource:
for example, the collective memory of earlier attempts to involve the
voluntary sector in implementing government policy – notably in the
Manpower Service Commission's programmes to reduce unemployment
– left many of the larger voluntary bodies wary about renewed
involvement, especially in the quasi-market universe the Government
was in the course of creating and the 'contract culture' prevailing there.

At local level, success would turn on the ability of the Government to
mobilise enough voluntary helpers in the 'little platoons' (in Edmund

Burke's phrase, to which ministers became hopelessly addicted). These 'active citizens' would be needed to staff the governing bodies and act as trustees of the new micro-quangoes. Involving sufficient numbers of these 'active citizens' and retaining their loyalties became problematic, especially once the recession began to impact upon previously prosperous areas and affect the past beneficiaries of Government policy in the Southern middle class. So, in turn, did the involvement of businesssmen, increasingly seen as the main source of practical help on implementation issues. Initially the business community was lured in to address the specific problem of urban regeneration, on the American model of public–private sector partnerships for renewal of cities (Deakin and Edwards, 1993). Coalitions of concerned businessmen were created to promote action locally and at national level: Business in the Community; the Per Cent Club. Royal and prime ministerial patronage was extended to these enterprises. Property developers featured prominently among the members of the boards of the Urban Development Corporations, created in large numbers at the end of the second term after the presumed successes of the first two experimental UDCs in the London and Liverpool Docklands. But as the third term continued, businessmen found themselves in demand for membership of other bodies; first of health authorities and later of the new Training and Enterprise Councils (TECs). As a result, the supply of competent and appropriately motivated individuals to discharge these functions began to come under increasing pressure.

Both inside and outside government, therefore, these and other implementation issues became progressively more significant as the third-term reforms were put in place. A further outcome of the new approach was a developing fragmentation in the responsibility for delivery of services and a consequent blurring of the lines of accountability as direct managerial control passed outside the public sector, as it has conventionally been defined. So, while these initiatives, when taken together, made up a coherent group of innovations informed at all stages by consistent policy objectives, as the reforms have evolved considerable variations have developed in different service areas. This in turn has set up tensions between centrally defined objectives and locally determined outcomes. The next section reviews individual initiatives and identifies their main characteristics and instances of cross-fertilisation between programmes.

THE THIRD-TERM INITIATIVES

Education

Of the various items scattered across the shop window of the Government's third-term manifesto, the proposal to legislate on education was clearly among the most controversial. This was partly a function of the conflicts that had arisen in the previous Parliament. Education had been a focus of concern well before the 1979 election. Anxieties about standards had been expressed in the form of a series of inquests into the performance of the system, starting with the 'Black papers' in the late 1960s, continuing through the Plowden Inquiry on primary education and Swann Report on ethnic minorities and coming into sharper focus in James Callaghan's 'Great Debate'. This was launched by the then Prime Minister at Ruskin College in 1976 in a speech that touched on many of the anxieties about standards in education and their implications for Britain's economic performance that later formed the central agenda for the education debates. As Duncan Graham subsequently commented: 'Callaghan did put his finger on the nub of the difficulties – a mixture of the things that were wrong and of a failure in communications' (1993, p. 4). At this point, the concerns he had identified were common to critics of all shades of opinion.

But any flavour of bipartisanship in the identification of issues to be addressed had disappeared by the end of the second term. A sustained attack had been launched on what was seen by the Government as producer control, exercised in schools by teachers and legitimated by the 'educational establishment' in the schools, teacher training and local education authorities. Although this assault was fought every inch of the way, teachers retaliating with strikes and LEAs resisting Keith Joseph's attempts to impose his priorities on their activities, the Government was generally successful in imposing their own way, abolishing the Schools Council, symbol of the establishment's control over the content of education and the teachers' national pay machinery. However, the Government had not by 1987 succeeded in substituting a new order of their own. The voucher as a potential device for empowering consumers of education by giving them an unrestricted choice of schools was dropped after brief and unsuccessful experiments. Other new devices had achieved marginal impact: principally the Assisted Places Scheme, enabling only a limited number of pupils from the state sector to attend private schools (5,000 were provided in all). Duncan Graham, subsequently to become responsible for implementation of the national curriculum, describes the Conservative Party at this point as falling under the influence of

> lobbyists who were continually ringing [*sic*] their hands, saying how awful it was that none of the country's children – apart from their own – could read or write, and that something had to be done, without having the slightest idea what it was that had to be done, or how intractable the problems were. (1993, p. 6)

But whatever their haziness on the detail, New Right think-tanks were determined not to lose sight of the basic objective – the need to break the hold of teachers over the manner and content of teaching. What was still lacking was the means – the leverage which would enable them to force an entry into the 'secret garden' of the curriculum. If, as Gilmour suggests, 'school education was largely spared the tuition of Thatcherism' during the second term (1992, p. 166) that was not because it had been removed from the agenda; ammunition was being stockpiled rather than fired off.

The Education Reform Bill, which became known as the 'Gerbil' (a term at first intended satirically, but later embraced as his own by the Bill's ostensible architect, Kenneth Baker) emerged from the Cabinet committee chaired by Margaret Thatcher before the 1987 election after the brief (if intense) period of consideration described earlier. As Nigel Lawson – who as usual has little time to spare either for his colleagues or their civil servants – smugly observes in his critique of the process of policy-making, this review left a number of details rather carelessly vague. In view of these continued uncertainties and the sweeping nature of what was proposed, 'the length and depth of the consultation process was insultingly brief' (Glennerster in Glennerster, Power and Travers, 1989, p. 13). This fundamental reform, which was justly compared in its impact to the Butler Education Act of 1944, was therefore introduced on the basis of superficial consideration of the issues on a narrow political base – policy made, in short 'on the hoof' (Gilmour's phrase). The contrast with the 1944 legislation, which was the product of lengthy consultation and taken through Parliament by ministers drawn from both main parties in the wartime coalition, could hardly have been sharper.

The 1988 Act introduced a series of fundamental changes in the governance of schools and institutions of higher education. At the head of the list is the introduction of a national curriculum for all maintained schools, setting out the levels of knowledge, skills and understanding that all pupils are expected to have reached by the ages of 7, 11, 14 and 16. Second, the relationship between LEAs and schools has been fundamentally altered. The act creates a new category of school, the grant-maintained schools. These have been allowed to opt out of local authority control and are funded directly (and at a level approximately 15 per cent higher) by the Department for Education. Opting out is on the basis of ballot among existing parents by simple majority and is irreversible in its outcome. In addition, a new system of self-management (including control over staffing budgets) is introduced for schools *en masse*, regardless of whether they have opted out or not. This new scheme of local management (LMS for short) greatly expands the responsibilities of head teachers and governing bodies. Access to schools was tilted in favour of parents by removing the right of local authorities to prescribe the total numbers of children at each school. All these measures were promoted as increasing parental choice. An additional element in the legislation was the invention of new City Technology Colleges (CTCs). These were designed as 'centres of excellence' to tap private money by appealing to those businessmen whose concern about standards of achievement in numeracy and literacy and fitness for employment were frequently cited in support of government policies. But the CTC programme ran into difficulties, falling far behind the initial targets as funds from the private sector proved harder to raise and suitable premises more difficult to find. Finally, the legislation provides for a national curriculum, the contents of which are prescribed by the Secretary of State, to be taught in all maintained schools.

These changes have substantially diminished the powers of LEAs. The largest and most obdurate of them, the Inner London Education Authority (ILEA), originally a Conservative creation, was finally abolished *pour encourager les autres*. Similar, if less drastic changes were introduced in higher and further education – a rolling process of reform, beginning in the 1988 Act with the removal of polytechnics from local authority control and the creation of a new entity, the Universities' Funding Council (UFC) to exercise more direct control over the universities through a revised system of financial support. This was intended to effect, as the junior minister reponsible admitted during the passage of the legislation, 'the nationalisation of higher education funding' (quoted in Letwin, 1992, p. 274).

The education reforms had a number of general characteristics which link them with the other third-term innovations. First, there is the simultaneous concentration and diffusion of power. Concentration in education is first and foremost on the person of the Secretary of State; but there has also been an important increase in functions of his department. Duncan Graham comments on the 'marked change of the attitude of civil servants after the introduction of the 1988 Education Reform Act, which they rightly saw as their first chance of having real power over state education' (1993, p. 13). The national curriculum represents the clearest possible case of the removal of authority from the periphery and placing responsibility at the centre. This – like most of the reforms – proved easier to conceive than bring to birth. There followed a tangled tale of implementation through the creation of new quangos for that purpose (another characteristic feature of third-term policy). Their failure to deliver what ministers wanted led to a further shaking up of structures and the introduction of new groups of 'trusties' (Graham, 1993). Another consequence of the reforms particular to the education field was the final surrender of the key to the secret garden of curriculum content that the teaching profession fought so hard to keep. Subsequent reform of the system of inspection by HMIs and the substitution of an inspectorate modelled on those devised for the privatised utilities (Ofsted) reflected their suspect status as accomplices to the 'professional conspiracy'. These changes left the field free at last for implementation of the alternative agenda for which the New Right had campaigned for so long. They also amply justified Glennerster's prediction that one result of the reforms would be 'to colonise yet another part of our social life for the political market place' (Glennerster et al.,1989, p. 13).

A second major change was the transformation of the situation of the consumers of education – conceived of as the parents at the time of taking decisions about their children's future. The right of opt-out by parental ballot devised by the Government was a powerful but one shot weapon – not merely is the result irreversible but its effect on the local system of education will also be permanent. As Gilmour summarises it:

> there will be increasing numbers of areas in which there are no schools where the local authority is in a position to exercise both its planning function and its control over admission. This will make life more difficult for many parents without giving them greater choice. They may be subjected to marketing techniques by the opted-out schools, but when a school is over-subscribed, it is the school that chooses its pupils not the parents that choose the school. This re-introduces the principle of selection. (1992, p. 168)

The general provisions for local management of all schools will also have an important longer-term impact. Both LMS and the provisions for opting-out place a high premium on the availability of sufficient 'active citizens' to implement the reforms and provide the detailed supervision of the operation of schools. The principal source of recruitment is among parents; but governors of grant-maintained schools are the subject of an unusual selection procedure – they are in the main a self-perpetuating group, sustained by cooption. The stipulation that members of the local business community must be included defines a specific status as privileged. These changes are of particular importance at a time when head teachers are in increasing need of support from their governors – especially those heads who have no special aptitude (or desire) to become entrepreneurs. It should be added that there have clearly been some who welcome the opportunities that the new status confers (Letwin, 1992, p. 243). Another crucial – and sometimes problematic – element in the new regime is the role of information as a means of securing standards both through the quasi-market version of competition and for enabling informed choices to be made between competing institutions through devices like the publication of league tables of pupils' examination performance.

The third major shift, already remarked upon, is the drastic reshaping of the role of local education authorities. Reform is transforming them into residual bodies, exercising only minimal control over the remnants of the local educational system (especially after additional legislation sent further education and sixth form colleges off to follow the polytechnics into the control of a new quango). Perhaps it is hardly surprising that there should have been discussion, at the time when the 1988 legislation was first being framed, of moving straight to abolition of local education authorities and making education explicitly a central function. Nigel Lawson's attempt during ministerial discussion of the legislation to draw a parallel with what he imagined to be the French system of central funding and control of all education (in reality long since modified) was advanced as part of a case for bringing an especially problematic area of public expenditure under firm (for which read Treasury) control. Although this approach was not adopted at the time, it is not difficult to read the writing on the wall.

The fragmentation of responsibility for the delivery of services during this transitional period is another characteristic of third-term institutional changes. So is the unresolved issue of the accountability of the various institutions that have been created at all levels of the system, over and above the control exercised by the Secretary of State, to whom the appointees to the new educational quangos are directly responsible. Among the functions at risk as a result of fragmentation are the means of expressing common concerns – the content and direction of education raises issues that extend beyond the interests of those who are currently parents. The protection of the position of minorities of all kinds in an increasingly competitive environment, and particularly those without proper access to the information that should enable them to make the right choices, may lack effective advocates, who can act as trustees for future as well as present interests. In this context, Gilmour compares the opting-out ballots to polling customers in a Marks and Spencer store on a particular Saturday on whether they want that branch to separate itself from head office in Baker Street (Gilmour, 1992, p. 170: location of headquarters presumably not coincidental!).

Health

If the education reforms were politically highly controversial, they were more than matched in that respect by the changes intoduced into the health service. As we have seen, the Prime Minister initially declined to include health service reform in the package of new policy proposals prepared for the 1987 election on the grounds that this would be too controversial. But the weight given to criticisms of the Government's performance in the health field by the Opposition during the election campaign clearly struck a chord with the electorate (to Nicholas Ridley's vividly expressed disgust). Their response made it clear that the Government's previous position – cautious managerial reform coupled with reassuring general statements, as a prelude to an agenda to introduce a more competitive working environment by gradual stages – was no longer sustainable. The Cabinet, Ridley says, 'were determined not to have to go through that experience again' (1992, p. 95). This perception of events precipitated another exercise in internal review under the direct supervision of the Prime Minister herself. This began with the Government under constant pressure from the professional lobby in medicine on the issue of adequate resourcing of the service, which reached a climax with a solemn protest from the Presidents of all Royal Colleges (Day and Klein, 1991, p. 44); and the continued drip of unfavourable publicity. In one especially painful episode the parents of an acutely sick child attempted to use the courts to obtain access to potentially life-saving surgery.

The Prime Minister's review, once embarked upon, evolved into another no-holds-barred exercise. Nigel Lawson, who claims the whole credit for precipitating the review through a 'post-prandial private talk' with Margaret Thatcher in January 1988 comments on how her radicalism grew as she advanced into the exercise: 'having been initially too nervous to do anything at all, once she had accepted the idea, [she] characteristically decided to go the whole hog and reform everything at once' (1992, p. 615). The reform package rested in part on earlier work: Roy Griffiths' report on management (1983), with its vivid image of Florence Nightingale with her lamp looking vainly for the person in charge and the review of funding and delivery of primary care. This had already been the subject of a White Paper (1986) and a particular focus of Treasury concern because of the perceived difficulty in controlling expenditure by GPs on drugs, which accounted for 46 per cent of the total budget.

The review drew upon material put together by the New Right think-tanks and in particular ideas that had been put forward by Alain Enthoven, a visiting American health economist, whose ideas about the creation of internal markets appealed to those who perceived the problem as being to enable the NHS to achieve, in Enthoven's words 'even more value for money if it is to make effective new medical technology available to all who can benefit from it' (1991, p. 61).

One of the most striking features of the review, compared to any earlier exercise in the health field, was the complete exclusion of the professional interest groups. In private, the language ministers used about the medical lobbies was almost as dismissive as that they employed about the teachers. The public (says Ridley with heavy sarcasm) 'believed doctors to be non-political, honest and impartial' (1992, p. 96). But to ministers they were simply another obstructive (and greedy) professional lobby. If they had anything to say, Nigel Lawson observed disingenuously, they could always submit memoranda (1992, p. 614). This meant that the decks were clear for the five-strong ministerial group (initially Margaret Thatcher, Nigel Lawson, his Chief Secretary, John Major, the Secretary of State at the DHSS John Moore and his deputy) supported by the ubiquitous Roy Griffiths and a political journalist on secondment to the Downing Street policy unit, to follow their own agenda. Among the initial alternatives considered was a shift to an insurance-based system along the lines of those in some other European countries and the United States; but the group rapidly reached the conclusion that the cost factor would rule this out. Inquiries they commissioned merely confirmed the well-established fact that if assessed simply in these terms the NHS is by far and away the most effective system yet devised.

Nevertheless, this did not deter Nigel Lawson from continuing to press cost-containment as a central issue for review; his argument is summarised in a private note to the review team of July 1988, reprinted in his memoirs: 'our objective has to be to see that, despite the absence of the price mechanism, the NHS provides health care as efficiently and effectively as possible – in other words, we get the best possible value for money' (Lawson, 1992, p. 616). But the political context in which the review was being undertaken required that a rather different set of objectives also be addressed: securing improved access to better quality services and a fairer distribution of resources. Reforms had to reconcile these varied goals; as Day and Klein put it, the Government's solution would need to 'combine the advantages of a national health service model (financial parsimony and social equity) and those of a market system (responsiveness to consumer demands)' (1991, p. 40).

The solutions that they devised, which were published in a White Paper in January 1989, rested on the principle of separation of the providing and purchasing functions within the system of delivery of health care. The changes took two specific forms: the District Health Authorities (after an internal structural overhaul) became purchasers of care; and hospitals, as the main providers were permitted to apply to withdraw from health authority control and become self-governing trusts within the health service, funded from general taxation but able to set their own conditions for employment of staff and sell their services wherever they could find a market for them. Contracts negotiated between purchasers and providers therefore become the principal motive force driving the new system of hospital care. Parallel changes allowed GP practices with large lists (the size limit being progressively reduced) to take control of their budgets and buy health care from them for their own patients. Thus, the GPs become proxy consumers and principal movers in the primary care system. The overall intention, at least as expressed in public, was to ensure that in future 'money followed patients' (*Working for Patients*, Cm 555, 1989).

Conspicuously absent from the White Paper, however, was any reference to provision of resources, although this had been the focal point of much previous debate, with rival figures illustrating the 'generosity' or 'meanness' of successive administrations being hurled to and fro across the parliamentary despatch boxes. It is clear from Mrs Thatcher's subsequent account that this was deliberate – she had decided to go for structural rather than financial reforms, largely because she feared that the Treasury would sacrifice the prospect of long-term radical change in favour of short-term cuts in costs (Thatcher, 1993, p. 614).

The only major financial change proposed was a tax concession for contributions to private health insurance schemes by or on behalf of the over-60s which the Prime Minister persuaded the Chancellor to make (according to his account) against his own instincts. Lawson duly introduced it, 'trying to conceal my embarrassment', in the 1989 Budget (1992, p. 617). By then he had also announced a substantial increase in the health budget, being 'sufficiently confident of the value of the reforms we were preparing' to justify himself in doing so (p. 619).

Many of the characteristics of the NHS reforms run parallel to those in education – as was often observed at the time. The attempt to reform the existing managerial culture, with the cheese in the trap being enhanced reponsibilities (and rewards) for individual managers, is one obvious example. This, in turn, has formed a crucial part of the attempt to break down the control exercised by the dominant professional group over the delivery of the service. This was a particularly difficult enterprise in the case of the doctors, whose professional autonomy in the clinical treatment of patients (sanctified in the NHS since Bevan's day) has been even more complete than that of teachers in the classroom. Part of the answer has lain, in both cases, in realigning the campaign by emphasising that the faults being addressed are those of 'bureaucracy', personified in the administrators in the intermediate organisations - the local education authority, and district and regional health authorities. Giving consultants and headteachers greater access to a share of the resources previously held by these agencies and the simulacrum (at least) of exercising some authority over their disposal has proved to be a powerful means of 'turning' senior professionals towards accepting the Government's objectives. The theme of devolution of control has been developed through the empowerment of small-scale producer enterprises (schools, GP practices) by giving them substantial responsibility for self-management. However, there has been a price to pay; in the hospital service, managers have now been given far greater control over the activities of the professionals. Medical audit is now compulsory and consultant contracts now specify in much greater detail what is expected of the holder (Day and Klein, 1991, p. 46).

The other outstanding characteristic of this group of reforms has been greatly enhanced power for the centre. The diminished role of the Local

Education Authority has no direct parallel in the health reforms. Rather, the change in health has been one in the character of the public institutions. The Regional Health Authorities have been left in place, hanging uncertainly between the districts and Department of Health (now separated from Social Security). District Health Authorities, with a major new role to discharge in the purchase of care have been purged by removal of the last foothold of elected representatives through their exclusion from membership – in their place, the Government has set out to promote local representation of a different kind, in order to enable DHAs to 'discharge their responsibilities in a business-like way' (Cm 555, 1989, p. 65). Appointments to the chairs of the reformed authorities have reflected this approach (and, critics add, the political allegiance of those appointed). The other means by which the centre can exercise surveillance – inspection and evaluation, has been substantially modified in the education field with the creation of OFSTED and, although previously conspicuous by its absence from the field of health, will now be provided there by the Audit Commission, as an extension of its role in local government.

A final common feature of the Government's approach to reform of the health and education systems has been their benevolent attitude towards the private sector – seen as a potential ally in the reform process and discreetly assisted with resources at the margin. The general expectation on which ministers appear to have proceeded has been that quality of service there will in the long run probably turn out to be higher than in the public sector and that policy should be based on that assumption. This was Margaret Thatcher's position, as reported by Ridley. According to him:

> she saw State provision [in health and education] as a free service necessary for those who could not afford higher standards, but she hoped that their numbers would dwindle as more and more families became able to afford to choose those higher standards in the private sector for themselves. She never believed it was either possible or desirable to bring standards in the public service up to the highest levels in the private sector: to do so would be enormously expensive. It would also destroy an area of choice, an ambition for which to strive, and restore an element of the dependency culture. (1992, pp. 80–1)

Other features of the health service reforms were particular to that area: the use of information technology as a key device in the process of setting up an internal market, for example. Most important has been the striking absence of any active role for the consumer of the service. Patients have been offered the now-customary Charter, in which a number of aspirations for improved delivery of service are set out; but these are not set out in the form of rights. More broadly, the health service reforms, especially in the case of hospital services, 'stopped well short of allowing consumer demand to drive the service' (Day and Klein, 1991, p. 46). This did not pass without criticism, even from the right, where it was represented, by the IEA as a failure to meet their declared objective of enhancing individual choice (Green, 1990). This criticism links to another concern: whether the new managerial culture that has been created, with managers trading with one another and lines of accountability stretching to a remote centre not anxious to become engaged in debate about the details of service delivery, might not be capable of being recaptured by producer interests. As Wistow comments: 'if managers have come to be the servants of Ministers rather than medicine, clinicians are some way from being the servants of either' (in Marsh and Rhodes, 1992, p. 115). The debate about the locus of final responsibility for the delivery of services continues; Paton comments that: 'Ministers have had to centralise ruthlessly in order to decentralise; but not ruthlessly enough to escape continued criticism' (in Deakin and Page, 1993).

Social care

By contrast, the reform of social care – still at the start of the third term the responsibility of the same government department, the DHSS, was far less politically contested. At the start of the 1987 Parliament, those involved had been waiting for the second shoe to drop. The speech that Norman Fowler made as Secretary of State at Buxton in 1984 had laid a heavy emphasis on modification of the role of local government to an 'enabling' function (see Chapter 5). A Green Paper had been promised; none was forthcoming. Instead, what followed was the Audit Commission's careful dissection of the failure of the community care system to deliver care effectively within the current distribution of responsibilities between local government, the health service, and voluntary organisations and the for-profit organisations encouraged into caring for the elderly by the perverse incentives provided by the social security system (*Making a Reality of Community Care*, December 1986). The outcome, the Commission concluded, was gross maldistribution of resources. In particular, informal carers (especially family members) who supply the vast bulk of care in the community setting appeared to be inadequately supported; only after a long fight through the European courts was the principle of an Invalid Care Allowance payable to immediate relatives finally secured. Pressure for change was intensified by a sequence of child care scandals and reports upon the failures of the existing system (Jasmine Beckford; the Butler–Stross Inquiry).

Given that there was by then general agreement that the situation could not be allowed to continue, the introduction of reforms became a matter of timing and allocation of responsibility for implementation, rather than an issue of principle. As in other policy fields, Sir Roy Griffiths was summoned to provide the conclusions. But when it came, his report (*Community Care: An Agenda for Action*, 1988) contained recommendations that were apparently far out of line with the general trend of policy-making in other social policy areas.

Sir Roy's conclusions were that a 'new focus for community care should be provided with a Minister clearly and publicly identified as responsible for community care'; a specific grant should be made to local authorities, 'to indicate that the primary responsibility for community care should correctly lie with the local authority', which should be distributed on the basis of an approved plan (para 22). A clear framework should be provided for coordination between local and health authorities, with the programme 'matched by parallel approval of those parts of the health service plans allocated and ring-fenced for community care' (para 23). At local level, the task of social service authorities should be to identify and assess needs and devise appropriate packages of care, based on services coordinated by a care manager. Sir Roy adds:

> This is a key statement. The role of the public sector is essentially to ensure that care is provided. How it is provided is an important, but secondary consideration and local authorities must show that they are getting and providing real value. (para 25)

A significantly different model, in short, though one with some detailed features in common with the pattern emerging in other service areas. In the circumstances, it was perhaps hardly surprising that it took ministers eighteen months before deciding to endorse the broad outlines of the Griffiths Report in their own White Paper, *Caring for People* (Cm 849, November 1989). In this document, the government accepted the essence of the Griffiths scheme without conceding the full means that he had proposed.

The focus of the Government's proposals were, as might have been expected, on the creation of a local market in care; but one adapted to permit local authorities to perform a facilitating and regulating role. This role was designed to incorporate a range of devices for stimulating variety in provision. These included encouraging new voluntary sector provision and setting up additional not-for-profit agencies to take responsibility on a contractual basis for existing functions of local government in the field of care (residential provision, in particular). In this 'mixed economy of care', the principal role of local authorities was to be the management and oversight of the process of delivering care, on behalf of clients. Comprehensive community care plans would be prepared, setting out the likely pattern of demand and the means proposed to meet it. Individual care packages would be devised for clients by social workers in local authorities acting on their behalf. The bulk of the formal care should be provided by other agencies, through a process of competitive tendering; this process and the monitoring and supervision of the outcomes would be the responsibility of local authorities. Where they cannot contract out a service they should act as residual provider: but they must maintain an internal division within the authority between the purchasing function and the actual provision of care, which would be confined principally to meeting the needs of 'people with high levels of dependency or particularly challenging patterns of behaviour' (1989, p. 22).

These proposals were given statutory effect, largely unamended, as a subordinate element in the health service legislation; but full implementation was delayed as a result of complications that arose over resource allocation, in part as a result of problems of transfer of budget items between departments, in part through the impact of the poll tax fracas, of which more later.

The further decentralisation of the management of social care services (albeit with a continued base within the public sector) alongside additional centralisation of control over policy and resources – and retention at the centre of discretion over the size and scope of funding (there was to be no 'ring-fencing' of the community care budget, as Griffiths had wished) – closely parallels developments in other service areas. So does the device of keeping the client at arm's length, with access to the quasi-market of care only through an intermediary acting for them. The evolution of a residual role for the public sector is also consistent with developments elsewhere. This was one of the distinctive features of the reforms in housing also put into effect at the beginning of the third term.

Housing

Policy in the first two Parliaments had concentrated on the extension of owner occupation through the promotion of council sales (the 'right to buy' introduced in the Housing Act 1980). As indicated earlier (p. 107), this had been one of the areas of unequivocal success, as measured by the expansion of the owner-occupied sector, which rose from 55 per cent of all dwellings in Great Britain in 1978 to 65 per cent a decade later (Hills, 1991, p. 138). But by the end of the second term, Nicholas Ridley, as the minister responsible, had reached the conclusion that a change of policy was necessary to enable the Government 'to weaken the almost incestuous relationship between some councils and their tenants' (1992, p. 87). The content of this new policy was based on an internal review, conducted by 'the usual ad hoc group' (p. 88) in the few weeks before the 1987 election. The Government's subsequent White Paper (*Housing: The Government's Proposals*, Cm 214) (no snappy title, for once) set out the basis of the new approach. On the assumption that owner occupation (even on the most favourable terms that could be contrived) was approaching the limits of what was feasible, the White Paper set out proposals for a revival of private renting; for individual tenants to change their local authority landlords ('tenants' choice') and for the creation of Housing Action Trusts (HATs) to take over responsibility *en bloc* for certain highly deprived housing estates. This policy has been described in shorthand as the 'demunicipalisation' of housing. The White Paper also contained proposals for strengthening the role of housing associations but changing their financial regime in such a way as to make them conform more closely to market disciplines.

Alongside these changes, incorporated in the Housing Act of 1989, went amendments in the system of housing finance: further restrictions on the ability of local authorities to engage in new building and tighter limits on the use of receipts from council house sales. The effect of these changes was by the end of the decade to drastically reduce local authorities' capacity to provide new homes. Taken together with the provisions for moving as much of the remaining stock out of the public sector as possible to other landlords, the role for local authorities was to be systematically reduced to catering for special needs, as the landlords of last resort.

Successful implementation of this tactic depended on two outcomes: the ability to bring about a revival of the private sector as a supplier of rented accommodation in adequate quantity and quality and success in persuading more tenants to opt to leave the local authority sector, whether through exercise of individual 'tenants choice' or by voting for HAT status in ballots (in which those not voting were deemed to have consented to change). In neither respect has the Government so far achieved any great success. Despite new financial incentives to potential investors through business expansion scheme (BES) funding, the private rented sector remained unattractive to investors or those making choices about their housing, compared with the overwhelming appeal of owner occupation, which enjoys both tax breaks and the added attraction of acquiring a potentially valuable capital asset. Rather than a return to private renting, the late 1980s saw a boom in house purchase of a size and scale never previously encountered, with property values in London and the South-East spiralling upwards to dizzy heights. In the light of the postwar history of the private rented sector the failure to reanimate it was only to be expected; but less predictable was the failure of tenants to respond to the opportunity to leave the public sector without having to take the risk of purchasing. Ballots under HAT schemes repeatedly produced large majorities in favour of remaining as local authority tenants. This seems to have been partly the result of the poor image of private landlords and property companies; but it was also partly the outcome of a concerted campaign by local authorities to improve standards and their responsiveness to tenant dissatisfaction. To that extent, government policies had an impact, if not precisely the one they had intended. But Ridley simply says, bluntly, that the HAT policy 'proved most unpopular and didn't achieve its objective' (1992, p. 89).

More effective than 'tenant choice' as originally conceived, or the HATs was a programme that emerged initially from within local government itself, of voluntary transfer of stock to housing associations (known as VST). These transfers accounted for much of the movement out of local authority tenure up to the 1992 election (Kemp in Marsh and Rhodes, 1992, p. 74); but the shift took place on terms which enabled provision to be made in a coordinated way.

Nevertheless, the general effect of the changes initiated in the third term was that local government housing departments, which had had high aspirations to become providers and facilitors of a comprehensive housing service for their neighbourhood were reduced to making marginal provision for highly deprived clients, operating under severe financial constraints. Housing is one of few areas in which public expenditure cuts in real terms have been made (Hills, 1991) – though this only holds true if provision for mortgage interest tax relief is excluded from the calculation, as Treasury-defined 'tax expenses'. The cessation of new building and the rises in council rents imposed by central government intervention led to a steady reduction in the availability of social housing at an affordable rent for people on low incomes. This in turn produced a rapid rise in the numbers of homeless families: the numbers of homeless households accepted by authorities doubled over the decade from 1979 to over 120,000 – and this figure excludes non-priority groups to whom the authorities have no statutory obligation, e.g. single people and those without children and under retirement age (Association of Metropolitan Authorities, 1990, p. 7). Given the lack of accommodation within their own reduced stock, the authorities' obligation to those families for whom they have accepted responsibility was mainly met by use of bed & breakfast accommodation, at absurdly uneconomic rates. The inability of the voluntary sector (especially after 1989 financial reforms) to provide cheap alternatives for those in special need in sufficient quantity and at an adequate standard, and the disappearance of acceptable 'bottom rung' accommodation in the private sector meant that for non-priority cases 'sleeping rough' on the streets became the other option. The hard core of former dossers were joined there as the 1980s progressed by young people of between 16 and 18 who had left home but were excluded from benefit by the 1988 social security reforms (Bridges Project, 1991) and patients discharged from long-stay hospitals under the community care policy. Begging on the streets became in most large cities a common feature of the urban landscape, especially in London. The results, Mrs Thatcher herself later censoriously commented, were deplorable: '. . . crowds of drunken, dirty, often abusive and sometimes violent men must not be allowed to turn the central areas of the capital into no-go areas for ordinary citizens. The police must disperse them . . .' (Thatcher, 1993, p. 603).

Ian Gilmour's verdict on the general housing policy over this period is harsh: 'once again the welfare state of the poor which depends on public expenditure was cut, while the welfare state of the better off which depended on tax expenditure or allowances was sharply inflated' (1992, p. 152). These contrasts were further highlighted by personal experience when some unlucky individuals were transported suddenly from the fortunate to the unfortunate category at the end of the decade, as a result of the collapse of the property market, high interest rates and the return of mass unemployment, which produced record rates of mortgage default and repossessions.

Social security and employment

Changes in other service areas during the third term have been less far reaching in intention and effect. The implementation of those social security reforms which came into force in 1988 were based on the legislative changes described in detail in Chapter 5; the structural modifications that had been made were substantial but, as demonstrated earlier, they were essentially changes in the methods of delivery, not in the basic concept of the function and purpose of the social security system. The contributory system remained in place, albeit in attenuated form. Means-tested benefits were increased in scope as an essential ingredient in the Government's programme to increase the scope of targeting, but some universal benefits continued in operation, notably child benefit. However, the level of benefit (already worth 7 per cent less in real terms in 1988 than it had been in 1979) was frozen for three successive years to 1991. The introduction of the Social Fund to replace the single-payment system stood out as the most significant change. This brought in the principle of loans to replace most grants, but on a cash-limited basis. The Social Fund's introduction and early period of operation was fraught with difficulties; it has proved easily the most expensive of the new benefits to run – a National Audit Office review found that over 30 per cent of its total budget was being devoted to administration. Despite the fact that it represents only a small fraction of the social security budget (0.36 per cent in 1990–1), the Social Fund has proved consistently controversial, because, as Jonathan Bradshaw puts it: 'it has left people in urgent need without support, increased their indebtedness and thrown extra burdens on the voluntary sector (and local authorities)' (in Marsh and Rhodes, 1992, p. 96). Gilmour concurs; he adds that it 'encourages debt, revived the pawnshop and causes totally unnecessary hardship for those already on the breadline' (1992, p. 134).

Implementation of the 1986 Act exposed the losers – of whom those who attempted to use the Social Fund were prominent but not alone. Government figures showed that after adjustments for the effects of inflation only 37 per cent of the recipients of the new income support system that replaced Supplementary Benefit had gained from the changes, while 20 per cent had experienced no change and 40 per cent had lost (Gilmour, 1992, p. 135). Some of these losses were inadvertent; others intended. Supplementary legislation in 1988 excluded the 16–18-year-old age group from entitlement to receive benefit, other than in exceptional circumstances. The rationale for this move was that a guaranteed place on a training scheme would be provided as an alternative and that parental provision would act as the safety net. As the DHSS put it at the time, the change was intended to avoid 'the damaging effects of moving straight from school into the benefit culture' (quoted by Lister in McCarthy, 1989, p. 114).

The introduction of the new social security regime in 1988 coincided with the most generous of all Nigel Lawson's tax reducing budgets, so that the economies achieved in terms of cuts in benefit rates for the poor coincided, as Ian Gilmour acidly observes, 'with a fall in a £100,000 a year executive's tax bill of £35 per day' (1992, p. 137). Even a rapidly expanding economy had failed to bring to a halt the hunt by what David Donnison calls the 'Treasury wolves' for economies in the social security budget; however, the long-awaited fall in the rate of unemployment after 1986 began to save the Government some money and reduced the political pressure on another part of the benefits front.

Reforms in the area of employment policy could therefore be undertaken in a less febrile environment. Previously, a series of employment schemes had tumbled out in quick succession to cope with the pressure of constantly rising unemployment, with confusingly similar names and overlapping objectives. Now the Government felt able to approach the task of improving the provision of training on the assumption that the supply-side reforms of the first two terms were feeding through and were about to produce the 'virtuous circle' of sustained growth, low inflation and public expenditure held to a steady proportion of GDP. The White Paper of February 1988 (*Training for Employment*, Cm 316) celebrated with lavish use of the term 'dramatic' the fall in unemployment and reductions in youth and long-term unemployment, setting them alongside 'the largest sustained increase in self-employment we have ever seen' and an economy which was 'creating a huge number of new jobs' (1988, p. 4). The task for Government, as it was now defined, was to create a route back to work for the remaining unemployed: this would be achieved by a mix of new training provision, incentives to return to work (through expansion of the Restart scheme, based on interviews and job counselling) and deterrence of those 'not actively seeking work as the law requires' or 'working in the hidden economy' (p. 39).

The decision of the TUC to withdraw from participation in training schemes to be undertaken by the proposed tripartite Training Commission, designated by the White Paper as the successor to the Manpower Services Commission, provided the opportunity to set in place a new structure based on the participation of employers, the Training and Enterprise Councils (TECs). These were launched in March 1989 and developed into a network of eighty self-governing organisations with board membership consisting of at least two-thirds serving chief executives, chairmen or top operational managers from the private sector. Once launched, the TECs took responsibility for delivery of the training programme on a decentralised basis, supported by staff from the Government's Training Agency and accountable to the Secretary of State for Employment.

These new structures were put in place just in time to confront the reappearance of a whole range of familiar problems precipitated by the sudden end of the Lawson boom, which rapidly reversed all the assumptions on which the 1988 White Paper had been based. However, even with the economic climate turning chilly, the Treasury was unable to resist imposing economies based on demographic changes (the fall in the numbers of young people entering the workforce) and past falls in unemployment. TEC directors were told that they should make good the shortfall by raising money from the private sector and expanding their income by obtaining grants from other Government programmes. *The Economist*, analysing these developments at the beginning of 1991, found widespread disillusionment among TEC directors, many of whom had concluded that 'the government is bluffing when it claims that TECs are intended to tackle Britain's persistent skills shortage. In fact, the TECs are little more than a device for luring the private sector into tackling unemployment' (5.1.91).

Local governance

Other third-term reforms form a outer ring of social policy initiatives, for example in criminal justice and the evolution of new community-based policies designed to address concerns about failure to deliver a lasting fall in the rate of recorded crime, despite generosity on the part of the Government in allocating resources unparalleled elsewhere in the public expenditure system.

Crime was one of the group of concerns that directed attention towards the inner cities. As we saw in Chapter 4, anxiety about public order after the 1981 disturbances (and later repetitions) was one of the root causes of much subsequent Government action. Margaret Thatcher's battlecry in the immediate aftermath of the 1987 election had been an exhortation to do something about 'those inner cities'. The something turned out to be an anthology of action being taken under other programmes, launched under the title *Action for Cities* (1988) – a glossy booklet stylistically halfway between White Paper and Central Office publicity handout and notable for its failure to make any reference to the role of local authorities in addressing the problems of concentrations of disadvantage. This was no coincidence, because the Action for Cities programme was based on the presumption that the stimulation of new activity should be entrusted to the private sector, with the logistic and financial support of decentralised units drawn from central government departments (notably the regional offices of the DTI and DoE) or created for the purpose. The working assumption was that the Urban Development Corporation (UDC) model first developed by Michael Heseltine in the docklands of London and Liverpool could be extended to cover the deprived inner areas of other major conurbations. By the time the return of recession demonstrated that most of the presumed achievements of the first UDCs were an artefact of general economic expansion and that their record in creating jobs and addressing skill shortages was poor (Deakin and Edwards, 1993), their successors were already designated. Operating alongside the half-empty office developments promoted by these new UDCs, the DTI task forces who were precipitated into inner-city areas suffering high unemployment to promote new entrepreneurial initiatives and 'lever' funds from the private sector to support them found themselves pedalling with less and less success up a progressively steeper incline. The succession of glossy documents on Government policy achievements (*Progress for Cities, People in Cities*) faltered and then ceased altogether as local unemployment rates turned up again and 'cranes on the horizon' lost their appeal as symbols of activity when their failure to bring new jobs with them became manifest. Local government, brushed on one side at the outset now found itself courted as a potential ally under the all-purpose rubric of 'partnership'.

But by then, partnership with central government was a difficult option to embrace. As described in the previous chapters, relationships between Whitehall and town halls had deteriorated rapidly after the Conservatives came to power; the main cause of conflict being repeated attempts by the centre (in practice, the Treasury) to bring expenditure by local authorities under control. As Nigel Lawson subsequently chose to put it, 'the tendency of local government to exceed the spending limits the Government made and on which its grant disbursements were based, became endemic' (1992, p. 565). The debate became a highly politicised process increasingly involving departmental ministers and backbenchers from all parties as well as the main protagonists in the dispute. Both of these characterised their opponents in extreme terms, as spendthrifts or tyrants; each appealed to (unwritten) constitutional conventions to justify their conduct. Against this background, central government hatched the scheme that would provide (it was believed) an effective check on the perceived in-built tendency of local authorities to overspend. This was the community charge, or as it was known to everyone except the Prime Minister, the poll tax – she would apparently 'drum her fingers on the table as if it were a piano' if this term was used (Lawson, 1992, p. 577).

The detailed history of the poll tax is tangled and vehemently contested; but the main outlines are now clear. Two precipitating factors led to its introduction; the pledge to replace the rates given by Margaret Thatcher in 1974 (as she now says, at Ted Heath's insistence) and the Scottish rates revaluation of 1985, the impact of which threatened to overwhelm the already enfeebled Scottish Conservatives – unless something was done before the next revaluation, due in 1990. But what?

The answer had been a long time brewing. Michael Heseltine's Green Paper of 1981 had been unenthusiastic about the range of possible alternatives: sales tax; income tax or poll tax. For a large part of 1985 the Cabinet sub-committee concerned with local finance mulled over the options again before deciding on a form of poll tax. This decision was taken on the advice of a task force convened by William Waldegrave, the junior minister at the Department of the Environment, in the teeth of the loudly expressed disapproval of the Chancellor. Nigel Lawson, who records that Department of Environment officials were privately astonished that the poll tax was being taken seriously, formally minuted his colleagues in May 1985 that this approach would lead to disaster and that a better way of reinforcing accountability would be for central government to take over sole responsibility for expenditure on education (1992, pp. 570–6). Nevertheless, the poll tax option was the centrepiece of Kenneth Baker's Green Paper for public discussion, *Paying for Local Government* published in January 1986, which proposed phasing in the tax over a period alongside the rates ('dual running') and replacing the system of non-domestic rates with a centrally determined uniform business rate indexed to inflation.

From this point the story becomes confused. The urgency of the political problem in Scotland precipitated early legislation, with an implementation date of 1989. This, internal critics of the tax hoped, might be used as a trial run (Nigel Lawson here taking the precise opposite position to the one he adopted on the health reforms). But at the Conservative party conference in October 1987, a revolt from the floor persuaded the Prime Minister and the Secretary of State for the Environment, Nicholas Ridley, that the poll tax should be introduced without any intervening stages and come into force in April 1990. After a turbulent passage through the House of Commons, in which Tory backbench opponents of the legislation for once made their objections felt, the Local Government Finance Act 1988 became law. 'The events that followed' Lawson observes, 'had a grim inevitability about them' (1992, p. 580). He adds:

> whatever theoretical arguments may be advanced in its support, no new tax can be introduced and sustained that is not broadly acceptable to the majority of the British people. The poll tax failed this basic test in the most fundamental way imaginable. (p. 583)

The tax failed other tests too. It proved difficult and expensive to collect (15,000 additional staff were required by local authorities to handle its introduction). Nicholas Ridley was unable to secure from the Treasury sufficient additional funding to smooth the introduction of the new tax. The rebate system was complex and difficult to understand. And, Ridley now alleges, 'many local authorities resolved to increase their expenditure by even more than usual, often deliberately in order to discredit the new system' (1992, p. 130). But most important of all, the poll tax's almost universal unpopularity further damaged the standing of the Conservative Party at a time when their handling of the economy was coming under increasingly severe scrutiny. It evoked mass protests both passive – the widespread withholding of payment – and active – demonstrations eventually boiling over into street violence. And finally, because the tax was so closely identified with the Prime Minister herself, the episode inflicted lasting – eventually fatal – damage to her reputation.

The brief inglorious history of the poll tax provides an appropriate coda to an account of the principal developments in social policy in the third term. The tax embodied many of the Government's main policy concerns: the desire to exercise central control over resources, regardless of the outcomes in terms of the experience of those at the receiving end of the policy process and the wish to put local authorities in their place and in so doing eliminate or drastically constrain the power-bases of political rivals. The language used by Mrs Thatcher about local authorities in her apologia for the poll tax episode is, even by her standards, extreme – she refers to the 'perversity, incompetence and often straightforward malice of many local authorities. Highminded talk of local democracy must not be allowed to obscure the lowlevel politics of the people we were up against' (Thatcher, 1993, p. 660). By their handling of the introduction of the tax, the Government alienated the professional networks (in this case local authority officers) who might have been mobilised to assist in the process. Instead, ministers attempted to use consumer power as leverage; but the choice provided was too circumscribed and the unfairness of the tax appeared too blatant, although there was some evidence of a rather shamefaced public welcome for very low local taxation levels where the system permitted it. But above all, the poll tax episode reflected the Government's style – persistence in the face of criticism; unwillingness to acknowledge the legitimacy of alternative positions. (It is reassuring, in a way, to discover that this attitude extended even to critics in the Cabinet itself.) And, finally, in its values, as Gilmour has it, the poll tax 'was the culmination of the Thatcherite market or rather supermarket philosophy. It graphically illustrated the Thatcherite attitude to institutions and their wish to give the market a monopoly' (1992, p. 219).

CONSTRAINTS ON CHANGE

The task of implementing the social policy reforms was crucially affected not just by obstacles thrown up within the field of welfare but also by a number of external constraints that became progressively more important as the third term continued.

Of these constraints, by far the most significant was the impact of the end of the brief phase of apparently successful economic management. The climate of general euphoria created in time for the 1987 election persisted after it and was reflected (as we have seen) in many of the Government's subsequent social policy documents (for example, the preface to *Action for Cities* and the *Training for Employment* White Paper). Fortified by plaudits from all sides (and the reluctant admiration of even some of his critics), Lawson continued on the tax-cutting path, injecting more and more spending power into the economy. The GDP grew by 4.4 per cent in 1987 and 4.7 per cent in the following year, when the Chancellor reduced income tax in his Budget by a further two pence overall and brought the top rate down from 60 per cent to 40 per cent. The vast increase in the availability of credit was fuelled by the liberalisation of the financial markets, which encouraged banks and building societies to compete for recipients for their largesse. Net lending trebled between 1984 and 1987; and in 1989 the net indebtedness of all households was 2.5 times greater than it was in 1982. Consumption reached dizzy heights; the most dramatic illustration (among many) was the rise in house prices, which increased by 30 per cent between 1987 and 1988 alone (Smith, 1992).

Boom conditions were not checked by the sudden crisis on the Stock Exchange in October 1987 (the first of the economy's sequence of 'black days') or by a succession of City scandals – though these all helped to add an authentic gamey high Victorian flavour to events, as Gilmour points out (1992, p. 63). No attempt was made to control credit until the twin pressures of a rapidly increasing balance of payments deficit and the reappearance of inflationary pressures forced the Chancellor to respond. He had been unable to persuade Margaret Thatcher to accept that entry into the Exchange Rate Mechanism was necessary to provide stability for the pound, their last exchange on the subject producing the memorable rebuke: 'I do not want you to raise the subject ever again: I must prevail' (1992, p. 918). Thwarted, Lawson continued with the alternative device of 'shadowing' the Deutschmark by holding constant the pound's exchange rate against the DM, cutting interest rates where necessary in order to do so. Faced with the prospect of the credit boom getting out of control, he turned again to this weapon (according to Ted Heath, his 'one club') but reversed direction, raising interest rates by stages to a peak of 14 per cent in May 1989. Under the pressure of these restrictions growth faltered and then came to an abrupt halt; but inflation continued to rise, reaching 8.3 per cent in May 1989.

By this stage, the Prime Minister had lost confidence in her Chancellor; she reappointed Alan Walters – a strident public critic of Lawson's policies – to serve from May as her personal economic adviser. By October, she had lost the Chancellor himself. Lawson's resignation is another patch of disputed terrain. Both protagonists have now given us lengthy accounts of this episode, Margaret Thatcher's hinging on her perception that Nigel Lawson was unable to face the consequences of the failure of what she presents as his personal economic policies. But it is beyond dispute that Lawson found continued public criticism of his position from the Prime Minister and elsewhere within Government insupportable. As Lawson put it in his resignation speech:

> for our system of Cabinet government to work effectively, the Prime Minister of the day must appoint Ministers whom he or she trusts and

then leave them to carry out the policy. When differences of view emerge, as they are bound to do from time to time, they should be resolved privately and, whenever appropriate, collectively. (1992, p. 1063)

A little more than a year later Margaret Thatcher followed him out of office. A large part of the reason for her departure was the failure to achieve the 'soft landing' for the economy for which the Treasury had hoped and which Nigel Lawson had confidently forecast in his resignation speech – mindful, perhaps, of Norman Lamont's private warning that 'no doubt unkindly it would be noted you had left when there were problems' (p. 963). In December 1989, John Major, the new Chancellor, had told the Treasury Select Committee: 'I do not in fact anticipate a recession' (Smith, 1992, p. 158). In his only budget in the following March, Major sought to maintain the *status quo*, adding incentives to saving, while interest rates remained at the 15 per cent level inherited from Lawson. The Budget was followed immediately by the implementation of the poll tax legislation, precipitating a rapid increase in costs of local services which fed into the cost of living. In August 1990, inflation broke through to double figures. In October, Major was finally able to persuade Margaret Thatcher to join the ERM, at the price of a cut in interest rates. She embarked on a strenuous defence of her policies, asking a business audience 'why, after years of sustained progress, of the right philosophy, of the right policies is this self-doubt assailing some of the business community – or perhaps more accurately the press?' (Smith, 1992, p. 174). But by then it was already too late for her; and too late for the economy. By the end of 1990 it was clear beyond any dispute that the newspapers were right – the economy had 'fallen off a cliff'. And it remained at the foot, stranded on the shingle, for the next two years.

It is still far too early to assess the consequences of the 1990–3 recession: the full impact will take a long time to work through. But three of the main implications for the economy are already clearly evident: the further damage inflicted on an already enfeebled manufacturing base, which had barely recovered from the effects of the previous recession; the return of mass unemployment, which turned rapidly upwards from a low point of 1.6 million in early 1990 and has returned to previous levels of around 3 million (June 1993); and the wholesale destruction of small businesses (whose creation had been proclaimed as one of the main achievements of the 1980s). The impact of these developments on individuals has been severe: job loss; homelessness; sickness and a range of traumatic consequences of unemployment, affecting in this recession a wider social and geographical spectrum of the country (Oppenheim, 1993).

Equally, if not more important have been the cultural and political effects of recession. The notion that a 'virtuous circle' (to use Lawson's favourite image) had been created and the endemic problems of the postwar economy had been resolved was decisively refuted by events (as Gilmour observed, the circle had simply been 'squared' – for a while). Once this illusion dissolved, what had happened could be seen as a simple reversion to the familiar postwar cycle of 'stop–go'. Indeed, on closer inspection the obvious parallel was with the most abrupt of these episodes, the 'Barber boom' of 1972–3 and its aftermath. This was especially striking because Margaret Thatcher (who was, of course, a member of the Heath Cabinet at that time) had constantly preached as Prime Minister the paramount necessity of avoiding any such repetition of that episode, using it to resist any change of policy during the political and economic crisis of 1981.

Moreover, the claim to have created a new climate of enterprise proved equally fragile – witness the laments that poured into David Smith's postbag after he had written about the consequences of risk-taking by small businesses at one end of the scale and the heartrending complaints from members of Lloyd's insurance syndicates when required to meet their obligations at the other. Even the Government's most enthusiastic propagandists recognised that something had gone wrong; Nicholas Ridley writes of the 'tragedy' that 'seemed to tarnish the good image of striking out on one's own' (1992, p. 255). The harsh reality of recession impacted not just on those who had borne the brunt of the 1980–2 episode but those who had been among the main beneficiaries of the following period. The 'sharp correction' (as economists put it) in house prices after 1990 spread panic in the ranks of homeowners who had overextended themselves – often with loans pressed upon them by banks anxious to invade the building societies' apparently lucrative territory.

Equally striking was the general drawing back from association with the policies of the later 1980s. Lawson's own political isolation increased rapidly (he left active politics at the end of the 1987–92 Parliament). In his subsequent account of his stewardship, he accepts that 'at one level my central mistake was undoubtedly to underestimate the strength and duration of the boom of the late 1980s and thus of the inflationary forces it unleashed' (1992, p. 989). But he places the blame for the boom itself on 'the imprudent reaction of the lending institutions to financial deregulation and the failure to foresee their folly', accepting only that he himself had 'overreacted' to the 1987 stock market crash and conversely reacted too slowly to the evidence of overheating (p. 991). Even so, he asserts, all would have been well had Margaret Thatcher not refused him entry to the ERM and declined to consider his proposals for an independent Bank of England, responsible for maintaining stable prices. These explanations have not been universally accepted. Lawson's former colleague Nicholas Ridley says simply of his resignation 'Nigel Lawson knew the economy was going badly wrong, and he knew he was entirely and solely responsible' (1992, p. 216). Perhaps as significant as the allocation of blame was the forfeiting of what had been one of the Government's strongest cards – their claim to competence in the management of the economy. Even the Government's erstwhile supporters in business and industry lost their enthusiasm for the policies that had been partly designed for their personal and professional benefit. Attempts were made to suggest that what had occurred was merely an inevitable stage in the business cycle or only part of a worldwide recession. But as the Governor of the Bank of England (Robin Leigh-Pemberton) admitted in 1991 before the Treasury and Civil Service Select Committee, the recession 'was somewhat homegrown on account of events which go back to the late 1980s' (Smith, 1992, p. 197). *The Economist*, one of the Government's most consistent allies, summed it up more bluntly: 'Mrs Thatcher's second recession was all her own work' (2.10.93).

The chief casualty of these events was Margaret Thatcher herself. The rapid decline of the economy in 1990 was matched by a drop in the popularity of the Conservative Government and her own personal standing. Her close involvement with the key third-term policies, especially the introduction of the poll tax, left her especially vulnerable. Her manifest lack of enthusiasm for the development of European policies, most famously expressed in her Bruges speech on the dangers of federalism, separated her from her senior colleagues. Her personal identification with Britain's economic performance as the touchstone of achievement during her period in office also became a liability when the 'miracle' proved to be only another of Nigel Lawson's over-enthusiastic after-dinner excursions (*Guardian*, 5 November 1992). The triumphalism of the beginning of the third term had hardened by mid-term into a style which made enemies unnecessarily – witness her treatment of Lawson and then of Geoffrey Howe, his predecessor as chancellor Howe's unexpectedly devastating resignation speech precipitated a contest for party leadership in November 1990 in which she found herself confronting another inveterate opponent in Michael Heseltine, out of office since his resignation over the Westland helicopter episode and therefore untainted by the third-term failures. A lacklustre campaign on her behalf left her facing a run-off with a margin too narrow to guarantee success. A characteristically belligerent statement in the immediate aftermath of the poll, modulated rapidly when she received the individually presented but suspiciously uniform advice of her Cabinet colleagues – that they would support her if she chose to stand but that she had little chance of success. Perceiving, as she later put it, that the Cabinet was not exactly composed of Polish cavalrymen, she opted for the prudent course and tearful resignation. But she remained strong enough to impose as a coda the successor of her own choosing on the Conservatives and the country: John Major, elected by the parliamentary party at her urgent prompting ahead of Heseltine and the Foreign Secretary, Douglas Hurd.

The record of the first period of the Major Government from November 1990 to the general election of 1992 can be briefly summarised. It was entirely dominated by the need to win the forthcoming election, in the face of a serious and virtually unprecedented difficulty – the political and economic cycles had been allowed to get wholly out of phase. Margaret Thatcher had left office with three of four major economic indicators less favourable than when she came in – inflation, unemployment and the balance of payments deficit had all moved in the wrong direction (productivity in industry is the exception). Growth from the second quarter of 1979 to the fourth quarter of 1990 averaged 1.8 per cent – lower than any period of similar length since the Second World War. Manufacturing output was less than 6 per cent higher when Mrs Thatcher left Downing Street than when she entered it (Gilmour, 1992, p. 70). Meanwhile, the poll tax had fulfilled all Lawson's predictions: it was compared by one despairing minister to a giant gorilla let loose with an insatiable appetite to roam about within Government – the latest victim being the funding of community care, whose introduction had to be postponed by two years. At vast cost in public expenditure the beast was finally caged; Michael Heseltine, brought back to the Department of the Environment for that specific purpose, unveiled in April 1991 proposals to return to a straightforward property-based tax.

Other problems defied such crude but effective political management. Repeated sightings of an end to the economic recession all proved deceptive – the phrase 'green shoots of growth' coined by the Chancellor, Norman Lamont, passed into the national vocabulary as a term of derision. The Government was reduced to trimming the fringes of existing social policies (notably in the Citizen's Charter), half-hearted gestures at continuity in economic policy (minor tax cuts in the 1992 Budget) and finally promises of increased public expenditure – the customary 'electoral Keynesianism', in the hope that the electorate would prove indulgent. When the general election finally came the Conservative manifesto promised more of the same from the same team (though crucially without the previous leader) modified in presentation to accommodate John Major's aspirations to create a 'classless society'. To the astonishment of most commentators, and confounding the opinion polls, the voters' response was favourable. The Conservatives were returned to Downing Street with a majority over all other parties of twenty-one.

In a sense, the outcome of the 1992 election provides its own verdict on the Conservative's third term in office: in a democratic system, however faulty the mechanisms may appear (especially to the losers) the voters must be presumed to know their own minds. It is fair to add that all the evidence suggests that the voters' verdict was not delivered on the social policies of the main parties. As in 1987, the electorate, when polled, preferred by a wide margin the policies of the Labour Party. This is consistent with much evidence from the intermediate period about individual perceptions of policies and choices between them (Jowell et al., 1990; 1992). But notwithstanding their unmistakable concern about the funding and management of public services, particularly the NHS, the voters nonetheless returned the Conservatives to power, as they had done in 1987. On this occasion, however, they did so not as a reward for services rendered through skilful financial management but in the hope that if returned the Government would somehow rediscover the competence they had apparently lost.

This task, together with the continued implementation of the third-term reforms – and in some cases their further expansion and development – were among the responsibilities that John Major's Government carried into the next Parliament, along with a great many other items of unfinished business. How he and his colleagues coped with them is another story, which lies outside scope of this study. Instead, to put these political developments in a wider perspective, this narrative concludes with a brief summary of the changing circumstances of citizens in general during the three terms of Conservative rule and the impact on them of some of the main developments that have taken place over the period up to the general election of 1992.

BRITAIN IN 1992

The picture can be painted in two different and contrasting styles. Most people were better off at the end of the 1980s than they had been at the beginning. Life has improved for the majority in a whole range of ways. For those in work, incomes rose by 25 per cent over the decade: more people own their own homes, use the private sector for health and education, see their children enter higher education, own shares, take foreign holidays and own electronic consumer goods. Self-employment doubled. Some of the gains were achieved through an expansion of credit, which doubled between 1981 and 1991; but the basic position was that wealth in the personal sector almost tripled (£806 billion in 1981 to £2,352 billion in 1989) over the decade, propelled mainly by the increase in house ownership and the value of homes and rise in share prices. *The Economist* in 1988 celebrated the change with a special cover story; it was entitled 'Bourgeois Britain Becomes Rich Again'.

But nearly all these bright achievements have a dark counterpart. The decade saw more people out of work than at any period since the war. Unemployment never came back down again to the rate inherited at the beginning of the Conservative period of rule – it remained at over 2 million for most the whole decade and over 3 million for twenty-six months – 'a record which would look even more appalling' Gilmour says, 'but for the government having fiddled the measurement some twenty-two times' (1992, p. 69) (see Figure A.8). A substantial proportion of those out of work – over 1 million of them, for much of the decade – remained so for more than twelve months, the point at which entitlement to unemployment benefit ceases and contact with the job market is usually lost. In this as in most other respects ethnic minorities have proved to be especially vulnerable (see Figure A.9). Increased home ownership also had its darker side: housing (both rented and for sale) became more costly and at the end of the decade there was a rapid growth in the numbers of repossessions, which increased fivefold between 1989 and 1991. Debt among students in higher education also increased. Small businesses went into receivership in large numbers. The private sector of health and education faltered; share prices fell back and both the proportion of shareholders in the population and the value of shares owned by individuals decreased.

Moreover, the real gains that had been made over the decade and retained by the end were not evenly shared. The reversal of the postwar trend towards greater equality of incomes had become marked by the end of the decade (see Figure A.13). The incomes of those in the bottom decile of earnings fell from 66 per cent of the median level in 1979 to 59 per cent in 1989; whereas the top decile rose from 157 per cent of the median in 1979 to 180 per cent in 1989. This shift was the direct result of changes in the tax system: direct taxation became less progressive, which particularly favoured those at the top end of scale, whose rate went down from 83 per cent (reached in steps) when the Conservatives came to power to a single 40 per cent band. Indirect taxation, which is regressive in effect, increased (Hills, 1988). Poverty became more widespread, whichever measure you choose (those at or below the Supplementary Benefit – Income Support level or those at 50 per cent of average earnings and below). By either test, around 12 million people were living in poverty in 1989 – approximately 20 per cent of the population. If the numbers of children in poverty are calculated the proportion is even higher – 3.1 million (25 per cent of the total child population) compared with 1.4 million in 1979. These trends reflect the growing feminisation of poverty; one-parent families, nine out of ten of which are headed by women are especially at risk (see Figure A.2). In addition, 'every indicator of poverty shows that black people and other ethnic minority groups are more at risk of high unemployment, low pay, poor conditions at work and diminished social security rights' (Oppenheim, 1993, p. 130).

Statistics will take us some way, but not far enough. People's perceptions of the circumstances in which they and others are living are also important. The gains made by the majority were sufficient over most of the decade to reassure them about the basis of policy – both in terms of believing that their own interests were secure and because the notion of 'trickle-down' offered some guarantee that increased prosperity would eventually be shared, at least by those who deserved to share it. If they had doubts about the durability of the 'miracle', the mass media were anxious to reassure them with a steady flow of reassuring stories.

Even so, the evidence from the British Social Attitudes Survey shows a continued high level of concern about unemployment and its consequences over the whole decade; and a selective anxiety about particular groups who had not shared fully in increased national prosperity – the elderly, in particular. To this extent, the majority did 'drool and drivel that they cared', in Margaret Thatcher's phrase. Some felt otherwise. The tax-cutting approach in the 1980s came as welcome release to some of the younger and more ambitious and especially those strategically placed to secure the maximum 'rewards for hard work'. First in the media and then the City, especially after the 'Big Bang' of deregulation, 'telephone number' salaries and a whole range of new wealth-conferring devices – golden hellos, handcuffs and parachutes designed to attract, retain and then speed the passage of the fortunate few – became commonplace. The phenomenon of the yuppie was born and strutted its hour on the public stage. The consumer boom created a whole sequence of millionaires in the service sector who surfed their way to fame and fortune on the crest of the boom, feeding off and accentuating the national feel-good mood.

The Government seems to have been uncertain at first how far they should go along with these highly publicised developments. At first, some ministers – Nicholas Ridley, John Biffen – thought that the flaunting of new wealth lacked class; the entrepreneurs should savour their liberty for its own sake and not require excessive material rewards as well. But Margaret Thatcher needed them, not just as symbols of the success of her policies and paradigm cases of socially responsible businessmen but as potential advisers to Government (and contributors to party funds) – with knighthoods as the honeytrap. So, as the decade advanced, the Government fell into line – first David Young's sermons, delivered in one case for the pulpit of a City church, asserted the moral value of wealth creation and dismissed criticism as merely the 'politics of envy'; then Kenneth Baker, a particularly well-oiled weathercock, producing more explicit justification for high rewards. True, Nigel Lawson, the main author of their good fortune, aims a posthumous kick at yuppies in his autobiography; but by then their hour was long past. Until recession returned in 1990, there was general acceptance in Government, if not outside, that the greater inequality that emerged over the decade could be defended as simply the natural consequence of the exuberance of market forces and their liberating effects. Not many reflected on the implications of J.K. Galbraith's gibe – why is it that if the rich receive more money it's justified as motivating them to work harder; but the poor earning more is deplored as doing the opposite?

Further evidence from the British Social Attitudes Surveys suggests that the majority of the British cast a jaundiced eye on these developments; their conclusion, supported by a succession of studies through the 1980s was that the population at large had resisted the attractions of the enterprise culture and distrusted the workings of the market. In sum, to the extent that the term has meaning, the British remained 'collectivist' in their general attitudes, disliking wide differential income differentials and looking to the State to redistribute resources through the community, if necessary through higher taxation, to assist the genuinely needy. But here was the rub; the surveys also showed a sharp differentiation between those thought worthy of help of this kind whose poverty was 'not their own fault' and who should therefore be assisted in the name of fairness – the quintessential English public virtue – and the 'undeserving' poor, reluctant to work and probably fiddling their benefit.

So at least one element in the Goverment's argument – the belief that over-generous benefits produce dependency – did strike a chord with the public; and may have been one of the factors 'screening out' the visible evidence of poverty. Many of the poor are not found in places where the 'average' citizen of Middle England is likely to encounter them, having been concentrated through much of the 1980s in severely impacted industrial towns based on obsolescent heavy industry like shipbuilding and steel, pit villages confronted with closures, and the satellite estates to which the poor in many larger towns and cities had been 'decanted'. But there has been one exception to this rule: the return of beggars in significant numbers to the streets of large British cities. Beatrice Webb once commented that one of the most striking social changes in her lifetime had been the disappearance of beggars from the London scene. To some people, their reappearance has been one of the highly visible emblems of the underside of the enterprise culture.

But even here a variant of the screening process has been at work. In Central London the office workers eating their lunchtime sandwiches learned to ignore the homeless stretched out on the grass in front of them; in the evening concertgoers barely notice those sleeping rough under Hungerford Bridge and pass by in ignorance of 'cardboard city' only yards away at Waterloo. When approached with a mumbled request for 'change', respectable citizens could console themselves by reflecting that the young and able-bodied among these beggars must be work-shy and their problems could be solved if, in one of the horrible bastard transatlanticisms then in vogue, they 'got off their butts' and looked for work. But respectable citizens had no desire either to understand the causes of homelessness or accept any share of responsibility for it. They did not wish to know that this was precisely what so many of the homeless had tried to do, especially by coming to London – in their misfortune, they are both paradigm cases and victims of the enterprise culture. So there were few objections raised when restaurant owners in the Strand proposed to flush the homeless (literally) out of the doorways in which they were sleeping so that they would not interfere with trade by frightening the tourists.

Nemesis awaited many of those who had been striking this kind of attitude in the saloon bars of the South-East. The second recession at the end of the 1980s took (as we have seen) a different path to its predecessor. The impact was less harsh in those areas that had suffered severely in the first recession but business closures and job losses cut a swathe through the retail and service sectors which had been engines of growth in London and the South-East. Then it was discovered that losing your job was not a form of moral laxity; and becoming homeless not invariably a device for jumping the housing queue. London-based journalists now discovered unemployment. They had been too idle to go out and look for it before, when it was far away in the North and Scotland – but now unemployment came to them, provoking a rash of stories about the injustices and hardships suffered by middle-class claimants encountering the State system of welfare, education (and even housing) at first hand for the first time. This discovery by 'comfortable Britain' of poverty had quite different overtones from the detached scrutiny that was the best that the poor could expect during the 1980s.

However poverty is defined, the poor have never been more than a relatively small and powerless minority in British society. But their greater visibility (in every sense) after the collapse of the Lawson boom at the end of the 1980s was a reflection not only of the failures of economic management that had added to their numbers but of a shift in public attitudes away from the values of the enterprise culture. These changes also help to provide a context for some of the claims made for the achievements of the Conservatives during their period in office, which will be examined in the final chapter.

7

TOWARDS THE MILLENNIUM

There will be time to audit
The accounts later, there will be sunlight later
And the equation will come out at last.

Louis MacNeice, *Autumn Journal*, xxiv.

THE TRIUMPH OF MARKET VALUES?

How far have the New Right reforms described in the previous chapter now set the agenda for social policy for the rest of the century? In a strictly practical sense, the scope for any substantial modification in the general direction of policy over the rest of the decade is quite limited, at least until the next general election – due in 1996 or 1997 at the latest. But is the proposition also true in broader terms? Have the Government's policies – especially those that have emerged over the last five years – already acquired the degree of legitimacy that would ensure that they remain substantially unchanged, even if the Conservatives leave office? This, after all, was what happened in the case of the Attlee Government's reforms, which were left in place by their successors, in order (in Churchill's phrase) to allow them sufficient time to 'bed down'. If so, the debate in social policy will for the foreseeable future be about modifications to the structures now being erected, not substantial challenges to the foundation of the whole enterprise. In this sense, the cliche may have come true: the Conservatives have indeed captured the high ground and are busy building upon it their 'city on a hill' (Willetts, 1992).

If this is right, what are the distinctive features of the new structure of welfare that has been constructed? As we saw in the opening section, the current group of policies have been freely described by their authors as 'revolutionary'. Kenneth Clarke has claimed that the Conservatives have completely changed 'old Attlee's welfare state'. Much of this is hyperbole, of course. Most of the third-term changes have been to do with the ways in which welfare in delivered: with the means, not the ends. Although market techniques are being adopted and the language employed is that of market transactions, the third-term shift has been concerned mainly with efficiency. It is about a change in the manner of what is being undertaken, not an abandonment of the principle of public support for welfare (Minford in Loney et al., 1991). True, there is also a barely concealed subtext about achieving reductions in expenditure, facilitated by efficiency savings made through the introduction of new management techniques; but this is standard Treasury talk, adjusted to the new environment. The project still lacks an animating principle: a grand design, à la Beveridge. Instead, what has been offered is a 'business-like' approach, flavoured with some customer-oriented trimmings, which can be successfully marketed as a vision of a better future for the consumers of that rather problematic product, welfare (Waldegrave, 1993). The rhetoric is diametrically opposed to that of Beveridge, with his lifelong suspicion of business values; but the substance is not yet so radically different.

There is, however, one significant exception – a concept around which an important part of the new agenda has been constructed. This concept has been heavily influenced by American models, as is often the case on the New Right, and has emerged over the whole lifespan of the Conservative Government, by gradual stages. It arose initially in part as a result of concern about the reappearance of what the Victorians called the 'dangerous classes' and was further intensified as a result of the specific anxieties generated by the inner-city 'disturbances' and the threat that these appeared to pose to the 'fabric of civil society'. It was strongly hinted at over a period of time in Margaret Thatcher's own pronouncements about welfare, notably in her speech to the General Assembly of the Church of Scotland (the so-called 'Sermon on the Mound'), in which she put the case to a sceptical gathering for the moral virtues of individualism and the enterprise culture. In shorthand terms, the idea was that the objective of welfare policy should be the 'remoralising' of the recipients of welfare. Only such a basic shift of values (it was argued) would put to flight once for all the problem of dependency, seen as the ultimate crux for Conservative policy on welfare (Ridley, 1992).

Specifically, a means had to be found to liberate the captive populations of the dependency culuture on the local authority housing estates and in particular the ultimate challenge to the enterprise agenda in social policy, single parents. As Nicholas Ridley perceived it, 'without husband, without job, and without effort, young girls could house, clothe and feed themselves at the taxpayers' expense, provided they had children' (1992, p. 91). While this impulse to dependency remained, solutions to the problem of funding the constantly expanding social security budget would always elude governments. Expectations would always march ahead of the capacity to satisfy them, especially when they were shaped by an indulgent public opinion and reinforced by the tireless propaganda of pressure groups. This was no longer a matter of more efficient delivery or better targeting of services. In Norman Fowler's Green Paper on social security (1985a) there had still been a strong emphasis on meeting the needs of families with children, even if he was severely criticised by Nigel Lawson for proposals that 'ran clean contrary to the moral sense of the nation' (1992, p. 595). But now ministers saw a clear need to address a problem to which, up to now, it had (in Ridley's words) 'proved impossible to find an answer'. The quest for a new set of moral values was to be Thatcherite social policy's Last Frontier.

As long as the cautiously pragmatic side of Margaret Thatcher's personality still dominated her approach to social policy – that is, up to the end of the second term (1987) – her personal views did not play a decisive part in determining policy, in this field. Moreover, there was an expectation immediately after the 1987 general election that the rising tide of employment, celebrated in many official publications of the time, notably the 1988 Training White Paper, would wash out many of the immediate problems and that private sector-led urban regeneration would reshape the inner-city landscape and provide the physical context for the moral tonic being administered to its inhabitants through the return of the enterprise culture (Deakin and Edwards, 1993).

A significant step in the journey towards the construction of the case for 'remoralisation' was taken in a widely publicised speech on poverty made by John Moore, when he was Secretary of State for Social Security and still a potential future Prime Minister (May 1989). Moore argued that the 'poverty lobby' had captured the agenda in the debate through the use of illegitimate tactics – mainly by redefining the meaning of poverty by the use of the concept of 'relative poverty'. They had done so for their own purposes, Moore said, in order to pursue 'the political goal of equality'. The lobby's intention was to divert resources to the poor, 'even though this would cripple the wealth of the country' and would not be in the interests of the recipients.

The answer, Moore went on to argue, could best be provided by capitalism through the benefits of economic growth from which the poor would achieve real gains. For 'by almost every material measure that it is possible to contrive . . . not only are those with lower incomes not getting poorer, they are substantially better off than they have ever been before' (1989, p. 13). In fact, the reverse was true. Despite Margaret Thatcher's claim in her valedictory speech in the following year, over her period in office the poor were becoming poorer in both relative and absolute terms (see Figure A.13). Worse, any prospect that wealth would trickle down to them in future through an expanding economy disappeared with the collapse of the Lawson boom at the end of the decade. If capitalism could not rescue the poor, other means would have to be found to address the problem.

Helpful ammunition was provided by the New Right's American allies. The most persuasive argument was the one made by the sociologist Charles Murray. This was first set out in his book *Losing Ground*, based on studies of the recipients of one of the major benefits in the American system, Aid to Families with Dependent Children (AFDC), and was subsequently extended to Britain in a lengthy article for *The Sunday Times* (26.11.89). Murray argued that much of the poverty encountered in major cities can be explained on behavioural grounds. This is particularly true of young males, with their high crime rates, propensity to father children outside marriage and then abandon them (never having themselves learned about or experienced fatherhood at first hand) and above all their reluctance to enter the labour force, or re-enter it, once having left. These were all threads in a single overall pattern: a basic unwillingness among the urban poor (or 'underclass') to accept responsibility for their own actions. The irresponsible poor should therefore be remoralised, through strict conditions placed on the receipt of welfare, in order that they should accept that responsibility.

Murray's views were communicated to the faithful through IEA pamphlets (Murray, 1990) and his argument repeated by British followers, who added to his indictment chronic fecklessness in use of money and to potential remedies deterrence, through the application of 'the disincentives, stigma and unpleasantnesses which arise naturally in local communities' (Digby Anderson, who doubled as the *Spectator*'s cookery correspondent, quoted in Oppenheim, 1993, p. 22). Finally the thesis reached ministers through seminars organised by the think-tanks, by which time it had become simplified to the point of caricature. Welfare is bad for the poor; it destroys their characters. Poverty restores the balance by providing the spur to work. Work is good for restoring character and provides incentives through material rewards, provided that these are not excessive (*Independent*, 21.5.90).

There are several problems with this thesis. First, is it soundly based in terms of the American evidence? This has been much debated, to inconclusive effect (Block, 1987). Second, is it applicable to the British situation? Some thought so – Norman Dennis and George Erdos writing 'from an ethical socialist position' harboured grave doubts about the capacity of the British working class to cope with problems that they face in the grossly delinquent behaviour patterns of young males who 'have been invited to remain in a state of permanent puerility [and] predictably behave in an anti-social manner' (1992, p. xxi). Some think not. The Policy Studies Institute found that little evidence could be assembled to support the case for the existence of an underclass in Britain with significantly different values from the majority on issues like work and crime (Smith, 1992). Third, even if it is accepted, can anything be done about it?

As it happens, some of the new policy initiatives taken in the course of the third term do lend themselves to being employed as a means to address these issues. Basic religious and moral values can be taught in schools, using the devices for controlling the curriculum that the 1988 Education Act has placed in ministers' hands. The Broadcasting Standards Council has been set up to protect the public from the excesses of moral laxity on television and radio. The churches have been exhorted to redirect their efforts towards instruction in morality rather than 'misconstruing' their role as critics of Government policy – witness the homilies by the then inner-cities minister (John Redwood) on the proper definition of the churches' reponsibilities (spiritual, not temporal) on inner-city policy. New institutions exist, though not yet in large numbers, as demonstrations of the potential rewards of enterprise, to motivate the young to take alternative paths, through the education system and into employment (the City Technology Colleges). Delinquent behaviour is to be harshly punished and severe penalties (including imprisonment) reintroduced for young offenders. Socially delinquent fathers who fail to take financial reponsibility for their children can be compelled to do so through the new Child Support

Agency. The system of welfare generally has been adjusted; loans substituted for grants, to provide incentives for individual responsibility in managing money. Deterrents have been introduced for those likely to lapse into long-term dependency on benefit – the 'Restart' scheme for systematic interviewing of the long-term unemployed: Britain's closest approximation to the 'workfare' schemes in the United States. But the New Right would wish to see all these devices as part of a broader project, to establish that empowerment through the market offers a better way. Michael Novak, another American academic, has put the case in its simplest and clearest form: democratic capitalism liberates through the moralising effects of making opportunities freely available to all.

So, taken on their own terms – and those of their most enthusiastic apologists (Letwin, Willetts) – Conservative administrations since 1979 have been engaged on three distinct but linked enterprises:

- more efficient management of the actually existing system of welfare, as exemplified by more effective use of public funds and improved standard of the services provided.
- the introduction of new machinery intended as a means towards these ends, modelled on market provision, using a variety of market-based devices and altering the basic relationship between the State and the recipient of welfare through a change in the way in which welfare is provided.
- the moral mission, to achieve a basic change in attitudes to welfare by remoralising the recipients of welfare and restoring a general sense of personal responsibility, through the substitution of market attitudes towards welfare for those of the traditional Welfare State. This – the 'hearts and minds' element in the project – has been particularly associated with Margaret Thatcher and her immediate political entourage.

ASSESSING THE OUTCOMES

To assess the success or failure of a project as elaborate and complex as that pursued by the Conservative Government between 1979 and 1992 involves making heroic assumptions about the outcomes of programmes, some of which are still in the early stages of evolution.

The simplest test of all to apply is the one most often invoked in political debate: the pattern of public expenditure. Taking the level of expenditure on social policy over this period, Figure A.7 on page 237 shows that the pattern of resources allocated to social policy programmes generally remained broadly stable throughout this period. There are some variations between different programmes: some, though not all of these can be explained by extraneous factors, like the demographic changes that have affected demand for some services. Others are the direct consequence of political decisions, like the sharp reduction in the proportion of resources allocated to public housing. But, in general, the Government sought to protect mainstream services like health and education, although the apparent rises in spending in these sectors are deceptive; increased costs at a time of rising demand means that the true volume of spending rose by very little. However, in spite of all the heated debates and the impact of economic pressures, especially at the beginning and end of this period, public spending on welfare, broadly defined, continued on a steady path, apart from the now customary accelerations in pre-election years.

It is when it comes to the use that has been made of these funds – the extent to which they have met the designated objectives of policy – that the picture immediately becomes more complex. One of the common features of almost all the reviews of the outcomes of public policy during the Thatcher period is that they have assessed the Government's performance on the basis of their own claims. But it is a proposition that scarcely requires elaborate proof that ideologies may set agendas but cannot guarantee delivery of the desired outcomes (Peacock in Wilson, 1991). The Thatcher administrations have been no exception to this rule. Implementation of their policy initiatives has involved a series of intermediate agencies, each with their own particular agendas and priorities. Even where new agencies have been specifically created for the purpose of implementing government policies passage through successive stages in the implementation process has on occasion substantially modified the outcomes – as in the case of the content of tests of attainment by pupils under the national curriculum (Graham, 1993).

Generally, those responsible for the management of the British system of government (in the broadest sense) tend to be unhappy when confronted with ambitious programmes; at least until recently, the civil service has preferred case-by-case administration (Weale in Wilson, 1991). However, one-party rule – now extending over fourteen years – has provided the stability which allows long-term changes to be introduced. Ministers are well aware that this has been an important precondition for their attempt to make permanent changes in the national policy agenda (Lawson, 1992), but less prepared to admit that it carries its own risks. Unlike other countries that have experienced long periods of one-party rule (Japan, Italy) the corruption that has resulted has not been financial; rather it has taken the form of an increasing tendency to confuse party and public interests. The assumption that there can be only one legitimate view on any major policy issue and that all opposition to it is based on factional interests and promoted on 'political' grounds is a constant motif in all recent ex-ministerial autobiographies. It also provides the justification for keeping the policy-making process sealed off behind closed doors, penetrable only by those who can be trusted to share the same basic assumptions.

The implementation of the new policy initiatives raises a whole series of other issues – many of which, at the time of writing (July 1993) remain unresolved. Clearly, it is far too early to reach conclusions about whether the third-term policies have been successful in achieving their objectives – although that has not inhibited critics and advocates alike from making sweeping and contradictory claims. The mandatory final pages of the politicians' autobiographies has been a particularly fertile source of optimistic assertions. In real life the impact of these policies will take several years to work their way through; and even then it will be difficult to distinguish their impact from that of other, extraneous effects. However, it is not too early to identify a number of points where issues have arisen which have problematic implications.

First, there is the question of how cultural change is achieved and what purpose it is intended to serve. How far is it possible to move in the direction of private sector practices within a context of a continuing public service? If it is both feasible and desirable to reproduce in the arrangements for the delivery of any service the totality of the private sector culture, then why is full-blooded privatisation not the logical objective of policy for all social policy programmes? Why have even quasi-markets if real markets are a realistic alternative? Nigel Lawson presents himself as a passionate advocate of privatising every conceivable Government activity, preferring 'the discipline of the market place' even to Treasury control of spending (1992, p. 391). Yet, even though 'there was no-one more zealous for privatization' than Lawson, he baulked at adopting this approach for the NHS. Exasperatingly, his explanation consisted solely of the claim that health was *sui generis* (p. 616; as he himself says of the civil service, always use foreign languages when you want to obfuscate). Instead, he and his Conservative colleagues devoted much time and energy during the debate on the health service reforms and their implementation to denying that the notion of privatising the health service had even crossed their minds. Yet if there are ways in which the private sector model is not universally appropriate, the Government has not been anxious to advertise them. This is especially surprising in the light of Margaret Thatcher's view (as expressed to Nicholas Ridley) that public services will always by definition be inferior to those provided by the private sector (see page 170).

Others have not been so coy. Ian Gilmour is once again among the sharpest dissenters. His criticism focuses on both the character of the choices presented – according to him, 'Thatcherites see the world as a prolonged pursuit of groceries whereby people choose education from Tesco and local government from Sainsburys' – and the consequences of employing market models of decision-making, i.e. increased centralisation and expansion of State powers (1992, pp. 170, 223). Like others, he is less than enraptured with the model of supermarket as a means of providing services. Defenders of traditional models of local service delivery have been at pains to stress ways in which the nature of the tasks addressed and the structure created to address them differ from those adopted in business. Uncritical adoption of private sector models (which often bear little resemblance to actual practice) 'prevents the development of an approach to management in the public sector in general or to the social services in particular based on their distinctive purposes, conditions and tasks', John Stewart writes (1992, p. 27). A variant of the same concerns has been expressed, in stately mandarinspeak, by the head of the Home Civil Service, Sir Robin Butler, who has drawn attention to the importance of sustaining at a time of rapid change 'the unifying charcteristics of the service which are not only its traditional strengths but its duties – the requirements of equity, accountability, impartiality and a wide view of the public interest' (Butler, 1988, p. 15).

As Butler's remarks imply, a second problematic issue is the question of accountability. The market-based procedures introduced into the public service appear to provide a means of securing both a line of accountability upwards and remedies for individual grievances. But in practice, both (it is argued) are deficient. Providing for accountability upwards is unsatisfactory, not only because the lengthy line to distant ministers is too long and too loose; but because the substitution of a system of contractual arrangements itself sets limits to accountability (Stewart and Walsh, 1992, p. 514). Those responsible at local level for overseeing new-style managers as they exercise their new-style responsibilities – the 'non-executive' board members of the new quangos – are themselves drawn from the *nomenklatura*, often without a base in the community and tending to share their managers' assumptions and values. The remedy, by analogy with 'pure' (super)market practices, therefore rests largely on complaints procedures, invoked by individuals. Improved responsiveness to complaints (where it is genuine, not simply presentational) is a welcome consequence of a customer-oriented approach; but it does not confer rights on users. Nor will it make new-style agencies more accountable for practices which lie beyond the capacity of individual complaints to resolve, like indirect discrimination and arbitrary rationing of positional goods.

This gap is the one of several intended to be filled by the 'Citizen's Charter' (1991), John Major's own particular contribution to the third-term reforms (and beyond). However, accountability does not feature among the seven key objectives established for the future of the public sector. Instead, Major's preface expresses a desire to 'drive reforms into the core of the public services' (like the stake into Dracula's heart?); while at the same time stressing that: 'The Citizen's Charter is not a recipe for more state action; it is a testament of our belief in people's right to be informed and choose for themselves' (HM Government, 1991).

Major also underlines the importance of securing standards and guaranteeing improved quality, and professes confidence that the public sector is capable of delivering services at the highest level. Yet at the same time privatisation is offered as a tried and tested alternative route (short cut, even) to the same desirable destination – the same ambiguity as before. Are those services that are to be denied the electric stimulus of market discipline also *sui generis*? Or are they, as some critics would argue, residual services whose attraction to potential private sector operators would be minimal and must therefore be left in the public sector as 'inevitably' of inferior quality?

Informed choice by citizens rests, as the Charter correctly implies, on the availability of the right information at the right time and place. But one of the other problematic features of the market model, which applies with equal if not greater force to quasi-markets too, is the asymmetry of access to information (both in quantity and quality). That is, in plain English, the contractor may know more than the customer and their knowledge may enable them to skew the terms of the deal in their own favour. This is often likely to be the case where deals are being struck between well-established providers of services and apprentice purchasers, as appears to have been the case in the NHS, where hospital trusts have had a distinct advantage in the earlier stage of their relationship with the District Health Authorites who purchase treatment from them. It may even be true in the case of those forms of quasi-market created within public sector institutions – the 'producer–provider splits' imposed by the Government on local authorities.

Availability of information to the service user may be even more problematic, for two reasons. First, there is an issue about accessibility. Second, there are problems about the quality of what is available. The regulatory agencies set up in the first two terms are now well into their stride and the Audit Commission, in particular, has performed important services through the running review of costs and efficiency of service delivery under the rubric of the 'three Es' (economy, efficiency and effectiveness). Nearly all of this information has been fed back into the system at institutional level, but may not be available at the level of individual users of the service. This becomes especially problematic when the service has been contracted out and 'commercial confidentiality' is invoked to justify not allowing the service user access to information with operational implications.

In such circumstances, users may have to rely on altogether less satisfactory measures, devised and provided on a comparative basis to introduce an element of competition into the quasi-market. The validity of this information has been the subject of hot dispute, especially in the case of the education 'league tables' comparing the examination performances of schools. The question here is not only one of access but of interpretation. Does information of this kind empower service users or mislead them?

Different issues have emerged around the themes of inspection and evaluation. This is familiar ground in British public policy; inspection is one of the oldest functions of government. Variations on this theme developed in the late 1980s as the models of the earlier privatisation of utilities were adapted, in part as a means of reforming those inspectorates thought to be especially prone to professional capture (specifically, Her Majesty's Inspectors of Education). The picture here has been one of pragmatic adaptation and variation service by service rather than a uniform policy; devices employed have ranged from wholly new agencies (education) through beefed-up versions of existing inspectorates (Social Services Inspectorate, HM Inspectors of Constabulary) to the introduction of an existing body, the Audit Commission, to an area in which inspection was previously virtually absent (health). In housing, by contrast only the private sector is regulated. The functioning of these bodies and their diversity suggests another set of questions on the purpose of inspection and who the outcomes of inspection are intended to benefit (Klein and Day, 1987). In passing, it is worth noting that one of the most effective of the inspectorates during the late 1980s in terms of achieving rapid change in institutions inspected was largely a one-man-band, HM Inspector of Prisons, Judge Stephen Tumim.

Two other potentially contentious issues have arisen as the introduction of the reforms has proceeded. First, the link between the new devices and the previous reforms in Government; the Financial Management Initiative (FMI) and the ministerial management systems, followed after the 1987 election by the devising of the 'Next Steps' strategy. Second, there is the official role that has been allocated to the Government's 'City Fathers' – to adopt Margaret Thatcher's term, first employed in the course of her attempt to summon the private sector to the rescue of the inner cities.

Reform in central government has been a theme of the Conservative administration from the outset which gathered pace through the 1980s but took a different form with the introduction of the 'Next Steps' policy – a measure devised within Government to achieve, in crude terms, a separation between the executive and policy-making arms of government through the creation of free-standing executive agencies operating within the public sector but as far as possible on private sector terms. This development raises a number of important issues in the context of the third-term reforms in welfare policy. Semi-independent agencies are in some respects very apt vehicles for the introduction of reforms; but their existence is sometimes difficult to reconcile with retention of central control and direction over policy. The attempt to separate out implementation qestions and devolve responsibility for them to managers was a particular feature of the NHS reforms, with the creation of a Management Board and appointment of a Chief Executive. The resulting politicisation of the role of senior managers was the exact opposite of what was intended; but the notion that controversial implementation issues could be floated off into limbo and become subjects of technical debate, if anything (safe from leverage exercised by 'pressure groups'), was never a realistic one. The result of the inevitable controversies that took place around the implementation of the third-term policies has been to identify senior officials and managers with particular policies and thereby promote the assumption that they have political as well as institutional loyalties. Exposure to cross-examination on the execution of policy before increasingly active House of Commons Select Committees – one of few independent sources of analysis of policy outcomes, which came to play an increasingly important role, by default, through the middle and later 1980s – further reinforced this trend. It would be too extreme to suggest that these developments were precipitating a crisis in the civil service; but they were seen as legitimate cause for concern. They also provided the context for calls for Government to face up to reality and go over to a contract system for employing senior civil servants, a device already adopted for chief executives of Next Steps Agencies (Mather, 1993).

Real politicisation has occurred not at the level of career civil servants – though Cecil Parkinson has provided a vivid picture of Margaret Thatcher 'auditioning' senior civil servants in his department and recording her private verdict with dots and lines drawn under their names identifying the sheep and goats (1992, p. 160). Rather, this has been promoted through the introduction of Government sympathisers into official posts in two forms. First, by their appointment as advisers (a familiar device, but far more significant in the 'closed' policy-making environment of the third term); and second, through the membership of the boards and committees of newly created agencies, starting with Urban Development Corporations and going on to a range of new quangos: new-style District Health Authorities, Training and Enterprise Councils, School Management Boards, City Challenge Committees, often in the process displacing representatives of elected bodies. The issue here is not so much the right of the executive to act in this way – the Government's approach is perfectly legitimate within the existing rules of the game, and not unknown in reverse, though hardly on so great a scale. Rather, it has been a question of the consequences in terms of the quality of those appointed – a policy of exclusion on political grounds has meant that the pool of those with time and talent is liable to be rapidly drained, with unhappy consequences in terms of the standard of services delivered.

Ministers have responded to these criticisms by arguing that they have created a new counterbalance to the power of the executive by conferring new responsibilities on individual citizens which have 'increased, not diminished, the individual's practical control over the public services provided to him or her' (Waldegrave, 1993, p. 4). But although one characteristic of the third-term initiatives has been the development of the 'hub–rim' relationships (to use Kenneth Baker's term) the most important change is not the devolution of responsibility but the gathering in of power. This has been conferred directly on ministers through the passage of legislation, the law serving as the legitimating device, and exercised by creation of the 'quangocracy', with appointed staff who share common values with ministers and owe no obligation except to them. The civil service have been the facilitators of this process and part-beneficiaries – reform has given new opportunities for younger civil servants to exercise their managerial talents. But the position on policy development has been rather different; once policy-making retreated behind closed doors during the preparations for the third-term reforms the role of ad hoc 'task forces' became more important (Lawson, 1992) and the scope for direct involvement by the New Right think-tanks correspondingly greater. The penetration of Whitehall on a semi-irregular basis has steadily developed over this period (see, for example, the role of Madsen Pirie and the Adam Smith Institute in developing the policies around the Citizen's Charter).

The 'mini-quangos' created by the Conservatives at regional and local level have partly filled the space once occupied by local government and have appointed boards with coopted rather than directly elected representatives. By 1993, they had taken over responsibility for the expenditure of £4.5 billion of public money formerly under the control of local authorities (*New Statesman*, 1.10.93). One of the outcomes of this change has been the emergence of what critics describe as a 'democratic deficit', mainly through weak accountability to the population that the new agencies are intended to serve. There have been some attempts to make this good: Urban Development Corporations have tried to do so by appointing liaison officers and setting up community trusts. The Government have also encouraged 'socially responsible' businesses (chiefly developers) to buy support in the community by hiring local labour and putting community facilities into new developments. But this is 'good times' stuff; and when the going gets tough in economic recessions developers get out, the projects disappear and the retreat is covered by clouds of meaningless rhetoric, inviting local people to 'share the vision' (Deakin and Edwards, 1993).

Generally, conclusions about the impact of cultural change at the point of delivery still remain mostly at the level of anecdote. Such as it is, the evidence suggests that the quasi-markets in social policy of the third term have had a very uneven impact (Le Grand and Bartlett, 1993). The introduction of market disciplines – value for money and competition as stimulus to improved performance – has been erratic both in scope and result. Either the new arrangements are not significantly more efficient than those they have replaced; or the reformed systems put the most vulnerable at risk by 'creaming off' the low-cost least vulnerable clients. Detailed outcomes have as often as not taken the form of superficial changes of style rather than substantial overhauls of the structure and organisation – with sensitivity to customer needs preached rather than practised. Managers have been readily persuaded that they should have freedom to manage but are often less sure what to do with it (and not always convinced that freedom is what they have actually been given). The record on their performance and the detailed impact of the structural changes made (especially those in health and education) is not yet clear enough to allow any firm conclusions to be drawn. Rival claims have already been referred to above; but – with the exception of certain surrogate indicators (hospital waiting lists; school exam results) customarily deployed by ministers in debate, whose deficiencies are well known – few performance measures that give reliable evidence on which to base conclusions about quality of service now being provided are yet available. The Charters that have been issued in most service areas still mainly present aspirations rather than setting up targets on which performance can be systematically measured, although the Audit Commission are engaged on work that will eventually fill this gap. The availability of information, crucial to the successful functioning of quasi-markets, should also improve as the impact of new-style inspection and regulation makes itself felt.

The evidence from the late 1980s might therefore suggest that the case for retaining a substantial role for elected local bodies was stronger than ministers were prepared to concede during the exuberant early days of their reforms, when the talk was of 'drawing a line under the failed municipal solutions of the past' (John Patten quoted in Deakin and Edwards, 1993). But this case has been compromised by weaknesses in earlier performance – what David Donnison calls 'the decay of once-humane left-wing ideals into a mere imperialism of the public sector' (1991, p. 172) – and a persistent absence of proper accountability to the community (as opposed to the collective electorate). Latterly, local government claims to have learnt and applied lessons from the experience of the 1980s, if sometimes under outside stimulus – for example, the impact of the Tenant Choice legislation on the practices of local housing departments or the activities of the Audit Commission. In some respects, local government was always more efficient than central government was prepared to allow; the 1980s were not barren years, as far as experiment and innovation go. Decentralisation of service delivery to smaller and more accountable units within local authorities is a good example of an innovation which was locally generated, not centrally imposed (Gaster, 1991). But even these important shifts in local government practice still leave a democratic deficit to be addressed. It should be added that William Waldegrave, the minister responsible for implementing the reforms based on the Citizen's Charter has vigorously denied that such a deficit has arisen. He argued that:

> far from presiding over a democratic deficit in the management of our public services, this Government has actually helped to create a **democratic gain**. We have not in any way altered or undermined the basic structure of public service accountability and hence to individual citizens. But we have made it useable. (1993, p. 18)

Another key issue has been the extent to which the whole range of policy has been successfully integrated – what has come to be known to its critics as the problem of fragmentation. In theory, centralisation of policy formulation should have reduced this danger, especially in the area of management of public expenditure. However, the manner in which this has been conducted has important implications for critics of the Government's performance. Continuous pressure has been exercised on levels of public expenditure in general and social programmes in particular. The outcome has been containment, at most, rather than reduction in spending, as we have seen. But this has not diminished the perception that Treasury interventions – both within central government and those involving other statutory bodies – have both reached a new pitch of intensity and strayed beyond the traditional role of controlling aggregate expenditure to involvement with the detailed content of programmes (Deakin and Parry in Deakin and Page, 1993).

Critics of the Treasury's role have latterly been joined in some of these reservations by former departmental ministers from the 'radical right', whose memoirs still resound with their resentment at being prevented from doing what they want to do. Witnesses include David Young ('Lord Spendmore' to the Treasury), who 'had been convinced for years that Sir Lewis Carroll had been Second Permanent Secretary to the Treasury' (1990, p. 286); and Norman Tebbit, who complains of occasions when 'junior Treasury officials delayed decisions while second-guessing my judgment on quite minor matters' (1988, p. 218). All of this looked quite different from Great George Street, as Nigel Lawson is quick to confirm in his insouciant account of his various interventions across the whole range of public policy – though he adds (correctly) that 'it would be foolish to imagine that my colleagues welcomed this interference' (1992, p. 586).

Good grounds for resenting this interference could certainly have been found not only in the manner in which it was being done (provoking though this must have been) but in the mounting evidence that the Chancellor – and the Treasury's – judgment on matters that did fall within their proper sphere of responsibility had become demonstrably fallible. The 1990–3 recession not only wiped out many of the material gains that had been secured during the course of the later 1980s, but also cast doubt on the thesis that a lasting cultural shift in favour of entrepreneurial values had taken place.

As for the other much desired cultural shift – the moral proclaimed with such vigour by Mrs Thatcher herself that would bring about the remoralisation of the victims of the 'dependency culture' and secure it in place by a revival of family values, evidence of success was also scanty. The suggestion that the encouragement of possessive individualism in the economic sphere and the attempt to reanimate the social cohesion of traditional communities might not be ideal partners began to be heard again on the right.

In all these respects, then, there was unfinished business at the end of the Conservative's third term and much less clarity about how it should be completed. Numerous questions were still left unanswered, both about what had been attempted and the style in which the attempt had been made. As *The Economist*, reflecting upon Mrs Thatcher's record in office, asked in some perplexity:

> Why was a politician, who celebrated the individual over the state such a ruthless centraliser of government power, and so careless of civil liberties? Why was a believer in small government such a ferocious defender of nanny-state middle-class entitlements such as tax relief on mortgage interest? (2.10.93)

STATE OR MARKET: WHAT FUTURE FOR SOCIAL POLICY?

All these unresolved issues have become even more important now that the social policy component has risen to top of the public agenda in such a striking way. It is instructive to compare T.H. Marshall's comment in 1961 that 'it is easy, when studying social policy, to exaggerate its effects, material and psychological' (p. 182) with David Donnison's assertion thirty years later: that social policy is 'not something to turn to only when economic problems have been solved. It is itself one of the problems, and at the same time an essential foundation for their solution' (1991, p. 146). But there should be no illusions about the likely outcome. Debate about the respective virtues and deficiencies of state-led and market-driven (*sic*) welfare falls at once into a set of familiar patterns. Discussion turns rapidly into a Punch and Judy exchange ('oh yes, you did'). The main weaknesses of the market are well known: externalities, free-rider problems and the inability to cope with public goods. But, as Glennerster puts it, to these have been added, on the basis of experience with the market philosophy in action over the 1980s, 'the concept of information failure in particular markets.... Uncertainty and inequalities of information between supplier and demander produce inefficient results, adverse selection and cream skimming' (Glennerster, 1993, p. 7).

The tendency of markets to slide towards monopolies dominated by cartels is also well-documented and likely to be particularly important in areas where the market is being newly introduced (or reintroduced after a protracted interval); hence the well-recognised need for inspection and regulation. Their strengths, for their advocates, cluster around the theme of liberty. To David Green, recent experience suggests that

> liberty is desirable not only to allow people to enter into mutually acceptable bargains, appealing only to the immediate interests of others and no more. It is also to set loose the enthusiasts and pioneers who pursue ideals outside themselves – people who seek to advance the common good. (1993, p. 90)

The main reservations that have been advanced about the role of the State are equally familiar. These include the tendency to expand to cater for 'egoistic' interests of bureau managers, to which public choice theorists have drawn attention (Buchanan, 1978; Niskanen, 1973) and the inherent tilt towards domination by producer interests. On coming into office at the beginning of the first Thatcher administration, Nigel Lawson reflected that 'civil servants and welfare administrators are far from the selfless Platonic Guardians of paternalist mythology; they are a major and powerful interest group in their own right' (1980, p. 9). At the end of his time in office, he was confident enough about the validity of this judgment to reprint that text in its entirety unchanged in his memoirs. The inflexible and wasteful style of state agencies and their encouragement of 'moral hazard' is also urged against them (Patrick

Minford in Loney et al., 1991). The defence of the public sector, as it was developed during the 1980s, also addresses these general issues, arguing that in terms of efficiency, standards of performance and above all accountability the record is far better than these critics have implied (Stewart and Walsh, 1992). In addition, Patrick Dunleavy's careful dissection of the 'public choice' criticisms leads him to conclude that many of the conclusions reached are 'simply anti-organisational rather than distinctly relevant to the complex organisational structures of the public service' (1991, p. 173).

There is also a more pragmatic position: that the State is no more than a convenient instrument, and 'fools will use it, when they can, for foolish ends, criminals will use it when they can, for criminal ends. Sensible and decent people will use it for ends which are sensible and decent' (Tawney, 1966, p. 172). The powers-that-be are simply overworked and worried gentlemen and 'Leviathan is a pantomime monster; inside its skin are people like us, who deserve our sympathy, with whom it is not difficult to do business because we have so much in commom' (Forrester, 1989, p. 67). However, this description does not altogether fit the experience of Treasury rule over the 1980s and its main characteristics.

CHOICES FOR CHANGE

Both agendas, the state-led and market-driven rest ultimately on the freely chosen involvement of individual members of society – what it is now fashionable to call 'empowering'. But there are different sorts of power, exercised in different arenas. In setting objectives, it is important to be clear about which one we are primarily concerned with – the political forum, the market-place or the community. This will help to determine whether the prior concern is with the circumstances of citizens, the position of consumers or simply the situation of individuals. All three have been debated – in different ways – over the course of the 1980s.

Some find the key to achieving change in the political arena, and the importance of equipping individuals with the capacity to assert their preferences there and satisfy their needs. For these purposes, the question of rights becomes crucial – in particular, the extent to which rights that have real content can be conferred on citizens and exercised by them. This is particularly controversial when social rights are at issue. The existence of political rights *per se* is not in dispute – though the form in which they are exercised may be – and civil rights are as important to the New Right as to the left, though there is much debate about the ways in which they should be invoked.

Social rights are criticised as a concept on the right because the notion of entitlements against the State for the payment of benefits or delivery of services touches the heart of the dependency issue. Talk of conferring them also raises the related question of social justice. This is unacceptable to the right because it is held to link two mutually incompatible concepts: justice, which is concerned with legal adjudication; and social redistribution, which is an arbitrary and potentially tyrannical act of public policy (Minford in Loney et al., 1991, p. 78). To the extent that it has any meaning (the argument continues) the concept of social rights also needs to be balanced by a stress on obligations and duties. A more practical objection is that it is often impossible to guarantee the delivery of the particular goods and services to which a right of access has been given, either because of their scarcity or where there are conflicting claims upon them. This is one justification for stopping short of such guarantees in the Conservative Government's Citizen's Charter. Critics say that this is one reason why the Charter's title is misleading; if it were a charter for citizens it would provide access to the kind of remedies that citizens should possess – rights against the State deriving from their status as full members of the society – and adequate precedural means for enforcing them (Coote, 1992).

However, the British are subjects, not citizens; our constitution (to the extent that it exists at all) is unwritten, descending from time immemorial in forms that have been determined by custom and practice and which our forefathers chose in their wisdom to keep that way. There are three reasons why this is important in the present context. First, if we are to 'take rights seriously' (in Ronald Dworkin's phrase) we ought to be able to establish what they are. But in the absence of a written constitution and with courts still functioning on the basis of common law and precedent with no explicit constitutional function (unlike most European countries), that is not always easy. Second, there has been an accumulation of evidence over the 1980s that suggests that the absence of rights has adversely affected the situation of individual citizens, especially the most vulnerable, pushed to the margin of society and seen as being, in Ruth Lister's phrase, 'beyond the bounds of common citizenship'. And, third, if our status as citizens is to be the determining factor in enjoying the exercise of our rights we need to be able to use that status to secure the outcomes that we want through the political system.

In principle, this should not pose a problem. Britain is a democracy in which all adult citizens over 18 have the vote. But that does not necessarily close the argument. Democracy has, from time to time, been a central issue in determining the development of welfare – witness Beveridge's explicit appeal to democratic values in his launching and campaigning for his Plan (Beveridge, 1943). But those wartime years were not normal times. In the pattern that has become established over the course of the last decade, the expression of preferences on social policy rarely feeds through directly into electoral process at national level. Rather, general elections have become a form of plebiscite on economic management and the likely benefits for voters as consumers, decided by rules which confer power absolutely on the winner by first-past-the-post of the plurality of seats in the Commons, even when (as has happened twice in the postwar period) this is not the party with the largest number of votes. A choice of this kind, taken once every five years on the basis of manifestos which do not constitute any form of commitment is a check of sorts, but hardly an adequate one.

So, clearly expressed preferences – for example, public views on the proper balance between levels of taxation and public expenditure – have gone unheeded or been dismissed out of hand. Instead, there has been an attempt to instruct the electorate in what Keith Joseph called their 'innocence' about what they should be thinking about welfare issues. This unwillingness to listen would be less important with a different style of government, in which decisions are reached by debate and policies reviewed before implementation. But the style of post-1979 administrations turned sharply away from that approach – Margaret Thatcher went so far as to describe advocates of consensus 'as quislings, as traitors' (Gilmour, 1992, p. 30). Instead, power has been concentrated and used, without inhibition, in the nearest approximation to a command polity seen in peacetime Britain. The alternative points of entry for citizen preferences expressed through the ballot box at local elections have been downgraded in significance and the legitimacy of the claims of elected local authorities to representative status not conceded. By 1992, it seemed quite conceivable that wholesale abolition of local authorities might come to feature on the Government's longer-term agenda (Patten, 1992).

Representative democracy is therefore not the easy route into expression of individual wants and needs that it might appear to be. But the constitutional reform agenda as it has emerged in public debate, initially through the activities of the pressure group Charter 88, has been of considerable importance in clarifying the issues that have arisen as a result: for example, about lines of accountability and the exercise of checks on power of the executive. Participatory democracy raises other questions: we will come to them shortly.

CHANGE AND THE MARKET

Constitutional reform is not a popular cause with the present Government. That is hardly surprising: a fox loose in the hen-coop is unlikely to have much interest in charters for chickens. Instead, they have preferred to conceive of empowerment as being about customer choice. Mostly, this is to be exercised in the market: empowerment there is simply and straightforwardly a matter of having sufficient resources to be able to afford the goods and services that individuals want for themselves and their families. The consumption politics of the later 1980s – the vast cuts in direct taxes of the Lawson Chancellorship, in particular – have been all about providing people with the means to satisfy these wants and creating new aspirations which in turn can be satisfied through the market – paid for in cash or through credit. Those sufficiently well rewarded have been given a head start in competing for 'positional' goods – high quality housing and education, in particular. A safety net with a coarse mesh has been retained only for those without the necessary resources – since empowering them with too much cash runs into problems of disincentives and the 'employment trap'.

During what is in conception, at least, only an interim period, the public services have remained part of this system; but their style of operation and management have been transformed by the creation of quasi-markets, which introduce competition as a device to improve quality and choice. The 'Citizen's Charter', which exemplifies it is actually a consumer's charter – a transplantation of private sector values as a less satisfactory substitute for moving the service in its entirety into the private sector. 'Market testing' of services identifies additional functions of Government that can be contracted out to the private sector. The right way forward for service delivery has been the 'supermarket' approach about which Ian Gilmour is so satirical. This postulates a choice of welfare goods on display in rival stores and competition as the means to force prices down and keep quality up. Issues that remain unresolved include access to adequate information for making choices, especially in the light of restrictions imposed by 'commercial confidentiality'; and questions of quality – the emergence of two-tier services based on access to cash may mean 'Kwiksave' welfare for the poor.

The 'social market' as a concept takes the combination of market devices and State agencies for social welfare a stage further. One problem here is the inability of the social market's advocates to settle on a common definition. Those who trace the origins of the social-market concept in Britain back to its origins in West Germany after the Second World War and stress the link with Christian Democrat assumptions there about the functions of welfare (Marquand, Skidelsky, Willetts) postulate a different and more positive role for the State than those who underline the market half of the equation (Thatcher, Ridley). Over the 1980s it has been the latter approach – a market economy in the full sense but 'with social obligations', to be met by the State only in cases where the market cannot deliver (Ridley, 1992, p. 78) which has predominated in Government policy. But this experience has not resolved the confusion about final ends; in the last resort, are the two concepts compatible, or are they like 'social justice' in the right-wing critique, oil and water? As we've seen, some Conservative politicians argue that they cannot be reconciled and that one of the two will incorporate or expel the other. So, too, from the opposite position would many local government critics, who suggest that the distinctive character of the public service and the services that it performs cannot be properly recognised by 'slapping on' the vocabulary and apparatus of the market – what is sometimes called 'marketisation'.

This concern about the implications of a switch towards market values, even if this remains partial and stabilises at the half-way point in some hybrid combination reflects a belief that some characteristics of the market in action are by definition unsocial – 'jugular' competition for profits and the elimination of competitors to improve market position, to take only the most obvious examples. If the four Chapter 1 tests are applied, the basic claim is that by expanding choice markets guarantee liberty. But as William Blake put it, 'one law for the ox and ass is tyranny' – those who enter the market with greater resources are likely to prosper at the expense of those who lack the strength to do so. Advocates of the market-driven approach would reply that the market is also concerned with equity: freedom to compete on equal terms is the basis for Arthur Seldon's claim that markets are more just, as well as being more efficient. It is their dislike of the egalitarian enterprise – equality imposed by state intervention – which led Margaret Thatcher to dismiss the notion that the pursuit of equality could make any contribution; as she put in when in opposition 'the promotion of greater equality goes hand in hand with the extension of the welfare state and State control over people's lives' (1977, p. 6). So, although equality of opportunity has been a standard (if sometimes contested) theme of British Conservatism over the postwar period (and goes back to de Tocqueville) it has become progressively less prominent as an objective over the 1980s. Rather, the emphasis has been on efficiency, with a side glance at the potentiality of reform to revive an active sense of community (an increasingly important element in third-term rhetoric).

Can the 'excluded middle' left by the implementation of the Conservative agenda be filled by developing community-based alternatives? In principle, a focus on that much misunderstood term 'community' may provide some common ground. The claim on the right is that the community is a seedbed of new innovation that fits snugly inside the market-choice paradigm (Willetts, 1992). A community-based approach even has something to contribute on the Conservatives' remoralisation agenda. In part this is nostalgia – a longing glance backwards to a rural England where social control based on traditional values could be exercised by squire and vicar and their agents (schoolmaster and policeman) in an obedient village community in which the young knew their place – or left. In part, in the American version, the neighbourhood is presented as the site of new opportunities for entrepreneurs and, in particular, newcomers to the city (Murray, 1990). In hard fact, the world of the urban poor in Britain during the 1980s, as seen from the bottom-up has been very different. The heroic struggles of some tenants' self-help groups on severely deprived local authority estates against problems of crime, poverty and drug abuse stand out in sharp relief as an example of what can be achieved against all the odds; David Donnison's account of the Scottish experience underlines how much depends on the involvement of a few outstanding individuals (mostly women). But as he also warns, the intensity of experience and activity over the short term may decay or even become distorted over longer periods (1991, ch. 6). Nor is the support that such groups require always forthcoming at the time and in the form that they most need it; this may be especially true of black groups and their particular needs which may not fit the template of the 'contract culture'. The problem of creating and sustaining a working relationship to statutory bodies may be particularly acute for groups catering for special needs which aren't universally accepted as valid. For example, the London Lighthouse, which has pioneered integrated provision of facilities for people with AIDS, continues to encounter problems in securing a stable basis of long-term support.

Sympathetic advocacy has its place here, of the kind that the Archbishop of Canterbury's Committee on Urban Priority Areas were able to provide in their report. At the same time it is important to 'keep cool heads' (as Donnison warns) and not go uncritically down the path towards entrusting all or even the bulk of provision to community-based action. An alternative signpost points towards a mixed or 'pluralistic' solution, combining the efficiency goal with a more democratic perspective and an egalitarian style.

This implies a more substantial role for formal voluntary organisations, a route which the Government has followed over the course of the 1980s. This has helped to generate a love–hate relationship between voluntary bodies and the Government. Voluntary organisations have been conscripted to take on service delivery functions in a number of policy areas – 'shaped to fit' the gap the Government has created by pushing aside local statutory bodies. Community care is a good example of a policy area in which this approach has been adopted. Yet the Government has exhibited some confusion about the nature of their new allies: are they to be seen essentially as volunteers (highly laudable), voluntary associations (good things in general) or pressure groups (thoroughly bad)? The first image has been reinforced by ministerial rhetoric: volunteers are portrayed as virtuously 'active citizens'. But there has also been a hankering to incorporate some larger organisations, especially the church-based groups, in the remoralisation project, and a corresponding disillusionment when they have preferred to continue to provide advocacy on their own terms.

So in practice, the Government has found it easier to deal with national organisations, even at the cost of a certain amount of pantomime about independence (see page 159). A sharper appreciation about the limits of what could be achieved developed in Government in the later 1980s, especially after the Home Office had undertaken its 'Efficiency Scrutiny' on central government's dealings with the voluntary sector (1990). In a White Paper issued immediately before the 1992 general election, with a preface by the Prime Minister, the Government reasserted its commitment to the independence of the voluntary sector and set out new goals for statutory–voluntary collaboration. But the White Paper blurs the issues by trying to introduce the concept of socially responsible business as part of the same process – a striking contrast with what William Beveridge had to say in his *Voluntary Action* (1948) about the 'business motive' as 'a good servant but a bad master' and another reminder of the wide gulf between Beveridge's values and those of his successors in the Conservative Government of the 1980s.

BEYOND THE RHETORIC OF CRISIS

Over the course of the early 1990s, discussions of the future of welfare have shown a tendency to revert to assumptions last advanced in the early 1980s: namely, that the costs involved will inevitably constitute an insupportable burden on an economy now seen as too fragile to sustain future expenditure at the present level. As Peter Lilley, Secretary of State for Social Security, put it when launching his version of a 'great debate' on the future of the social security system:

> The message that underlying growth in social security has exceeded, and will continue to exceed, growth in the economy is an uncomfortable one. But it must be faced . . . it is not possible for the system to continue indefinitely to grow more rapidly than the economy as a whole. (Department of Social Security, 1993, p. 3)

The significance of this message was unmistakable, especially coming at a time when the British economy had just experienced a prolonged period of 'negative growth'. Other arguments are also adduced, many of them very similar to those advanced in the previous 'crisis' debate: demographic pressures, the problem of higher unemployment, social change (in particular, the growth in the numbers of single parents). However, the demographic pressures are not in fact as great as this implies, at least until the next century – as the Department themselves comment, 'the numbers of pensioners will rise very little before 1999/2000' (this was a point also made by Norman Fowler in the course of the last 'crisis' debate); and unemployment is at least in part a function of policy priorities and successful economic management, not a given. Forecasts of increased expenditure on social security are highly sensitive to projections about economic growth: the Department of Social Security's 'Case 2' forecast (p. 13), made on the basis of a 2.5 per cent annual increase in GDP and unemployment reduced by three-quarters of a million has expenditure on social security almost static as a proportion of GDP – the Government's current standard measure – at the end of the century. These forecasts are of particular interest, given how rapidly previous 'crisis' talk evaporated in the mid-1980s when the secret of steady growth was apparently discovered, followed by three years of increase in the GDP at the level of the DSS forecast (and higher) and an equivalent drop in the level of unemployment, before Lawson's Midas touch deserted him.

However, even if the immediate sense of crisis once again subsides – and there are reasons for believing that the effects of the second Conservative recession will take longer to dispel – a more general problem remains. All recent governments have shown a well-developed tendency to view each and every issue through the prism of its public expenditure implications. Clearly, the cost of welfare policies must always be a legitimate element in the political discussions and a central concern for ministers in charge of spending departments, who will need to be able to present and defend policy proposals convincingly in those terms. But the discipline of identifying the cost factor has too often been used not to define choices but to cut off debate. Successive Chancellors of different parties – notably Nigel Lawson but to some degree all those who have held the post – have been eager to use the authority which successive Prime Ministers have given them to assert the inevitable primacy of economic goals. This concentration on costs (narrowly conceived, in money terms) inevitably distorts the decision-taking process.

A second leading characteristic of the debate over the past decade has been that it has been extraordinarily parochial. Assumptions about the unparalleled generosity of the British system of welfare and the unique character of the problems that face us survive largely unchallenged and even, on occasion, stoked up by ministerial rhetoric, impervious to all evidence to the contrary. It is proper that the experience of other countries should be treated with caution as a source of new policy initiatives; different histories and cultures ensure that structures and values differ, often in crucial respects. Yet debates about the future of welfare have been part of the common experience of all Western countries over the past decade. Moreover, the second half of the decade has seen the tentative beginnings of the emergence of a European social policy, based on initiatives taken by the European Commission in the field of employment and symbolised by the inclusion of the Social Chapter in the Maastricht Treaty on European Union. Yet only in the case of the United States has there been any significant attempt at systematic transfer of experience. Misled by the possession of a common language, politicians on both sides of the Atlantic have attempted to transplant ideas and policies which, in A.H. Halsey's phrase, have often proved too soggy on arrival after the crossing to be of any practical use. The experience of the attempt to devise a British equivalent to 'workfare' schemes is only one example among many across the whole range of welfare services.

Ideas generated by transatlantic think-tanks (filtered through their local associates) have nevertheless received a ready hearing, especially during the closed phase of policy development just before and during the third term of the Thatcher Government. By contrast, other sources of new ideas have not been welcomed. The departure from office of Margaret Thatcher might have been the moment when that changed. Without the force of her personality and deeply-felt convictions it is doubtful – as others closely involved acknowledge – whether the third-term reforms on social policy would have acquired the momentum or taken the distinctive shape that they did. But in view of the electoral impact of the health service reforms and the catalogue of detailed difficulties that emerged in the course of implementation elsewhere (even leaving on one side the extreme case of the poll tax), the occasion of her departure from office might have been taken to review the content and style of policy, especially given John Major's early attempts to establish a more conciliatory approach. There are examples of consensus legislation during this period (Children Act 1989, Criminal Justice Act 1991); and the setting up of a Royal Commission on Criminal Justice broke the pattern of closed internal review established during the Thatcher years. But in most key respects, the bandwagon of the third-term reform has rolled on since along the same tracks; drawing on the same narrow spectrum of ideas and exhibiting the same determination not to take account of criticisms from outside the charmed circle, let alone alternative analyses which suggest different principles on which the system of welfare could be founded.

The most conspicuous example of these exclusions is the feminist critique of welfare, now well developed with a substantial literature and important lessons to teach on how policy and provision interact, especially in the area of informal care. Yet feminist accounts of the objectives and outcomes of new social policies have been treated with a mixture of caution and condescension, descending in the case of some ministers to crude caricature. It is, of course, precisely the fact that feminism provides a view from an entirely different perspective and one not capable of being assimilated into the conventional frame of reference that gives the critique its particular strength, which requires consideration in its own right and on its own terms.

Much the same is true of other types of dissent from the orthodox position – for example, the black perspective that treats the established fact of endemic discrimination by individuals and institutions, public and private, on racial grounds not as a peripheral phenomenon but a central fact about British society, its values and the hierarchies of power and prestige within it, that the Thatcher episode – for all its self-proclaimed radicalism – did so little to change. Or there are those critics who have been asking fundamental questions about the continued viability of current modes of economic organisation. Although the reappearance of mass unemployment has been traumatic in its effects in the field of welfare, the assumption that has developed over the course of the decade has been that society can adapt without excessive dislocation to the existence of continued high levels of unemployment. But the longer-term social and financial costs of such an adaptation remain a matter of speculation; and the measures that would be needed to address the consequent problems have barely even been sketched. The implications for the future organisation of welfare remain to be explored and unorthodox perspectives from outside the political mainstream have potentially important insights to offer, if only such exploration were to take place.

However, this is not likely to take place while the present Government remains in power. One of the leading characteristics of this period of Conservative rule has been the confident assumption that answers to the main questions are already known (although they were a little slow in appearing in the social policy field) and that any debate that may be necessary can therefore be concentrated upon questions of implementation. One of the missing elements in this argument is the question of public consent, assumed to have been conferred by electoral mandate. Not merely has any other evidence been dismissed as irrelevant or positively misleading, including the sequence of findings on public attitudes towards welfare contained in successive British Social Attitude Surveys; even the outcomes of the exercise of local choice built into recent legislation on housing and education have been questioned or in extreme cases set aside on the ground that they do not represent real preferences. As Ian Gilmour puts it:

> the market was God to Thatcherites except when the consumers wanted a non-Thatcherite product. Then, provided the electoral dangers could be contained, their wants were ignored. They might want improved social services; what they were going to get was more tax cuts (at least if they were quite well off), since that was what was better for them. (1992, p. 175)

But despite this bland assumption that politicians know what is good for the electorate better than they do themselves and that the Government therefore possess a mandate to force them to be free (the kind of approach that the same politicians once denounced as 'paternalist') important issues of principle remain unresolved. Put in its most basic form, there is still fundamental disagreement about the objectives that any system of welfare should be designed to meet. Further, this would still be the case whether the system was based on provision by the State, the market, through informal care or by any combination of the three. Such disagreement goes far beyond the choices implied in Lenin's once-notorious query, 'who-whom?' – or, translated into this context, who benefits from welfare and at whose expense? That is an important question; but it does not go far enough. More important still is the question of who *should* benefit and why. And to answer that question directly involves deciding which set of values should determine policy in this field.

While this revised text was in the course of preparation, the new leader of the Labour Party, John Smith, took the decision to establish a Commission on Social Justice to address these questions. The remit for the exercise was broadly drawn and members of other political parties included; in its preliminary reports, the Commission has laid great stress on the importance of recognising that welfare policies raise central and not subordinate questions about the relationship between the State, the citizen and the collection of formal and informal associations that lie between them (Commission on Social Justice, 1993a and b). If carried through to the preparation of the Commission's main report, this approach should help to illuminate areas which have too often remained in obscurity. Welfare, if viewed in the round, is not simply a transaction between the State and its poorest citizens administered through bureaucratic agencies, but a complex network of relationships involving substantial transfers of resources through the tax system and burgeoning occupational welfare schemes as well as direct provision of services and income support. The growth of the 'middle class welfare state' which until recently has proceeded largely unremarked – although the sums involved easily match the scale of expenditure on what is conventionally regarded as 'welfare' – comes into focus if this broader perspective is adopted.

TOWARDS A NEW SOCIAL POLICY?

Four different values were paraded for inspection at the beginning of this survey. Impatient readers might be forgiven for wondering at this point whether the author will ever be prepared to flop off the fence and declare his own preferences. Given that the basis of the argument throughout has been that to be effective social policies cannot be merely exercises in technical analysis (important though these are in context) but must be informed by a clear vision of the kind of society they are intended to sustain, that is a legitimate expectation. Any attempt to meet it must be subject to qualification; for reasons perhaps sufficiently stressed already, there cannot be a single clear-cut choice between them. As the Commission on Social Justice remarked in their first report, *The Justice Gap*, it is important 'to guard against all-or-nothing assumptions. It is not true that either we have a complete top-down theory or we are left only with mere prejudice and subservience to the polls.' Some values will inevitably conflict with one another, although 'reflection may not eliminate all conflicts, but it can help us to understand them, and then arrive at policy choices' (1993b, p. 7).

Fortified by this comforting assertion, I would suggest that, at least for the present, the most important of the four values is equality, in part because it has been the most neglected over the past decade. If this is the case, there are some central problems of implementation to be faced. A strategy of equality, if it is to be more effective than it was when attempted (admittedly with all manner of reservations and restrictions) during the immediate postwar period, necessarily involves direct and sustained use of the powers of the central State. This would almost certainly imply not merely intervention through changes in the level and pattern of taxation and redistribution of the resulting resources but other forms of positive intervention designed explicitly to promote the interests of those who face insuperable disadvantages in current circumstances. Some of these interventions could take the form of legislation to extend the range of entitlements; but the effectiveness of such new departures would rest on the extent to which machinery exists, at central or local level, to ensure that they reach those for whom they are intended.

As we have already seen, there are two familiar objections to such an approach. The first, from the right, is that intervention of this kind is simply illegitimate; it fractures the implied contract between State and citizen by invading areas of personal choice and responsibility and comandeering private resources to do so. The second is that the effectiveness of such a strategy would depend on the efficiency of State institutions – precisely the area where left and right agree that performance has been grossly deficient over the whole postwar period.

But in the classic case for equality made by R.H. Tawney sixty years ago – some parts of which have now lost their force – there is an additional element that may be helpful. The project as he defines it is concerned not merely with the ending of the grosser forms of inequality, which he dismisses as a relatively straightforward technical operation (Tawney, 1964, p. 29). It is also about the creation and maintenance of a common culture, in which mutual aid and 'fellowship' (an awkwardly stiff Edwardian term for what the late twentieth century prefers to call, without much greater precision, community) replace the 'tadpole' values of a competitive capitalism which seeks to retain the loyalty of its citizens by offering them a one-in-a-thousand chance of turning into a prosperous frog. The importance of such a common culture, for which greater social and economic equality provides the keystone, is the central element in any case for a revised collectivism.

Like many of the terms employed in the current debate, the concept of collectivism has been drained of most of its meaning by recent abusage. But it can still be defined by reference to its polar opposite: unconstructed individualism and the approach to social policy that this implies, encapsulated in Margaret Thatcher's well-known comment that 'there is no such thing as society'. Capitalism may indeed be, in Nozick's phrase, a 'transaction between consenting adults'; but the conclusion that follows – that when it ends badly for one of the participants (let alone the bystanders or their families) this cannot be helped – is unacceptable. A system that leaves no place for exchanges of other kinds – and indeed mocks the notion that moral transactions can occur even within a market framework which do not involve direct financial gain – is incompatible with the kind of approach based, however loosely, on a revival of Tawney's values.

Now that welfare has been allocated a place at the centre of Government policy, rather than at the margin, what function should it be expected to perform? Traditionally, conservatism in its paternalist mode regards welfare as a statutory version of philanthropy – a means of discharging society's moral obligations to the poor. Such an approach is defensible in its own terms; but incompatible with an approach which views equality based on common citizenship as the main objective of policy. As Richard Titmuss commented in reintroducing Tawney's *Equality* to the British public in 1964, the Conservative prescription means that 'in the natural process of market levitation all groups will stand expectantly on the political right, as the escalator of growth moves them up' (Tawney, 1964, p. 18). The alternative is explicitly egalitarian;

but equality not just as an end in itself and welfare not solely as the means to achieve it, important though it may be in achieving redistribution of resources. Rather, the closer integration of society and minimising of the risk of alienation are the ultimate objectives (Deacon, 1993). In such a perspective, access to welfare becomes, in an image worn down by repeated use, the 'badge of citizenship'. But it cannot perform that function if there are not one but several badges, for admission by different doors and when the services to which they provide access and the treatment clients receive there are different. The fragmentation of welfare services and variations in quality between different segments helps to entrench these differences (essentially, differences of class). In certain areas of welfare, this process of differentiation is already well under way, as the more successful schools and hospitals 'opt out' of the State system, gliding down a slipway lubricated by the lavish application of public funds. So, although the quality of service received by clients using State welfare services provided the New Right with one of its most powerful arguments their policies in office have in their outcomes confirmed the shift towards a two-tier system of welfare, with the lower tier reserved for the poor. To be fair, equality of standards of provision was never on their policy agenda – witness Margaret Thatcher's illuminating comments to Nicholas Ridley about the impossibility of providing State services that match the quality of the private sector (see page 170).

Another model for providing welfare – sometimes known as 'Hobbit socialism' – stresses the equal status of all those involved in the transaction; client (or consumer) and worker dissolve and roles are exchanged spontaneously, as the need arises. There is much that is attractive in this image of welfare as a gift freely shared; it taps the still strongly implanted roots of concern for the stranger in need which forms part of the Christian inheritance that most of the left are now too embarrassed to acknowledge openly (Ignatieff, 1984, p. 139). At the same time, it is often naive and limited in its application, lacking the analytical capacity to address the issues that arise when (for example) rising unemployment destroys the social, as well as the economic base of communities and Hobbesian questions of survival in a nasty and brutish world confront the hobbits.

The challenge is how to retain the valuable elements in this attempt to work outside conventional structures without slipping back into the style of corporate socialism which generated such deep disillusionment in the 1970s; or giving unnecessary hostages to economic determinism, with its automatic assertion that priority should be given in all circumstances to the state of the economy.

The orthodox answer has been to attempt to uncouple means and ends; in other words, to view the use of State bureaucracies (local or central) to deliver services, privatisation of some and contracting with voluntary or for-profit agencies to provide others, or the devolution of responsibility to the community or to individuals merely as a choice between different techniques, any or all of which may be appropriate in particular circumstances. Ownership of the agency that provides the service is in this approach a secondary question; what matters is the quality of what is provided. This is the approach through 'welfare pluralism', one version of which is reflected in the reforms of social services that were introduced during the third term. In political terms, it implies the possibility that a new Middle Way can be driven between competing models of welfare to left and right.

Yet choices between different modes of delivering welfare imply consequences which go beyond straightforward issues of efficiency. To rely in the search for alternatives to the market upon State institutions whose credibility has been severely impaired, or upon informal solutions where the responsibility rests on voluntary bodies staffed and even run largely on good will, or on simply passing the burden down the line to the carer of last resort, the woman in the household, involves making sweeping assumptions about the availability of resources and the capacity of institutions to change and adapt – for which evidence is still lacking.

One alternative route into this difficult area is through placing greater emphasis on the value that has a central place in Tawney's scheme, but has been ostentatiously set on one side by the right: democracy. For all that it figures so prominently in party liturgies, translating the principle of greater democracy in welfare into practice is not a simple matter. Democracy implies conferring a capacity to make real choices, with the corollary that those choices may not always be to the liking of those who believe they know best. There are difficult and important issues about how the constituencies that make these choices shall be defined, on the basis of neighbourhood, or by interest or circumstance, and by whom. Something of the tension that these problems can produce is visible in the behaviour on those on the left and right alike, who would clearly prefer, like the one-time dictator of Pakistan, Ayub Khan, a 'guided' democracy. Much talk about enfranchising minorities and empowering communities has ended with carefully structured agendas and hierarchies of representation through which vested interests can preserve their control over events. On the other extreme, compulsory democracy can too easily lead to sterile repetition of arguments over progressively less significant issues, so that the local people in whose name the debate was joined in the first place slip away and abandon the field altogether to the compulsive attenders of meetings, with their not always entirely disinterested motives. Bertrand Russell was not altogether wrong when he observed that: 'a fanatical belief in democracy makes democratic institutions impossible' (quoted in Pym, 1985, p. 96).

Yet with all its deficiencies, democracy may still provide the most helpful way out of the impasse. A social policy based on democracy would have something important to contribute through making institutions more accountable for meeting the needs of their users, which neither the advocates of choice through the market nor the dwindling band of State centralisers can match. This implies creating a system in which citizen choice is not exercised just through the ballot box and one in which the need for free and unbiased circulation of information on which difficult and complex choices can be made is fully satisfied. If that need is met, the retention at the centre of the function of resource allocation and power to review the standards of services provided poses less difficulty. Effective democracy suggests smaller rather than larger units of government, but with closer linkages between them, so that the effects of the separation of functions between the elected and non-elected sectors that now causes such difficulty at local level is reduced to the minimum.

Accountability should be a key virtue in such a reformed system. I have referred earlier to the debate that has taken place over market-based accountability (see page 160). The difficulty that defenders of the reformed system have not satisfactorily confronted is that, whatever its merits in providing improved access for individual complainants, if conflicts of interest arise between users and providers when those in charge are appointees rather than elected their response will be determined by the attitudes of those who appointed them – that is, directly or indirectly, ministers. Nevertheless, it is important that accountability should be exercised not only through the process of election or through the machinery of local political parties but by making better provision for those chosen as representatives to deal directly with those who choose them.

Since welfare issues, especially in health and social services, are increasingly liable to become matters of local controversy the processes of accountability are certain to become increasingly significant. Here, the move towards decentralisation of local government services may help to provide solutions by developing new forms of representation evolving from local neighbourhood forums. A system which places stress on democracy ought always to be open to change; and especially to the value of new ideas that come from the locality, where the context in which social policy has to be applied is often better understood than it is at the centre. Such a system would not be dogmatic about forms of cooperation between different agencies and individuals with different perspectives and loyalties; producers will participate, but not dominate. Above all, a democratic model of welfare would give the maximum possible scope for people to manage and where they freely choose to do so provide their own services: tenant cooperatives, self-help groups for those facing particular problems, even social service agencies. It would provide technical advice and financial assistance for those that require it; but it would not make such participation a condition of receiving help.

That such an approach is Utopian goes almost without saying; though, as Oscar Wilde once remarked, a map of the world on which Utopia does not appear is not worth having. Demoralisation, not all of it produced by lack of resources, is now well advanced in many of the areas where some form of new intervention is now essential. These are too often precisely the areas where voluntary associations are at their weakest, and the stresses on those who might otherwise play an active role as individuals strongest. Faced with such formidable practical problems, to invest in such solutions would be an act of faith; but it is worth remembering that the title of the report produced by the Archbishop's Committee on urban priority areas after two years spent in close contact with precisely these issues was 'faith in the city'.

The social policy literature, perhaps surprisingly for what is often taken to be – a dry and statistical subject – is full of recurrent images. One, in particular, that reappears again and again over fifty years, is that of the garden. The originators of the new welfare policies portrayed themselves as gardeners planting the seeds; their successors saw their task as good husbandry: nurturing the plants and filling up the empty beds. Clement Attlee (who described himself as a 'rough gardener') claimed to have learnt from politics the importance of ruthless weeding. Other critics preferred to prune; or the more belligerent to eliminate parasites. Tory wets discussed the draining of the soil. Monetarists, like Milton Friedman, compared their universe to a Japanese garden, small and perfectly formed – or deformed, their critics might say. Richard Titmuss registered his scepticism about the concept of care in the community by referring to it as 'that everlasting cottage-garden trailer' (Titmuss, 1968, p. 104).

Probably this says no more than that the British, of all classes and both genders, have a well-developed national passion for a pursuit in which they can freely express in visible form their own individual creativity and impose where and when they wish a little order, however fleeting, on their surroundings. But I believe that it is not a coincidence that it is those postwar social policies that have run with this grain – the homely, perhaps at times constricting, British version of New Jerusalem that has grown up half-planned and half-spontaneously in the garden cities (public and private) and suburbs – that have succeeded in keeping the loyalties of their inhabitants, where the tower blocks of the municipal housing empires and the mansion blocks of the developers have failed. A willingness to accept the implications of that lesson would be an important step towards a new approach to social policy, which might then come closer to being, as the philosopher R.G. Collingwood once put it, 'a nursery-garden where policies were brought to maturity in the open air, not a post office for distributing ready-made policies to a passive country' (1944, p. 103).

APPENDIX

Introduction

The main body of the text is intended as a narrative account of the events in the political arena; and, as such, I have not burdened it with an additional apparatus of tables or detailed analyses of data. However, there are some issues on which readers may want to have further information or where the argument could helpfully be amplified by reference to data in tabular form. This appendix has been prepared to meet these needs. The data have been drawn largely from official Government sources although this, as attentive readers of the text will know, does not automatically guarantee their reliability as a basis for reaching conclusions on official policies. Information has been assembled in four groups. First, there is a brief section dealing with some demographic and social changes, both past and in prospect, that are of particular importance for the evolution of social policy. A second group covers developments in the economic arena: public expenditure – the focus of much debate during the 1980s – growth, levels of inflation and a collection dealing with the contested issue of unemployment (using both official counts and those employing earlier definitions). A third group provides information about levels of income, distributions and the extent of poverty. Readers should be able to judge for themselves the validity of rival claims made about the diffusion of wealth within this society. Finally, another group presents data about attitudes, drawn from the independent British Social Attitudes Survey and on a social issue that I judge to be of particular significance: homelessness.

All selections of this kind are bound to be to some extent arbitrary and this one is no exception. I leave it to the good sense of readers to decide when and how best to use this information.

DEMOGRAPHIC AND SOCIAL CHANGE

Table A. 1 Age and sex structure of the population
United Kingdom

Percentages and millions

	Under 16	16–39	40–64	65–79	80 and over	All ages (= 100%) (millions)
Mid-year estimates						
1951	24.8	31.4	31.6	9.5	1.4	50.3
1961	25.6	31.3	32.0	9.8	1.9	52.8
1971	25.5	31.3	29.9	10.9	2.3	55.9
1981	22.2	34.9	27.8	12.2	2.8	56.4
1991	20.3	35.2	28.7	12.0	3.7	57.6
Males	21.4	36.5	29.1	10.7	2.3	28.1
Females	19.3	34.0	28.3	13.3	5.1	29.5
Mid-year projections[1]						
2001	21.3	32.6	30.5	11.4	4.2	59.2
2011	20.1	30.0	33.7	11.7	4.5	60.0
2021	19.5	30.5	31.9	13.6	4.5	60.7
Males	20.2	31.6	32.1	12.7	3.4	30.0
Females	18.7	29.5	31.6	14.5	5.7	30.7

1 1989-based projections.

Source: Social Trends, 3, 1993.

percentage of population in 0–19, 20–59 and 60+ age bands

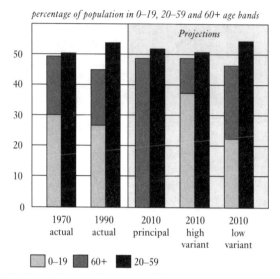

Figure A.1 Population Age Structure, 1970 to 1990–2010 (*Source*: Policy Studies Institute, 1992)

Great Britain

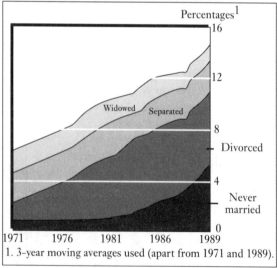

Figure A.2 Proportion of all families with dependent children headed by lone mothers: by marital status (*Source*: Office of Population Censuses and Surveys)

ECONOMIC PERFORMANCE

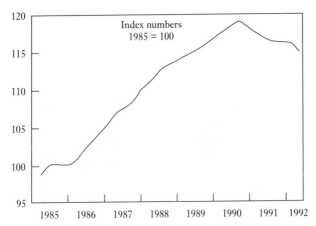

Figure A.3 Gross domestic product (GDP) at 1985 market prices (*Source*: Treasury Economic Brief, Autumn 1992)

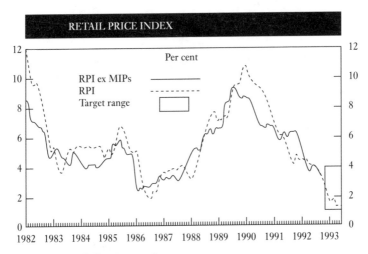

RPI and RPI excluding mortgage interest payments

Figure A.4 Retail price index 1982–93, including and excluding mortgage interest payments (*Source*: Treasury Economic Brief: Autumn 1993)

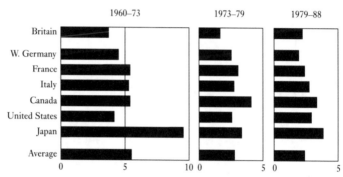

| | 1960–73 | 1973–79 | 1979–88 |

Economic circumstances have differed greatly in the three periods 1960–73, 1973–79 and 1979–88; but in all three of them economic growth in Britain was well below the average of the 'Group of Seven' countries.

Figure A.5 International Economic growth rates, gross domestic product: average percentage growth per year of 'Group of Seven countries (*Source*: Policy Studies Institute, 1992)

PUBLIC EXPENDITURE

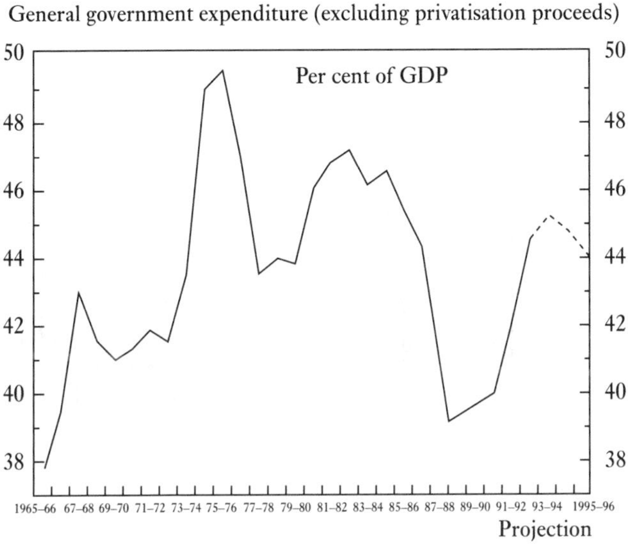

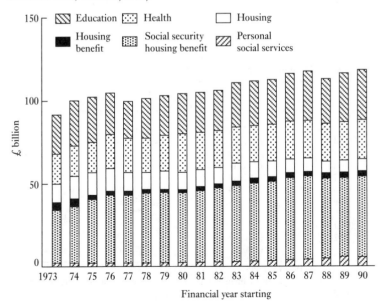

General government expenditure (excluding privatisation proceeds)

Per cent of GDP

1965–66 67–68 69–70 71–72 73–74 75–76 77–78 79–80 81–82 83–84 85–86 87–88 89–90 91–92 93–94 1995–96

Projection

Figure A.6   Trends in Government spending (*Source*: HM Treasury, *Autumn Statement 1992*, HMSO, 1992)

Education   Health   Housing

Housing benefit   Social security housing benefit   Personal social services

£ billion

1973 74 75 76 77 78 79 80 81 82 83 84 85 86 87 88 89 90

Financial year starting

Figure A.7   Public spending on welfare in the United Kingdom in £ billion 1973–90 (1990–1 prices) (*Source*: Glennerster, 1992)

238   *Appendix*

UNEMPLOYMENT

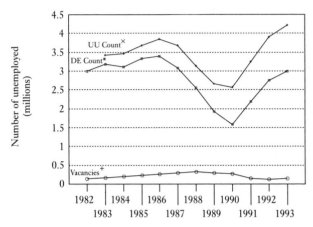

× Unemployment unit count.
* Department of Employment count from 1985, covers benefit claimants only.
+ From 1985 vacancy figures include self-employed vacancies in addition to those for employees.

Figure A.8 UK unemployment and vacancies, 1982–93 (not seasonally adjusted) (*Source*: Unemployment Unit Working Brief, June 1993)

Table A.2 UK unemployment & vacancies (not seasonally adjusted)

	Unemployment (DE Count[††])	Unemployment (UU Count)	[†]Vacancies
Apl. 1982	3,007,800	n/a	116,000
Apl. 1983	3,169,900	3,414,400	140,800
Apl. 1984	3,107,700	3,493,400	155,100
Apl. 1985	3,272,600	3,672,500	173,900
Apl. 1986	3,325,100	3,781,200	197,700
Apl. 1987	3,107,100	3,670,500	240,000
Apl. 1988	2,536,000	3,165,300	282,200
Apl. 1989	1,883,600	2,659,200	216,800
Apl. 1990	1,626,300	2,534,500	193,600
Apl. 1991	2,198,400	3,276,700	119,000
Apl. 1992	2,736,600	3,882,700	117,000
Apl. 1993	3,000,500	4,173,400	124,100

[††] From October 1982 unemployed count covers claimants only.
[†] From 1985 vacancy figures include self-employed vacancies in addition to those for employees.

Table A.3 UK long-term unemployment: unemployed for greater than 12 months (not seasonally adjusted)

	April 1986	April 1990	April 1991	April 1992	Jan 1993	April 1993
Men	1,033,036	425,536	447,571	693,967	855,853	892,730
Women	323,473	114,189	107,486	146,882	174,430	182,337
All	1,356,509	539,725	555,057	840,849	1,030,283	1,075,067

Source: Unemployment Unit Briefing, June 1993.

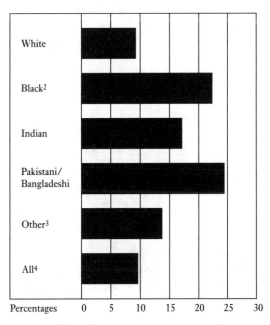

1. Unemployed based on the ILO definition as a percentage of all economically active.
2. Includes Caribbean, African and other black people of non-mixed origin.
3. Includes Chinese, other ethnic minority groups of non-mixed origin and people of mixed origin.
4. Includes ethnic group not stated.

Figure A. 9 Unemployment rates[1]: by ethnic origin, Spring 1992 (*Source*: *Social Trends* 23, 1993)

POVERTY AND INCOME DISTRIBUTION

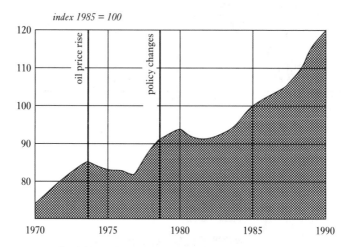

Figure A.10   Real disposable income per head, 1970–90 (*Source*: Policy Studies Institute, 1992)

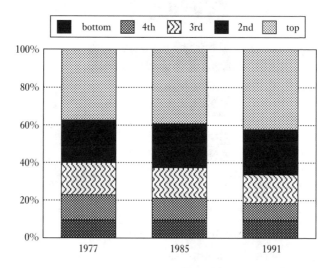

* All figures use Government equivalence scales, which take account of household size. All figures are after taxation, including indirect taxation, and benefits.

Figure A.11   The changing distribution of income in the UK* (*Source*: Commission on Social Justice, 1993b)

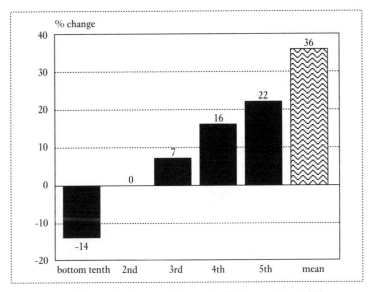

Figure A.12 Change in income of bottom half of population 1979 to 1990–1 (*Source*: Commission on Social Justice, 1993b)

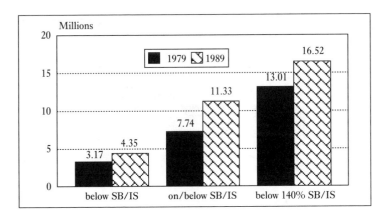

Figure A.13 Numbers of people in poverty in 1979 and 1989 (*Source*: Commission on Social Justice, 1993b)

PUBLIC ATTITUDES TO WELFARE

Table A.4   The debate on public spending vs. taxation

Suppose the government had to choose between the three options on this card
*Which do you think it should choose?**

	1983 %	1986 %	1989 %
Reduce taxes and spend less on health, education and social benefits	9	5	3
Keep taxes and spending on these services at the same level as now	54	44	37
Increase taxes and spend more on health, eduation and social benefits	32	46	46

*Figures for three years only are shown but the trend is consistent over the six readings.
Source: R. Jowell et al., *British Social Attitudes* (Gower, 1990).

Table A.5   Priorities for extra Government spending*

	First priority		Second priority	
	1983 %	1989 %	1983 %	1989 %
Health	37	61	26	23
Education	24	19	26	36
Help for industry	16	2	13	5
Housing	7	7	13	15
Social security benefits	6	5	6	9

*Defence, public transport, roads, police and prisons and overseas aid attracted no more than 4 per cent support in any year and so are omitted from this table.
Source: R. Jowell et al., *British Social Attitudes* (Gower, 1990).

Table A. 6 Images of the Welfare State

	1983	1989
% agreeing that		
The Welfare State makes people nowadays less willing to look after themselves	52%	39%
The Welfare State encourages people to stop helping each other	37%	32%
People receiving social security are made to feel like second class citizens	48%	53%
Social workers have too much power to interfere with people's lives	47%	36%

Source: R. Jowell et al., *British Social Attitudes* (Gower, 1990).

HOMELESSNESS

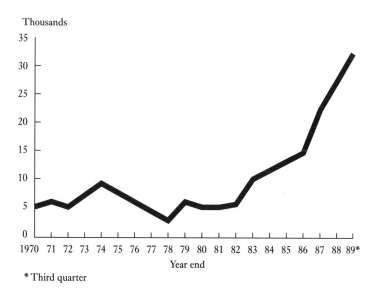

Thousands

* Third quarter

Figure A.14 Homeless households in temporary accommodation at year ends (England) (*Source*: DHSS and DOE homelessness statistics)

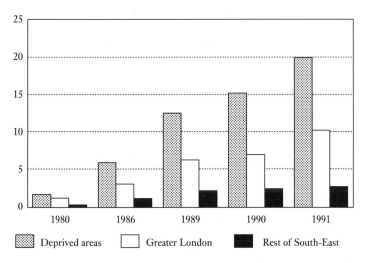

Figure A.15 Households in temporary accommodation: London and South-East region, end-June, per 1,000 households (*Source*: *Urban Trends* 1, 1992)

BIBLIOGRAPHY

Abel-Smith, B. (1966) *Labour's Social Plans*, London, Fabian Tract, 369.

Archbishop of Canterbury's Commission on Urban Priority Areas (1985) *Faith in the City: A Call for Action by Church and Nation*, London, Church House Publishing.

Ashby, P. (1984) *Social Security After Beveridge: What Next?*, London, Bedford Square Press.

Association of County Councils and National Council of Voluntary Organizations (1981) *Working Together*, Association of Municipal Authorities, London, Bedford Square Press.

Association of Metropolitan Authorities (1990) *Homelessness Programme for Action*, London, Association of Metropolitan Authorities.

Audit Commission (1984) *The Impact of Local Authorities' Economy, Efficiency and Effectiveness of the Block Grant Distribution System*, London, HMSO.

Audit Commission (1985) *Good Management in Local Government, Successful Practice and Action*, London, Local Government Training Board.

Audit Commission (1986a) *Managing the Crisis in Council Housing*, London, HMSO.

Audit Commission (1986b) *Making a Reality of Community Care*, London, HMSO.

Banham, J. (1986) 'Paying for local government', *Lloyds Bank Review*, 161, July.

Banting, K. (1979) *Poverty, Politics and Policy: Britain in the 1960s*, London, Methuen.

Barnett, C. (1986) *The Audit of War*, London, Macmillan.

Bell, D. (1962) *The End of Ideology*, New York, Free Press of Glencoe.

Belloc, H. (1927) *The Servile State*, London, Constable (new edn).

Beltram, G. (1984) *Testing the Safety Net*, London, Bedford Square Press. Summarised in *New Society*, 16 August.

Benn, A.W. (1981) Introduction to R.H. Tawney, *The Attack*, Nottingham, Spokesman.

Berthoud, R. (1985a) 'Welfare benefits', *Catalyst*, 1 (3), Autumn.

Berthoud, R. (1985b) *The Reform of Supplementary Benefit*, London, Policy Studies Institute.

Beveridge, Sir W. (1942) *Social Insurance and Allied Services*, Cm 6404, London, HMSO.

Beveridge, Sir W. (1943) *Pillars of Security*, London, George Allen and Unwin.

Beveridge, Sir W. (1944) *Full Employment in a Free Society*, London, Allen & Unwin.

Beveridge, Sir W. (1948) *Voluntary Action*, London, George Allen and Unwin.

Block, F. (1987) *The Mean Season: The Attack on the Welfare State*, New York, Pantheon Books.

Blunkett, D. (1985) 'Values matter in politics', *Observer*, 22 December.

Blunkett, D. and Green, G. (1983) *Building from the Bottom: The Sheffield Experience*, London, Fabian Pamphlet, 491.

Bosanquet, N. (1983) *After the New Right*, London, Heinemann Educational.

Bradley, I. (1981) 'Industrial influence in Britain, past and present', in R. Harris and A. Seldon (eds) *The Emerging Consensus*, London, Institute of Economic Affairs.

Bridges Project (1991) *Excluding Youth*, Edinburgh, Centre for Social Welfare Research.

Brittan, S. (1983) *The Role and Limits of Government: Essays in Political Economy*, London, Temple Smith.

Brown, C. (1985) *Black and White Britain*: the third PSI Survey, Aldershot, Gower.

Brown, J. (1990) *Villains or Victims?*, London, Policy Studies Institute.

Buchanan, J.M. (1978) *The Economics of Politics*, London, Institute of Economic Affairs.

Budd, A. (1978) *The Politics of Economic Planning*, London, Fontana.

Butler, D. and Stokes, D. (1971) *Political Change in Britain*, Harmondsworth, Pelican.

Butler, R.A. (1971) *The Art of the Possible*, London, Hamish Hamilton.

Butler, Robin (1988) *Government and Good Management: Are they Compatible?*, London, Institute of Personnel Management.

Cairncross, F. (1985) 'Review of Social Security Green Paper', *London Review of Books*, 20 September.

Central Statistical Office (1993) *Social Trends*, 23, London, HMSO.

Channon, 'Chips' (1967) *Diaries*, R. Rhodes James (ed.), London, Weidenfeld & Nicolson.

Clarke, D. (ed.) (1950) *Conservatism 1945–50*, London, Conservative Political Centre.

Coetzee, S. (1983) *Flat Broke*, Birmingham Welfare Payments Group.

Collingwood, R.G. (1944) *An Autobiography*, Harmondsworth, Penguin.

Commission on Social Justice (1993a) *Social Justice in a Changing World*, London, Institute for Public Policy Research.

Commission on Social Justice (1993b) *The Justice Gap*, London, Institute for Public Policy Research.

Conservative Party (1976) *The Right Approach*, London, Conservative Central Office.

Conservative Party (1977) *The Right Approach to the Economy*, London, Conservative Central Office.

Conservative Political Centre (1958) 'The future of the Welfare State', in I. Macleod, *The Political Divide*, London, Conservative Political Centre.

Coote, A. (ed.) (1992) *The Welfare of Citizens*, London, Rivers Oram Press.

Crosland, Tony (1956) *The Future of Socialism*, London, Cape.

Crossman, R.H.S. (1966) *Socialism and Planning*, London, Fabian Society.

Crossman, R.H.S. (1976) 'The role of the volunteer in the modern social service', in A.H. Halsey (ed.) *Traditions of Social Policy*, Oxford, Blackwell.

Crossman, R.H.S. (1977) *Diaries*, J. Morgan (ed.), London, Fontana.

Day, P. and Klein, R. (1991) 'Britain's health care experiment', *Health Affairs*, Fall, 39–59.

Deacon, Alan (1993) 'Richard Titmuss 20 years on', *Journal of Social Policy*, vol. 22, pt 2, April 1993, 235–43.

Deakin, N. (ed.) (1986) *Policy Change in Government*, London, Royal Institute of Public Administration.

Deakin, N. and Edwards, J. (1993) *The Enterprise Culture and Inner Cities*, London, Routledge.

Deakin, N. and Page, R. (eds) (1993) *The Costs of Welfare*, Aldershot, Avebury.

Dean, M. (1983) Review of H. Glennerster (ed.) *The Future of the Welfare State*, *Guardian*, 18 April.

Dennis, Norman and Erdos, George (1992) *Families without Fatherhood*, London, Institute of Economic Affairs Health and Welfare Unit.

Department of Social Security (1993) *The Growth of Social Security*, London, HMSO.

Dilnot, A.W., Kay, J.A. and Morris, C.N. (1984) *The Reform of Social Security*, Oxford, Clarendon, for Institute of Fiscal Studies.

Donnison, D. (1982) *The Politics of Poverty*, Oxford, Martin Robertson.

Donnison, D. (1991) *A Radical Agenda*, London, Rivers Oram.

Duke of Edinburgh (1985) *Inquiry into British Housing*, London, National Federation of Housing Associations.

Dunleavy, P. (1991) *Democracy, Bureaucracy and Public Choice*, Hemel Hempstead, Harvester Wheatsheaf.

Durbin, E.F.M. (1940) *The Politics of Democratic Socialism*, London, Routledge & Kegan Paul.

Durbin, E.F.M. (1942) *What Have We to Defend?*, London, Routledge & Kegan Paul.

Durbin, E.F.M. (1949) *The Economics of Democratic Journalism, Problems of Economic Planning: Papers on Planning and Economics*, London, Routledge & Kegan Paul.

Durbin, Elizabeth (1985) *New Jerusalems*, London, Routledge.

Edwards, J. (1986) *Positive Discrimination*, London, Routledge.

Enthoven, A. (1991) 'Internal market reform of the British National Health Service', *Health Affairs*, Fall, 60–70.

Field, F. (1982) *Poverty and Politics*, London, Heinemann.

Finer, H. (1946) *Road to Reaction*, London, Dennis Dobson.

Forrester, D. (1989) *Beliefs, Values and Politics*, Oxford, Oxford University Press.

Fowler, N. (1991) *Ministers Decide*, London, Chapman.

Franey, R. (1983) *Poor Law*, Poverty Pamphlet 58, London, Campaign for Homeless and Rootless (CHAR).

Friedman, M. (1970) *The Counter Revolution in Monetary Theory*, London, Institute of Economic Affairs.

Friedman, M. and Friedman, R. (1980) *Free to Choose*, Harmondsworth, Penguin.

Gamble, A. (1984) 'The lady's not for turning: Thatcherism mark III', *Marxism Today*, June.

Gaster, L. (1991) 'Quality and decentralisation: are they connected?', *Policy and Politics*, 19 (4), October, pp. 257 –67.

Gilbert, B.B. (1970) *British Social Policy 1914–39*, London, Batsford.

Gilmour, I. (1992) *Dancing with Dogma*, London, Simon & Schuster.

Glennerster, H. (1992) *Paying for Welfare, the 1990s*, Hemel Hempstead, Harvester Wheatsheaf.

Glennerster, H. (1993) 'Paying for welfare: issues for the nineties', in N. Deakin and R. Page, *The Costs of Welfare*, London, Avebury.

Glennerster, H., Power, A. and Travers, T. (1989) *A New Era for Social Policy: A New Enlightenment or a New Leviathan?*, STICERD Pamphlet WSP/39, London.

Golding, P. and Middleton, S. (1982) *Images of Welfare*, Oxford, Martin Robertson.

Goldman, P. (ed.) (1958) *The Future of the Welfare State*, London, Conservative Political Centre.

Graham, D. (1993) *A Lesson for Us All*, London, Routledge.

Green, D. (1985) *Working Class Patients and the Medical Establishment*, Aldershot, Gower/Temple Smith.

Green, David G. (1990) *The NHS Reforms: Whatever Happened to Consumer Choice?*, London, Institute of Economic Affairs Health and Welfare Unit.

Green, D.G. (1993) 'Chasing a chimera', *Fabian News*, 105 (2), March/April 1993.

Griffiths, B. (1985) *Monetarism and Morality: An Answer to the Bishops*, London, Conservative Political Centre.

Griffiths, Sir R. (1988) *Community Care: Agenda for Action*, London, HMSO.

Griffiths, Roy (1983) *National Health Service Management Inquiry*, London, Department of Health and Social Security.

Hadley, R. and Hatch, S. (1981) *Social Welfare and the Failure of the State*, London, Allen & Unwin.

Hailsham, Lord (1976) 'Elective dictatorship', *Listener*, 21 October.

Halsey, A.H. (1976) *Traditions of Social Policy*, Oxford, Blackwell.

Halsey, A.H. (1986) 'Building the New Jerusalem on the post-industrial ruins', *Listener*, 29 May.

Harris, R. and Seldon, A. (1977) *Not for Benevolence...*, London, Institute of Economic Affairs, Hobart Paper.

Harris, R. and Seldon, A. (1979) *Overruled on Welfare*, London, Institute of Economic Affairs.

Hayek, F.A. (1944) *The Road to Serfdom*, London, Routledge & Kegan Paul.

Hayek, F.A. (1973) *Economic Freedom and Representation Government*, London, Institute of Economic Affairs.

Hayek, F.A. (1976) *Law Legislation and Liberty*, vol. 2, London, Routledge & Kegan Paul, p. 64.

Hayek, F.A. (1978) *New Studies in Philosophy, Politics and Economics and the History of Ideas*, London, Routledge & Kegan Paul.

Heald, D. (1983) *Public Expenditure*, Oxford, Martin Robertson.

Healey, Denis (1990) *The Time of my Life*, Harmondsworth, Penquin.

Heath, E. (1986) Employment Institute Lecture, *Charter for Jobs Bulletin*, 3, July.

Heclo, H. and Wildavsky, A. (1974, revised edn 1981) *The Private Government of Public Money*, London, Macmillan.

Higgins, J., Deakin, N., Edwards, J. and Wicks, M. (1984) *Government and Urban Poverty*, Oxford, Blackwell.

Hills, J. (1988) *Changing Tax*, London, Child Poverty Action Group.

Hills, J. (ed.) (1991) *The State of Welfare*, Oxford, Clarendon Press.

Himmelfarb, G. (1984) *The Idea of Poverty*, London, Faber.

Hirschman, A.O. (1970) *Exit, Voice and Loyalty*, Cambridge, Mass., Harvard University Press.

Hirst, P. (1992) 'Sidestepping the State', *Australian Legal Review*, September 1992.

HM Government (1972) *Education: A Framework for Expansion*, Cm 5174, London, HMSO.

HM Government (1977) *Policy for the Inner Cities*, Cmd 6845, London, HMSO.

HM Government (1978) *Royal Commission on the National Health Service*, Research Paper 5, 'Patients' attitudes to the hospital service'.

HM Government (1979) *The Government's Expenditure Plans 1980–81*, Cmd 7746, London, HMSO.

HM Government (1981) *Alternatives to Domestic Rates*, Cm 8449, London, HMSO.

HM Government (1985a) *Reform of Social Security*, Cm 9517, London, HMSO.

HM Government (1985b) *Reform of Social Security: Programme for Change*, Cm 9518, London, HMSO.

HM Government (1985c) *Reform of Social Security*, Background Papers, vol. 3, Cm 9529, London, HMSO.

HM Government (1985d) *Reform of Social Security: Programme for Action*, Cm 9691, London, HMSO.

HM Government (1986) *The Reform of Personal Taxation*, Cm 9756, London, HMSO.

HM Government (1988) *Training for Employment*, Cm 316, London, HMSO.

HM Government (1989) *Caring for People*, Cm 849, London, HMSO.

HM Government (1989) *Working for Patients*, Cm 555, London, HMSO.

HM Government (1991) *The Citizen's Charter*, Cm 1599, London, HMSO.

HM Government (1993) *Raising the Standard: Britain's Citizens Charter and Public Sector Reforms*, London, HMSO.

HM Treasury (1984) *The Next Ten Years: Public Expenditure and Taxation into the 1990s*, Cmnd 9169, London, HMSO.

HM Treasury (1986) *The Reform of Personal Taxation*, Cmnd 9756, London, HMSO.

Hobhouse, L.T. (1911) *Liberalism*, Oxford, Oxford University Press, reprinted 1964.

Hobsbawm, E. (1983) 'Labour's lost millions', *Marxism Today*, October.

Hogg, Q. (1948) *The Case for Conservatism*, Harmondsworth, Penguin.

Holland, S. (1975) *The Socialist Challenge*, London, Quartet Books.

House of Commons Social Services Committee (1986) Session 1985–6, *Reform of Social Security*, London, HMSO.

Howell, D. (1986) *Blind Victory: A Study in Income, Wealth and Power*, London, Hamish Hamilton.

Ignatieff, M. (1984) *The Needs of Strangers*, London, Chatto & Windus.

Institute of Economic Affairs (1964) *Rebirth of Britain*, London, Pan Books.

Institute of Economic Affairs (1981) *The Emerging Consensus....?*, London, Institute of Economic Affairs.

Jackson, P. (ed.) (1985) *Implementating Government Policy Initiatives. The Thatcher Administration. 1979–83*, London, Royal Institute of Public Administration.

Jacobovitz, Sir I. (1986) *From Doom to Hope*, London, Office of the Chief Rabbi.

Jacobs, E. and Worcester, R. (1990) *We British*, London, MORI.

Jewkes, J. (1948) *Ordeal by Planning*, London, Macmillan.

Johnson, P. (1985) *The Historical Dimensions of the Welfare State Crisis*, London, Suntory Toyota International Centre for Economics and Related Disciplines, Welfare State Programme 3.

Jordan, B. (1991) 'Want (Social Security)', *Social Policy and Administration*, 25 (1), March, 14–26.

Joseph, Sir K. (1979) *Stranded on the Middle Ground*, London, Conservative Political Centre.

Joseph, Sir K. and Sumption, J. (1979) *Equality*, London, John Murray.

Jowell, R. and Airey, C. (1984) *British Social Attitudes: The 1984 Report*, Aldershot, Gower.

Jowell, R., Brook, L., Prior, G. and Taylor, B. (1992) *British Social Attitudes, Ninth Report*, Aldershot, Gower.

Jowell, R., Witherspoon, S., Brook, L. and Taylor, B. (1990) *British Social Attitudes, Seventh Report*, Aldershot, Gower.

Kaldor, N. (1983) *The Economic Consequences of Mrs. Thatcher*, London, Fabian Tract, 486.

Kedourie, Elie (1989) 'Perestroika in the university', London, Institute of Economic Affairs Health and Welfare Unit.

Keegan, W. (1984) *Mrs. Thatcher's Economic Experiment*, Harmondsworth, Penguin.

Keynes, J.M. (1931) *Essays in Persuasion*, London, Macmillan.

Keynes, J.M. (1936) *The General Theory of Employment, Interest and Money*, London, Macmillan.

Keynes, J.M. (1972) 'How to pay for the war', 1940, in *The Collected Words of J.M. Keynes*, London, Macmillan, vol. IX.

Kinnock, N. (1985) *The Future of Socialism*, London, Fabian Society Pamphlet, 509.

Klein, R. and Day, P. (1987) *Accountabilities*, London, Tavistock.

Klein, R. and O'Higgins, M. (1985) *The Future of Welfare*, Oxford, Blackwell.

Land, H. and Rose, H. (1985) 'Compulsory altruism for some or an altruistic society for all', in P. Bean, J. Ferris and D. Whynes (eds) *In Defence of Welfare*, London, Tavistock.

Lawson, N. (1980) *The New Conservatism*, London, Centre for Policy Studies.

Lawson, N. (1984) 'Mais Memorial Lecture', *Sunday Times*, 24 June.

Lawson, N. (1992) *The View from No. 11*, London, Bantam Press.

Le Grand, J. (1982) *The Strategy of Equality*, London, Allen & Unwin.

Le Grand, J. (1990) *Quasi-Markets and Social Policy*, Bristol, School for Advanced Urban Studies.

Le Grand, J. (1991) *The Distribution of Public Expenditure on Health Care Revisited*, STICERD Pamphlet WSP/64, London, LSE.

Le Grand, J. and Bartlett, W. (1993) *Quasi-markers and Social Policy*, Basingstoke, Macmillan.

Letwin, S.R. (1992) *The Anatomy of Thatcherism*, London, Fontana.

Liberal Industrial Inquiry (1928) *Britain's Industrial Future*, Tonbridge, E. Benn.

Lilley, P. (1993) Preface to *Department of Social Security report on spending on social security*, London, HMSO.

London–Edinburgh Weekend Return Group (1980) *In and Against the State*, London, Pluto.

Loney, M., Bocock, R., Clarke, J., Cochrane, A., Graham, P. and Wilson, M. (1991) *The State or the Market*, London, Sage.

Lowe, R. (1993) *The Welfare State in Britain Since 1945*, Basingstoke, Macmillan.

Mack, J. and Lansley, S. (1985) *Poor Britain*, London, Allen & Unwin.

McCarthy, M. (ed.) (1989) *The New Politics of Welfare*, Basingstoke, Macmillan.

MacKenzie, N. and J. (eds) (1983) *The Diaries of Beatrice Webb*, London, Virago.

Macleod, I. and Powell, E. (1954) *The Social Services: Needs and Means*, London, Conservative Political Centre Research Series.

Macmillan, H. (1938) *The Middle Way*, London, Macmillan.

Macmillan, H. (1969) *Tides of Fortune*, London, Macmillan.

Manning, N. and Page, R. (eds) (1992) *Social Policy Review 4*, Kent, Social Policy Association.

Marquand, D. (1985) 'Fire, fire be it in Noah's flood', *Government and Opposition*, 20 (4), Autumn.

Marquand, D. (1988) *The Unprincipled Society*, London, Fontana.

Marsh, D. and Rhodes, R. (eds) (1992) *Implementing Thatcherite Policies*, Buckingham, Open University Press.

Marshall, T.H. (1961) *Social Policy*, London, Hutchinson.

Mather, G. (1993) 'Responsibility, accountability and standards in government', London, European Policy Forum.

Meacher, M. (1985) 'The good society', *New Socialist*, June.

Middlemas, R.K. (1979) *Politics in Industrial Society*, London, André Deutsch.

Mill, J.S. and Himmelfarb, G. (1974) *On Liberty*, Harmondsworth, Penguin.

Minford, P. (1984) 'State expenditure: a study in waste', *Economic Affairs*, April–June.

Mishra, Ramesh (1984) *The Welfare State in Crisis: Social thought and social change*, Hemel Hempstead, Harvester Wheatsheaf.

Moore, John (1989) 'The end of the line for poverty', speech to Greater London Area Conservative Political Centre (TS), 11 May.

Morgan, K. (1991) *The People's Peace: British History 1945–1989*, Oxford, Oxford University Press.

Morgan, K. O. (1991) *The People's War: British History 1945–1989*, Cambridge, Cambridge University Press.

Mount, F. (1985) 'First principles: a view from the right', *Marxism Today*, July.

Murray, Charles (1990) 'The emerging British underclass', London, Institute of Economic Affairs Health and Welfare Unit.

National Consumer Council (1984) *Of Benefit to All*, London, National Consumer Council.

National Consumer Council (1986) *Measuring Up: Consumer Assessment of Local Authority Services*, London, National Consumer Council.

Next Five Years Group (1935) *The Next Five Years: An Essay in Political Agreement*, London, Macmillan.

Niskanen, W.A. (1973) *Bureaucracy, Servant or Master?*, London, Institute of Economic Affairs.

Northcott, J. et al. (1992) *Britain in 2010*, London, Policy Studies Institute.

O'Connor, J. (1973) *The Fiscal Crisis of the State*, New York, St. James' Press.

Offé, C. (1984) *Contradictions of the Welfare State*, London, Hutchinson.

Oppenheim, C. (1993) *Poverty: The Facts*, London, Child Poverty Action Group.

Owen, D. (1984) *A Future that Will Work*, Harmondsworth, Penguin.

Parkinson, Cecil (1992) *Right at the Centre*, London, Weidenfeld & Nicolson.

Patten, John (1992) speech to Conservative Political Centre, in National Council for Voluntary Organisations, *Bulletin*, Winter.

Pimlott, B. (1984) *Fabian Essays in Socialist Thought*, London, Heinemann.

Plant, R. (1985) 'Welfare and the values of liberty', *Government and Opposition*, 20 (3), Summer.

Pliatsky, Sir L. (1986) 'Can government be efficient?', *Lloyds Bank Review*, 159, January.

Policy Studies Institute (1992) *Britain in 2010*, London, PSI.

Political and Economic Planning (1960) *Growth in the British Economy*, London, Allen & Unwin.

Powell, E. (1961) *The Welfare State*, London, Conservative Political Centre.

Powell, E. (1964) 'Is it politically practicable?', in Institute of Economic Affairs, *The Rebirth of Britain*, London, Pan.

Prior, D., Stewart, J. and Walsh, K. (1993) *Is the Citizens Charter a Charter for Citizens?*, London, LGMB.

Prior, J. (1986) *A Balance of Power*, London, Hamish Hamilton.

Pym, F. (1985) *The Politics of Consent*, London, Sphere.

Rentoul, John (1989) *Me and Mine*, London, Unwin Hyman.

Riddell, P. (1984) *The Thatcher Government*, Oxford, Martin Robertson.

Ridley, N. (1992) *My Style of Government*, London, Fontana.

Robinson, R. (1986) 'Restructuring the Welfare State: an analysis of public expenditure, 1979/80–1984/5', *Journal of Social Policy*, 15 (1), 1–21.

Robson, W.A. (ed.) (1942) *Social Security*, London, Allen & Unwin.

Robson, W.A. and Crick, B. (1970) *The Future of the Social Services*, Harmondsworth, Pelican.

Rose, H. (1984) 'Property of the professionals', *New Statesman*, 22 October.

Rose, R. (1985) *The State's Contribution to the Welfare Mix*, Centre for the Study of Public Policy, University of Strathclyde, Paper 140.

Rose, R. and Abrams, M. (1960) *Must Labour Lose?*, Harmondsworth, Penguin Special.

Ryan, A. (1974) *J.S. Mill*, London, Routledge & Kegan Paul.

Savage, S. and Robins, L. (1990) *Public Policy under Thatcher*, Basingstoke, Macmillan.

Seldon, A. (1981) *Churchill's Indian Summer*, Sevenoaks, Hodder & Stoughton.

Silburn, R. (1985) *The Future of Social Security*, London, Fabian Society.

Sinfield, A. and Fraser, N. (1985) 'The real cost of unemployment', Newcastle, BBC North-East.

Skidelsky, R. (1992) *J.M. Keynes: The Economist as Saviour*, London, Macmillan.

Smith, David (1974) *Black and White Britain*, Second PSI Survey, Aldershot, Gower.

Smith, D. (1992) *From Boom to Bust*, Harmondsworth, Penguin.

Social Democratic Party (1986) *Merging Tax and Benefits: Attacking Poverty*, London, SDP.

Spencer, H. (1969) *The Man versus the State*, D.G. MacRae (ed.), Harmondsworth, Penguin.

Stewart, J. (1992) *The New Magistracy*, London, European Policy Forum.

Stewart, J. and Walsh, K. (1992) 'Change in the management of public services', *Public Administration*, 70 (4), Winter 1992, 499–513.

Stewart, M. (1977) *The Jekyll and Hyde Years, Politics of Economic Policy Since 1964*, London, J.M. Dent.

Stowe, Kenneth (1992) 'Good piano won't play bad music', *Public Administration*, 70 (3), pp. 387–94.

Tawney, R.H. (1931) *Equality*, London, Unwin, revised edn, 1964.

Tawney, R.H. (1964) *The Radical Tradition*, Harmondsworth, Penguin.

Tawney, R.H. (1981) *The Attack*, Nottingham, Spokesman Books.

Taylor, R. (1986) 'Tories' way with figures', *Observer*, 3 August.

Taylor-Gooby, P. (1985) *Public Opinion Ideology and State Welfare*, London, Routledge & Kegan Paul.

Taylor-Gooby, Peter (1991) *Social Change, Social Welfare and Social Science*, Hemel Hempstead, Harvester Wheatsheaf.

Tebbit, N. (1988) *Upwardly Mobile*, London, Weidenfeld & Nicolson.

Thane, P. (1982) *The Foundations of the Welfare State*, London, Longman.

Thatcher, M. (1977) *Let Our Children Grow Tall, Selected Speeches 1975–77*, London, Centre for Policy Studies.

Thatcher, M. (1993) *The Downing Street Years*, London, Harper Collins.

Titmuss, R. (1950) *Problems of Social Policy*, London, HMSO.

Titmuss, R. (1958) *The Irresponsible Society*, London, Fabian Tract, 323, reprinted in *Essays on the Welfare State*, London, Allen & Unwin (also 1963).

Titmuss, R. (1968) *Commitment to Welfare*, London, Allen & Unwin.

Titmuss, R. (1970) *The Gift Relationship*, London, Allen & Unwin, and Harmondsworth, Penguin, 1973.

Townsend, P. (1979) *Poverty in the United Kingdom*, Harmondsworth, Penguin.

Townsend, P. and Abel-Smith, B. (1965) *The Poor and the Poorest*, London, Bell & Hyman.

Townsend, P. and Davidson, N. (1982) *Equalities in Health, the Black Report*, Harmondsworth, Penguin.

Tyrrell, R.E. jun. (1977) *The Future that Doesn't Work: Social Democracy's Failures in Britain*, New York, Doubleday.

Ungerson, C. (1985) *Women and Social Policy, a Reader*, London, Macmillan.

Waldegrave, William (1993) *Speech to Public Finance Foundation*, 5 July (TS text).

Walker, P. (1991) *Saying Power*, London, Bloomsbury.

Wapshott, N. and Brock, G. (1983) *Thatcher*, London, Futura.

Ward, S. (1985) *DHSS in Crisis*, London, Child Poverty Action Group.

Watson, G. (1957) *The Unservile State*, London, Allen & Unwin.

Webb, S. and Webb, B. (1920) *A Constitution for the Socialist Commonwealth of Great Britain*, London, The Authors.

Whitelaw, W. (1989) *The Whitelaw Memoirs*, London, Aurum Press.

Whybrew, R. J. (1988) *Britain Speaks Out*, London, Gallup.

Willetts, D. (1992) *Modern Conservatism*, Harmondsworth, Penguin.

Williams, S. (1981) *Politics are for People*, Harmondsworth, Penguin.

Wilson, T. and D. (eds) (1991) *The State and Social Welfare*, Harlow, Longman.

Winch, D. (1972) *Economics of Policy: A Historical Survey*, London, Fontana.

Wootton, B. (1945) 'Working-class associations, private capital, welfare and the state in the late nineteenth and early twentieth century', in N. Parry, M. Rustin and C. Satyamara (eds) *Social Work, Welfare and the State*, London, Edward Arnold.

Young, D. (1985) Speech delivered at St. Lawrence, Jewry, 6 November, Department of Employment press release.

Young, D. (1990) *The Enterprise Years*, London, Headline Press.

Young, H. (1990) *One of Us*, London, Pan.

Young, H. and Sloman, A. (1982) *No, Minister: An Inquiry into the Civil Service*, London, BBC.

Young, H. and Sloman, A. (1986) *The Thatcher Phenomenon*, London, BBC.

Young, K. (1986) 'The Welfare State at 40', *Listener*, 10 July, 11–12.

INDEX